Career Development Activities
for the Elementary Grades:
Relating Academic Areas to the World of Work

By
Miriam McLaughlin and Sandra Peyser

Career Development Activities for the Elementary Grades

Copyright, 2001 Educational Media Corporation®

ISBN 1-930572-08-5

Printing (Last Digit)
9   8   7   6   5   4   3   2   1

Library of Congress
Catalog Card Number 2001088035

All rights reserved. No part of the material protected by this copyright notice may be reproduced or utilized in any form or by any means, electronic or mechanical, including photocopying, recording, or by any information storage and retrieval system, without the written permission of the copyright owners.

Permission is granted to practicing school counselors and teachers to duplicate and/or modify the handouts, and other materials included in this book for use in their own school building.

Publisher—
Educational Media Corporation®
PO Box 21311
Minneapolis, MN 55421-0311

(763) 781-0088

Graphic Design—
Earl R. Sorenson

Production Editor—
Don L. Sorenson

Table of Contents

Chapter I	Language Arts Activities	11

Journalist	Activity 1	In the News	12
Elementary School Teacher	Activity 2	Planning a Lesson	13
Lawyer	Activity 3	Two Sides to Every Story	14
Professional Athlete	Activity 4	Let the Games Begin	16
Parole and Probation Officer	Activity 5	Get a Job	18
Air Traffic Controller	Activity 6	Right Turns	20
Writer	Activity 7	Words, Words, Words	21
Secretary	Activity 8	Get Me to the Meeting on Time	23
Animal Trainer	Activity 9	Friends and Helpers	24
TV Repairer	Activity 10	Tuning In	25
Automobile Assembler	Activity 11	Parts of a Puzzle	26
Stagehand	Activity 12	On Stage	27
Maintenance Mechanic	Activity 13	Mr. Fix-it	28
Clergy	Activity 14	I Do	30
Child Care Worker	Activity 15	Playtime	32
Motorcycle Repairer	Activity 16	Zoom!	34
Actor	Activity 17	On With the Show	35
Seismologist	Activity 18	Move the Dishes	36
Electrical Engineer	Activity 19	Lights Out	37
Aerospace Engineer	Activity 20	Up, Up and Away	38
Crane Operator	Activity 21	On the Job	39
Janitor	Activity 22	Clean as a Whistle	41
Hospital Administrator	Activity 23	Decisions, Decisions, Decisions	42
Service Station Attendant	Activity 24	Out of Gas	44
Electrician	Activity 25	Lights On!	46
Veterinarian	Activity 26	Going to the Dogs	47
Sound Engineer	Activity 27	Noisemakers	50
Clothing Salesperson	Activity 28	Listen Up	52
Dental Lab Technician	Activity 29	Following Directions	54
Mail Carrier	Activity 30	Lots of Letters	56
Librarian	Activity 31	A Visit to the Library	58
Computer Repairer	Activity 32	On Line	60
Press Operator	Activity 33	Going to Press	62
Automobile Mechanic	Activity 34	Car Parts	63

Educational Media Corporation®, Box 21311, Minneapolis, MN 55421-0311

Chapter II	Mathematics Activities	65

Restaurant Manager .... Activity 35.... Food for Sale 66
Architect .... Activity 36.... A House for Little People 68
Truck Driver .... Activity 37.... On the Road 70
Shipping and Receiving Clerk .... Activity 38.... Fill the Order 71
Travel Agent .... Activity 39.... Lets Go! 72
Newspaper Carrier .... Activity 40.... Money Makers 73
Cosmetologist .... Activity 41.... Cuts and Curls 75
Waitperson .... Activity 42.... Let's Eat Out 77
Floral Designer .... Activity 43.... Rose Petals 79
Interior Designer .... Activity 44.... Best Room in the House 81
Petroleum Field Worker .... Activity 45.... Looking for Oil 82
Elevator Mechanic .... Activity 46.... A Little Lift 83
Buyer .... Activity 47.... Fashions to Buy 85
Bricklayer .... Activity 48.... Brick by Brick 86
Accountant .... Activity 49.... Dollars and Cents 88
Drywall Worker .... Activity 50.... Dollhouses 90
Bulldozer Operator .... Activity 51.... Out of My Way 91
Cashier .... Activity 52.... Making Change 93
Drafter .... Activity 53.... First Draft 96
Carpenter .... Activity 54.... Hammer and Nails 98
Bus Driver .... Activity 55.... Ride the Bus 100

Chapter III — Social Studies Activities — 101

Real Estate Salesperson	Activity 56.... New Family in Town	102
Camp Counselor	Activity 57.... Summer Fun	104
Law Enforcement Officer	Activity 58.... Keeping Safe	105
Tourist Information Specialist	Activity 59.... The Good Old Days	107
Commercial Fisher	Activity 60.... Gone Fishin'	108
Telephone Installer and Repairer	Activity 61.... On the Line	110
Mayor	Activity 62.... Key to the City	111
Farm Worker	Activity 63.... On the Farm	112
Ship's Crew Member	Activity 64.... Ship Ahoy	113
Surveyor	Activity 65.... Over the Meadow and through...	114
Taxi Driver	Activity 66.... Finding Your Way Around	115
Chauffeur	Activity 67.... A Road to the Stars	116
Home Health Aide	Activity 68.... Helping Hand	117
Social Worker	Activity 69.... Where to Go	118
Civil Engineer	Activity 70.... Bridge Builders	120
Construction Laborer	Activity 71.... Pick Up Sticks	122
Roofer	Activity 72.... Tippity Top	124
Landscape Architect	Activity 73.... Parks and Playgrounds	126
Railroad Engineer	Activity 74.... All Aboard	127
Astronaut	Activity 75.... Off in Space	129
Engineering Technician	Activity 76.... Building Zones	131
School Principal	Activity 77.... Head of the Class	132
Aircraft Mechanic	Activity 78.... Good Working Order	134
Tool and Die Worker	Activity 79.... Making It	135
Forester	Activity 80.... Do you want to be a Forester?	137
Heating and Cooling Systems Mech.	Activity 81.... Hot and Cold	139

Educational Media Corporation®, Box 21311, Minneapolis, MN 55421-0311

Career Development Activities for the Elementary Grades

Chapter IV	Science Activities	141

Park Ranger	Activity 82.... Birds, Bees, Flowers and Trees	142
Pilot	Activity 83.... Flying High	143
Meteorologist	Activity 84.... Weather Words	145
Gardener	Activity 85.... How Does Your Garden Grow?	146
Oceanographer	Activity 86.... Oil and Water	149
Plumber	Activity 87.... Water Water Everywhere	151
Optometrist	Activity 88.... How Far Can You See?	152
Astronomer	Activity 89.... Shining Stars	154
Bakery Worker	Activity 90.... Bake Me a Cake	156
Furniture Worker	Activity 91.... Table Talk	158
Chemical Lab Technician	Activity 92.... Experimenting	160
Biomedical Engineer	Activity 93.... The Human Body	162
Laundry and Dry Cleaning Worker	Activity 94.... Mr. and Mrs. Clean	163
Biologist	Activity 95.... Leaves and Flowers	164
Chemist	Activity 96.... Pollution	165
Geologist	Activity 97.... The Good Earth	166
Steel Worker	Activity 98.... On the Beam	167
College Teacher	Activity 99.... College Courses	168
Forest Technician	Activity 100.. Save a Tree	169
Machinist	Activity 101.. The Wonderful Machine	170
Medical Technologist	Activity 102.. Looking and Learning	172
Welder	Activity 103.. Heat and Fire	174
Optical Technician	Activity 104.. Experiments with Light	175

Chapter V	Music and Art Activities	177

Clothes Designer	Activity 105.. Lookin' Good!	178
Musician	Activity 106.. I've Got Rhythm	179
Graphic Designer	Activity 107.. Make a Pretty Picture	180
Painter	Activity 108.. What Color Will You Use?	181
Photographer	Activity 109.. Hold that Pose	182
Radio and Television Announcer	Activity 110.. On the Air	183
Telephone Operator	Activity 111.. This is the Operator	184
Autobody Repairer	Activity 112.. Paint Job	185
Jeweler	Activity 113.. Creative Jewelry	186
Artist	Activity 114.. Rainbow of Colors	187
Computer Graphics Specialist	Activity 115.. Take a Byte	188
Clothing Pattern Maker	Activity 116.. Patterns	189
Broadcast Technician	Activity 117.. You're On	191

Chapter VI — Physical Education, Health and Safety Activities — 193

Military Officer	Activity 118 .. Forward March	194
Chef	Activity 119 .. What's Cookin'?	196
Dietitian	Activity 120 .. Eat Healthy	197
Emergency Medical Technician	Activity 121 .. What Would You Do?	199
Pharmacist	Activity 122 .. Read the Prescription	200
Dentist	Activity 123 .. Smile	202
Dental Hygienist	Activity 124 .. Take Care of Your Teeth	204
Respiratory Therapist	Activity 125 .. Take a Deep Breath	206
Security Guard	Activity 126 .. Guard Duty	209
Nurse	Activity 127 .. A Need for Nurses	211
Robotics Technician	Activity 128 .. The Production Line	213
Military Enlisted Personnel	Activity 129 .. Balloon Ball	215
School Counselor	Activity 130 .. Negotiating and Mediating	216
Preschool Teacher	Activity 131 .. Learn a Skill	220
Firefighter	Activity 132 .. To the Rescue	221
Physical Therapist	Activity 133 .. On the Go	223
X ray Technologist	Activity 134 .. Hold that Pose	225
Physician	Activity 135 .. Jeopardy	227
Receptionist	Activity 136 .. First Impressions	229
Psychologist	Activity 137 .. What Do Psychologists Think	231

Chapter VII — Computer Skills Second Language — 233

Desktop Publisher	Activity 136 .. Computer Whiz	234
Computer Programmer	Activity 137 .. Summertime	236
Flight Attendant	Activity 138 .. Coffee, Tea, or Milk	238

Bibliography — 240

Introduction

Why is career development so important at such a young age? In part, the answer lies in our changing economy. Technology has completely altered the way we do business, made some jobs obsolete and created many other career opportunities. Most important, perhaps, is that these changes have made clear the link between education and the world of work. Jobs today require more education and more skills than ever before. At one time young adults with little or no education or skills could become mechanics, farmers or factory workers and earn a living wage. Now mechanics need to understand computers, farmers need to know how to operate a business and factory workers have, in many places, been replaced by sophisticated robots operated by highly skilled technicians.

Even with all these changes, there are still traditional jobs available for students who do not choose to attend college. For example, as long as there are elevators there will be a need for elevator repair people. And bulldozers may be improved, but they still will require people to operate them. Demand for service workers is steadily increasing. Restaurants are continually advertising for staff, as are shops, grocery stores, hospitals, and nursing homes. The world of work offers ever broadening opportunities for young adults.

The longest phase of our lives is spent in the world of work. Children in elementary schools have just fifteen years or so to prepare for their lives as working adults. The more thought, planning, and preparation that occurs prior to adulthood, the more likely these children will have successful, rewarding careers. Preparing for the work world includes learning life skills such as good communication and responsibility. Students need to explore work to understand the skills they will need to do the variety of jobs available to them.

Like so many other aspects of child development and learning, schools have been charged with helping children become aware of and understand the world of work. Classroom teachers, already overwhelmed by the pressures of performance standards and myriad initiatives, have little time left to focus on career development. *Career Development Activities for the Elementary Grades* is designed to address this problem by providing career activities that are tied to major subject areas. Using this book, teachers and counselors can expose students to specific careers while teaching math, English, science or social studies. Students can see how knowledge of school subjects applies in the work world.

Counselors who are providing career development programs, a major component of the National Counseling Standards, can use these activities during classroom guidance. They can also help teachers incorporate these activities into the regular curriculum.

Career Development Activities for the Elementary Grades is unique in its approach to career development. This book offers students a chance to explore a variety of specific careers, such as Hospital Administrator, Cosmetologist and Civil Engineer. Most children talk about becoming a Doctor, an Astronaut, a Teacher, or a Police Officer; but, how many know what a Lab Technician, or a Stagehand, or a Maintenance Mechanic does?

Activity Design

The activities in *Career Development Activities for the Elementary Grades* are designed for grades three through six, but can be adjusted for other grades and age groups. For example, the same activities can be used with more capable second graders and less advance seventh graders with a few modifications.

Each activity has two levels of difficulty. The second level, Part Two, of each activity, is more challenging and builds on the activity in Part One. Teachers and counselors can choose the appropriate part of the activity based on the skill level of the class, or combine Parts One and Two into one activity.

Most activities are assigned to one subject area. However, some cover more than one. For example, the Mayor addresses both Social Studies and Art. The Elementary School Teacher uses both reading and writing.

Directions in each activity are written to the children. Teachers and counselors can provide children with their own book or copy the individual activities as needed. Depending again on the skill level of the class, teachers and counselors can also do the lesson with the children, reading the instructions aloud.

Accompanying each activity is a summary description of the career and a teacher's guide with instructions and suggestions for implementing the lessons. Also process questions are offered at the end of each activity. These questions are important to determining accountability, checking on the learning that has occurred and bringing closure to the activity.

About the Authors

Miriam McLaughlin

Miriam McLaughlin is a consultant with the Comer School Development program and a free-lance trainer and writer in the area of student support services. She wrote the American Lung Association's *Alternative To Suspension* Program, and served as writer and editor for the *Not On Tobacco* Program. She is co-author of the training manuals *D.A.R.E to Parent* and *The Race to Safe Schools*. She has also co-authored *Peer Listening in the Middle School, Warm Ups & Wind Downs: 101 Activities for Moving and Motivating Groups, Character Education Activities for the K-6 Classroom, Addiction: The High That Brings You Down,* and *TLC • Tutoring • Leading • Cooperating: Training Activities for Elementary Students.* Currently, Mrs. McLaughlin is co-author of a weekly career development article for an on-line parent's magazine.

Mrs. McLaughlin is a nationally recognized trainer in peer programs, dysfunctional families, parent involvement in schools, and risk and resiliency. She is also a master trainer for the American Lung Association

Sandra Peyser

Sandra Peyser is a retired school counseling consultant for the state of North Carolina, currently doing private consulting. She has served as an elementary teacher, counselor, and peer program supervisor. She has contributed to the field of career work by doing state training workshops. Ms. Peyser is the co-author of seven books including *WarmUps & Wind Downs, Character Education Activities (K-6)* and two peer helping books. She is a native of Miami, Florida and lives in Raleigh, North Carolina.

Chapter I

Language Arts Activities

Career Development Activities for the Elementary Grades

Journalist

Journalists write stories for newspapers, magazines, television or radio. Usually the stories are about important current events. Most of the stories are of general interest, like sports and politics. Journalists spend time doing research, talking to people who may be involved in the events and writing the stories. Radio and television journalists may read their stories on the air.

Journalists often write about interesting or famous people. They interview these people to get the information they need for their stories. Journalists work with a deadline. They must have their stories completed by a certain time.

Activity 1

In the News

Subject Area: Reading and Writing
Materials: Paper for an interview sheet, pens or pencils
Time: 30 to 60 minutes

Part I

Background:
- Explain the concept of *open-ended questions* to your class. Have them practice asking open-ended questions.
- Explain that the word *deadline* means the time the story is due to be printed or aired.

Procedure:
1. Think of someone you know about whom you would like to write a story. You could choose a family member, a friend, a teacher, or another adult as your subject.
2. Write that person's name at the top of your interview sheet.
3. With your class, brainstorm 10 or more questions you could ask the person to get information for your story. Avoid questions that only need a "yes" or "no" answer. For example, if you ask someone, "Do you like your job?" the person only needs to answer yes or no. You will get much more information by asking, "What do you like about your job?"
4. Write the questions you want to ask on your interview sheet.

5. Interview the person you have chosen. Write the answers to the questions you ask in the space provided on your interview sheet.

Process Questions:
1. What was hard about interviewing someone?
2. What are some deadlines that you have to keep in your life?

Part II

Background:
- You may want your students to find examples—in newspapers or magazines—of stories written from interviews.
- Have your students submit a first draft of the story to you for editing (correcting).

Procedure:
1. Using the information you have written on your interview sheet, write a story about the person you interviewed. Write at least three paragraphs.
2. After completing the story, show it to the person you interviewed to check for facts. Correct any errors.

Process Questions:
1. How did the person you chose react to your story?
2. Why is it important to check facts?

Miriam McLaughlin and Sandra Peyser

Chapter I

Elementary School Teacher

Elementary school teachers need to know about many different subjects. They also need to understand the different ways children learn. Children learn new skills and learn about themselves and the world with the help of their teachers. Elementary school teachers are among the most important people in a child's life.

Activity 2

Planning a Lesson

Subject Area: Reading, Writing
Materials: Paper, Pencils, Crayons, Markers, other materials for a lesson
Time: 30 to 45 minutes

Part I

Background:
- Use topics your class has studied or is studying. You may wish to add to or change the topic list.
- Working through the process as a class will help your students understand the look, listen, and do process.
- To enhance this activity, your students could work through the listen and do process also.

Procedure:
1. Everyone learns differently. For example, one student may be able to learn how to use a computer just by listening to someone explain how to use it. Another student may be able to learn by reading the directions that come with the computer. Someone else may need to sit at the keyboard and try it out before understanding how a computer works. Elementary school teachers must make sure that all the students in the class learn the lesson, no matter how they learn best. They do this by teaching the same lesson in different ways. Students learn by looking, listening, and doing.

2. Pretend you are an elementary school teacher. You want to teach one these topics:
   READING, MATH FACTS, WORD ENDINGS, VOCABULARY, TIME, MONEY, WRITING, STATES AND CAPITALS.

3. Choose a topic from the list and think of something your students could **look at** to learn about this topic.

   For example: if very young students were learning the alphabet, they could look at pictures of the letters or blocks with the letters on them.

4. Now, decide what your students could **listen to** to learn about the topic. *For example:* they could listen to the "Alphabet Song" to learn the alphabet.

5. Now choose something students could **do**. *For example:* to learn the alphabet, they could practice writing the letters.

6. Write your ideas on a piece of paper.

Process Questions:
1. Why is it helpful to provide different ways of learning the same material?
2. Which way do you learn best?

Part II

Background:
- This part provides an opportunity for cross age or same age peer tutoring. For same age peer tutoring, choose a subject area in which your class needs reinforcement. Partner the students and have them teach each other the concepts.
- For cross age peer tutoring, partner your students with a younger class. Ask that teacher for lesson topics that would be helpful to their students. Have your students choose and plan the lesson topic. Pair your students with the younger students for a tutoring session.

Procedure:
1. Decide on a person to be your student. The teacher will assist you with this choice.
2. Working by yourself or in a small group, follow the instruction in Part I to teach to your student.
3. Teach the lesson to your student.

Process Questions:
1. How did it feel to help someone learn something new?
2. How can you be sure your partner learned the lesson?

Career Development Activities for the Elementary Grades

Lawyer

Lawyers study the laws of the state and the country. They explain the laws to people and advise them about their responsibilities and their rights within the law. When people challenge laws or break them, lawyers represent these people in courts in front of judges and juries. Judges are also lawyers. They make many of the decisions in court based on what they know or have researched about the law and what the lawyers tell them during a hearing or trial.

Activity 3

Two Sides to Every Story

Subject Area: Reading
Materials: None
Time: 30 minutes

Part I

Background:
* This activity works well in small groups or with a whole class.

Procedure:
Working on your own, read each of the following incidents, one at a time. Identify both sides of each story and write on a piece of paper what those sides are. Decide who broke the law or rule and what law or rule was broken. Write your answer on the paper.

Incident 1.
One morning, Jane borrowed Allen's pencil from his book bag while he was working on a project on the other side of the classroom. The lead in her pencil was broken, and no one in the class was allowed to go to the pencil sharpener except at lunchtime or after school. Jane meant to put the pencil back right away, but forgot until she saw Allen looking through his bag later in the day. Allen was very angry when she finally gave the pencil back and he accused Jane of stealing.

What are the two sides to this story?

Who broke a law or rule and what was the law or rule?

Incident 2. James and his friends were playing a game of basketball. James' brother had loaned them his brand new basketball for the game. Suddenly, one of the boys took a wild shot and the ball went over a tall fence. The fence had signs on it saying 'No Trespassing' and 'Keep Out'. James climbed over the fence anyway to get his brother's basketball. Someone called the police and reported James for trespassing.

What are the two sides to this story?

Who broke a law or rule and what was the law or rule?

Incident 3. Joanne was hurrying down the hall and bumped into Tanya. Tanya dropped her books and papers all over the floor. Joanne was afraid she would miss her bus, so she started to move away. Tanya wanted Joanne to stay and help pick up the mess, so she grabbed Joanne's sleeve. Joanne pushed Tanya away and then Tanya pulled harder at the sleeve and ripped Joanne's jacket.

What are the two sides to the story?

Who broke a law or rule and what was the law or rule?

Process Questions:
1. *Why is it important to know both sides of a story before deciding who is right and who is wrong?*
2. *Tell about a time when both sides were partly right or partly wrong.*

Miriam McLaughlin and Sandra Peyser

Chapter I

Part II

Language Arts Activities

Background:
- You may wish to research the laws in your state about petty theft and minors drinking alcohol. It is important to note when discussing the seatbelt issue, that laws in many states are different but we must obey the laws of the state we are in, even if we are just driving through. Note: in Massachusetts, people over thirteen years old do not have to wear seat belts.

Procedure:
Work with your small group to do this activity. Read each situation and discuss it, using the questions that follow each situation. Have a volunteer make notes about your discussion.

Incident 1. William and Michael are good friends and spend a great deal of time together. William's father recently lost his job and William told Michael that their family was really worried about money. One day at school, Michael saw William take some money from a student's desk. The very next day Michael saw William reaching into the pocket of a coat that was hanging on the back of a chair. Michael knew that it was not William's desk or William's coat, but he didn't say anything about it to anyone.

Did William break a law? If so, what law?
What should Michael have done?
What would you do?

Incident 2. Susan, Danielle and Linda are in the fifth grade. One Saturday night the girls had a sleep over party at Susan's house. Susan's parents were next door playing cards with the neighbors. They told the girls to call if they needed anything. When Danielle saw beer in the refrigerator she tried to talk the other girls into drinking some. She insisted that no one would ever know and that it would be fun. Finally, the other girls agreed and they all drank some beer.

Were the girls breaking the law by drinking beer at Susan's house? If so, what law?
What should Susan have done?
What would you do?

Incident 3. Sam and Vanessa Johnson are adults who were driving from Massachusetts to North Carolina. Just as they crossed the North Carolina border, they were stopped by the police for not wearing their seatbelts. Vanessa explained that wearing seatbelts is not a law in Massachusetts. The North Carolina State police gave them a ticket and they had to pay a $25 fine anyway.

Were the Johnsons breaking the law? If so, what law?
What is the law about seatbelts in your state?

Share the conclusions your group came to about the situations with the class.

Process Questions:
1. *How are the rules at school like the laws of states?*
2. *What are the consequences for breaking a law? a rule at school?*

Educational Media Corporation®, Box 21311, Minneapolis, MN 55421-0311

Career Development Activities for the Elementary Grades

Professional Athlete

Professional Athletes earn money playing sports. They play their sports in high school and college and must demonstrate their skills before they have the opportunity to become professionals. Some athletes play professional sports as part of teams like football or hockey teams. Others compete by themselves, like tennis players and golfers. It takes many years of practice and dedication and a little luck to become a professional athlete.

Activity 4

Let the Games Begin

Subject Area: Reading, Writing
Materials: Handout, pens or pencils
Time: 30 minutes—one week

Part I

Background:
- You may wish to include other sports on the list.
- Enhance this activity by having your students write their sports vocabulary words on the board for the class. Note the repetitions, spelling, and how different words might be used.

Procedure:
1. All athletes have some equipment they must use to play their sports. On the handout is a list of athletes and a list of different kinds of equipment and locations that are a part of their sports. See if you can match them up.
2. Choose a sport from the list, or choose one that you like to play or watch.
3. Make a list of words associated with the sport you chose. The word might be another piece of equipment, the location where the sport is played or words used in play.
4. These words are the vocabulary used in the sport.
5. Write a short paragraph about the sport you chose using at least three of the vocabulary words.

Process Questions:
1. What are some other ways people can use athletic ability besides becoming professional athletes?
2. What are some ways that adults and children in your community enjoy sports?

Part II

Background:
- You may wish to provide the names of famous athletes yourself, thereby ensuring the availability of biographies in the media center.
- Oral book reports are appropriate for this activity if the students are reporting on different athletes.

Procedure:
1. Professional athletes are often very famous. Write the name of a famous athlete who interests you on a slip of paper and give the paper to your teacher. If too many students choose the same famous athlete, your teacher may ask you to choose another.
2. Read a biography or autobiography about the athlete you chose.
3. Write a book report that answers the following questions:
    * How did this person become interested in the sport?
    * How long did the person play the sport before becoming a professional athlete?
    * With so many people wanting to be professional athletes, what caused this person to succeed while many others failed?

Process Questions:
1. Can you guess how many men and women who start out to become professional athletes actually make it?
2. What else do you need besides athletic ability to become a successful professional athlete?

Chapter I Language Arts Activities

Handout—Activity 4

Let the Games Begin

1. Here is a list of athletes and a list of different kinds of equipment and locations that are a part of their sports. See if you can match them up.

Baseball Player	pole
Hockey Player	saddle
Golfer	rink
Basketball Player	tee
Ice Skater	track
Equestrian	racquet
High Jumper	parallel bars
Runner	pool
Tennis Player	hoop
Gymnast	puck
Swimmer	bat
Football Player	50 yd. line

2. Choose a sport from the list, or choose one that you like to play or watch.

3. Make a list of words associated with the sport you chose. The word might be another piece of equipment, the location where the sport is played or words used in play. These words are the vocabulary used in the sport.

4. Write a short paragraph about the sport you chose using at least three of the vocabulary words.

Career Development Activities for the Elementary Grades

Parole and Probation Officer

Parole and Probation Officers help people who are leaving prison to adjust to every day life. They help former prisoners find jobs, places to stay, and other kinds of assistance they may need. They talk to these people about what kinds of behavior they expect and check regularly to make sure that the former prisoners do not break any laws. Parole and probation officers help these people stay out of trouble.

Activity 5

Get a Job

Subject Area: Reading
Materials: Newspapers, classified section, worksheet, pencils or pens, tape
Time: 30 to 60 minutes

Part I

Background:
- You may wish to bring classified ads to your class and divide them up to ensure that your students are working with a variety of ads.

Procedure:
1. Find five want ads from the classified section of a newspaper. Choose job advertisements from different categories so that they are not all alike. (The categories are usually at the top of the columns of ads.)
2. Tape each ad in the space provided on the worksheet or a piece of paper and answer the questions below the ad.

Process Questions:
1. Brainstorm some jobs that people might do in prison.
2. Why might it be difficult for a person who has been in prison to get a job?

Part II

Background:
- Compare and contrast the differences in salary, skills, and so forth as students share their groups findings.

Procedure:
1. Working with your small group, go through two columns of the "Help Wanted" section of a newspaper to find the following information. (As much as possible, each group should work on different parts of the "Help Wanted" section.)
   - What are the column headings (e.g., clerical, trades, professional)?
   - What jobs are the most commonly advertised?
   - What are the five most common characteristics used to describe the kind of person wanted for the jobs (e.g., responsible, hard-working)?
   - What is the most common level of education required by the jobs listed?
   - If pay is listed, what are the three top paying jobs?
2. Share your group findings with the whole class.

Process Questions:
1. Which of the people described on the worksheet would have the easiest time getting a job? Which will have the hardest? Why?
2. Discuss possible discrimination against people who have taken money or sold drugs?

Miriam McLaughlin and Sandra Peyser

Chapter 1 — Language Arts Activities

Worksheet–Activity 5

Get a Job

Part I

Tape Ad Here

How much education is required to get this job?
- High School?
- College?
- Advanced Degree?
- Technical Training?
- None?

What skills does the job require?

_____
_____
_____

What does the ad say about personal characteristics?

_____
_____

Does the ad mention how much money this job pays? If so, how much does it pay?

_____

Are there any special requirements for this job? (eg. drivers license, must be 21)

_____
_____

How to people apply for this job? (Write and send resume, go to the place of business in person, call on the telephone.)

_____
_____

What is the deadline for applications?

_____

Part II

Working with your group, decide what kinds of jobs might be available for the people listed below.

- Angel Rivera is thirty years old and has a high school education. When she was in prison, she answered the phone for the warden and typed business letters on a computer.

- Kim speaks distinctly and is a very patient person. She had a driver's license before prison and worked as a cook. Kim went to prison for stealing money from a bank.

- William Jones is a twenty-five year old body-builder. He kept very fit during his years in prison. He also learned first aid and CPR during that time. William never finished high school. Before prison, William worked for a landscaper, mowing lawns and planting trees and shrubs. He went to prison for seriously injuring another person.

- Lee Saunders is thirty seven. She has a college degree in English, and did a great deal of writing while she was in prison. Before she went to prison, she was the vice president of a small manufacturing company in charge of finances. Kim went to prison for selling drugs.

- Michael Taylor is twenty nine. He has been in training school or prison since he was a young teenager. In prison, Michael has been working on getting a high school degree, but he is not yet finished. He wants to change his life and help other boys stay out of trouble. Michael was a gang member who was involved in several shootings.

Career Development Activities for the Elementary Grades

Air Traffic Controller

Air traffic controllers direct planes through airspace. They tell the pilots when and where to take off and land and the altitude at which they can safely fly their planes. Air traffic controllers work from radar screens that tell them where the planes in their areas are located and how near they are to other planes. They must be able to concentrate, make quick decisions and give clear directions.

Activity 6

Right Turns

Subject Area: Reading
Materials: Blindfolds, Materials for obstacles
Time: 20 to 45 minutes

Part I

Background:
- Help your students choose a place for this activity. Make sure it is safe (does not require crossing streets or parking lots) and that the route to get there is indirect.
- Make sure your students understand that the directions are detailed. Your students should not assume, for example, that the person reading the directions knows where the door is located that exits the classroom.

Procedure:
1. With your small group, write the directions from your classroom to the playground or the corner of the street your school is located on. Write the directions as if the person reading them is standing in the middle of your classroom and has no idea what to do next.
2. Swap directions with another small group.
3. Choose someone in your group to read the directions aloud slowly, while the rest of the group follows the directions exactly. (Do what the directions say to do, no more or less.)
4. After completing the directions return to the classroom.
5. Tell the class whose directions your group was following, any problems with the directions and what part of the directions were very clear.

Process Questions:
1. Share some of the experiences of the small groups.
2. What happened to some of the people who did not hear or understand the directions?

Part II

Background:
- This activity should take place in a gym or on a level playground. Obstacles should be large enough for students to feel with parts of their bodies other than their feet.
- There should be an adult supervising each obstacle course. A student, waiting his or her turn, can count the number of times the blindfolded person bumps into an obstacle while moving through the course.

Procedure:
1. Help your teacher set up three obstacle courses of chairs and large trash cans or other large objects in a big space.
2. Partner up and decide who will give directions first.
3. Blindfold the other partner and place that person at the beginning of one of the obstacle courses.
4. Someone who is waiting to do a course should count the times obstacles are bumped.
5. The other partner must direct the blindfolded person around each obstacle. The blindfolded person must pass behind and in front of each obstacle in the course without bumping into anything.
6. The direction giver must proceed slowly and give very precise directions, e.g., STOP, BACK UP, ONE STEP, TURN RIGHT and TAKE TWO STEPS.
7. The partners with the least total bumps are the champion direction givers.

Process Questions:
1. How is going through an obstacle course blindfolded like an airplane flying through a fog?
2. Why does the air traffic controller have to give precise directions?

Chapter I Language Arts Activities

Writer

Writers may be story tellers who use words to tell their tales. Writers are sometimes poets who create pictures with their words. Some writers work on the information that we read everywhere: on signs, in advertisements, and in the directions that come with games and toys. They are responsible for creating the books and magazines we read. Good writers know about sentence and paragraph structure and are good spellers too.

Activity 7

Words, Words, Words

Subject Area: Writing
Materials: Story Map, pencils or paper, library books
Time: 45 to 60 minutes

Part I

Background:
- You may want your students to write a paragraph about each picture instead of a story.

Procedure:
1. Find two pictures in a magazine of scenes that you like. They could be pictures of the beach, the mountains, a race car course or any others that appeal to you.
2. Then find two pictures of people you like.
3. Glue the pictures of the people on to the backgrounds.
4. Choose one of the pictures and write a short story about what is happening to the people in the scene.
5. Share your story with the class.

Process Questions:
1. Why does a story have a beginning, a middle and an end?
2. How can you make characters in a story more interesting?

Background:
- A story map pulls together all of the elements of a story in a graphic presentation. Story maps help students construct meaning as they understand not only the story elements but their relationship to one another. A story map typically includes the setting, characters, problems, events, and resolution of a story. Story maps make students think about how to plan and organize stories, and they help to eliminate unnecessary or unrelated details that cause the story to become boring and episodic.
- The questions in a story chart form the basis of understanding most stories. They will help the students to reconstruct stories that they read and to construct stories that they write.

Procedure:
1. Bring in a book you have read recently.
2. With your class, review the story map and sequence chart activity sheets.
3. Fill out the story map according to the story in your book.
4. Working with a partner or small group, explain your book using your story map and sequence chart.
5. Use the story map again to write your own story. It can be a story you make up or something that happened to you.
6. After you have filled in your story map, write your story.

Process Questions
1. Where do writers get their ideas?
2. Why do writers need to know about sentence structure and punctuation?

Career Development Activities for the Elementary Grades

Handout—Activity 7

Words, Words, Words

Story Map

Title: _____

Setting: _____

Characters: _____
_____
_____

Problem: _____

Event 1 _____
Event 2 _____
Event 3 _____
Event 4 _____

Solution: _____

Story Chart

Characters:
Who or what is the story about? _____

Setting:
When and where does the story take place? _____
_____

Problem:
What is the problem? _____
_____

Events:
What happens in the story? _____
_____

Solution:
How does the story end? _____

Chapter I

Secretary

Secretaries help organizations to run smoothly. They make appointments, keep files of letters and information, and maintain and order supplies. Most secretaries have good typing and computer skills and know how to operate a variety of office machines. In some organizations, secretaries greet people and answer the telephone in addition to their other duties. Secretaries should be good spellers and have good penmanship.

Language Arts Activities

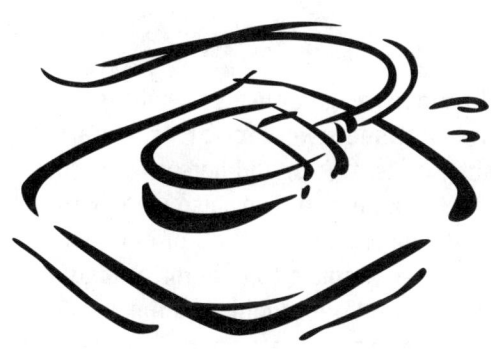

Activity 8

Get Me to the Meeting on Time

Subject Area: Reading, Speaking
Materials: Paper, pens or pencils
Time: 30 to 45 minutes

Part I

Background:
- Discuss the fact that more and more men are in the position of secretary or office assistant.

Procedure:
1. Pretend you are a secretary. Think of a name for your boss.
2. With your class, brainstorm the kinds of activities bosses do each day.
3. It is your job to keep your boss' calendar. On a blank calendar page, write your boss' name at the top. For each day of the week, fill in an appointment he/she may have or a meeting he/she will be attending.
4. Be sure to include the time and place of the event.

Process Questions:
1. Why is it important for a secretary to keep an accurate calendar?
2. How do you keep a calendar on a computer?
3. How would a homework calendar help you in school?

Part II

Background:
- Make sure that students understand how voice mail works.

Procedure:
1. You will be answering the phone for your boss. What is important when you answer the phone for someone else?
2. Write out a phone greeting including the boss's name, and your name.
3. Also write out a greeting you would leave on a voice mail if you are away from your desk.
4. Find a partner and practice answering a phone call from a customer.
5. Use good phone manners.

Process Questions:
1. Why is it important for a secretary to answer the telephone in a pleasant, professional tone of voice?
2. Why must a secretary take accurate messages?

Calendar For:
Name_____ Month_____

Sunday	Monday	Tuesday	Wednesday	Thursday	Friday	Saturday

Educational Media Corporation®, Box 21311, Minneapolis, MN 55421-0311

Career Development Activities for the Elementary Grades

Animal Trainer

Animal trainers teach animals to behave in certain ways. A few trainers work for circuses, training elephants, lions, tigers, and horses to perform tricks for the audience. They also work with dolphins and whales in some parts of our country, teaching these animals to perform. Seeing eye dogs used by the blind are taught by animal trainers to lead and to watch for traffic and obstacles blind people cannot see. Still other trainers work with pets, usually dogs, teaching them to mind their owners and follow commands.

Activity 9

Friends and Helpers

Subject Area: Reading, Writing
Materials: Magazines, pictures of animals
Time: 45 to 60 minutes

Part I

Background:

Depending on the abilities of the small groups, you may want to do the brainstorming as a class.

Procedure:

1. Brainstorm with your class the different ways that animals can be trained to help people. Think about other countries where people use animals to help them with work. In some countries where there are deserts, for example, people ride camels. In some jungle areas, elephants are used to lift and haul heavy loads.

2. Cut out pictures of two animals.

3. Choose something you could teach each animal to do that would be helpful to someone. In your description include what the animals are fed and where they sleep.

Process Questions:

1. If you have a pet or would like a pet, what would you train it to do?

2. How have dogs been trained to help handicapped people? Are other animals trained to help handicapped people?

Part II

Background:

To shorten this activity, brainstorm the use of horses throughout the history of America with the entire class. The groups can then use that information to do their timelines.

Procedure:

1. Working in your small group do a time line showing how horses have been trained to serve our country at different points in history.

2. Draw the time line on chart paper beginning with 1492 and ending with the year 2000. The time line should take up the length of the chart paper. Mark years 1500, 1600, 1700, 1800, and 1900, and 2000 on evenly spaced segments of the time line.

3. Draw pictures showing how horses were used at different points in our history. Be sure you draw the pictures at the correct places on the time lines. Make a small mark on the time line and write the date if the horse was used in an event like a war. For example, horses helped people fight battles during our history. If you are drawing a horse in the American Revolution you would put that picture by the part of the time line marked 1700s. You may have to use an encyclopedia or other reference books to check your dates.

4. Post your time line and ask for a volunteer from your group to explain it to the class.

Process Questions:

1. Discuss the saying, "A dog is man's best friend".

2. Animals are not used as workers much today in the United States. What countries still rely on animals for heavy work?

Chapter 1 — Language Arts Activities

TV Repairer

Television repair people fix television sets. They must be familiar with different kinds of television sets and how they work. They use meters and other tools to help them identify the problems. Some television repair people will go to your house to make repairs, and others have shops where you can take a television when it is broken.

Some people think television is a bad influence on young people, but others believe it is educational. We do know that people spend a great deal of time watching television and depend on the repair person to keep their televisions operating.

Activity 10

Tuning In

Subject Area: Reading, Writing
Materials: None
Time: 20 to 30 minutes

Part I

Procedure:

Working on your own, see if you can solve the following problems. You can use the Hint List.

a. Usually your television gets 40 different channels. Today you can only get 3. What do you think might be wrong? _____

b. You get a clear picture on the TV but no sound. What might be wrong? _____

c. When you turn on the television, nothing happens. What might be wrong? _____

d. The remote control will not do anything. You have to use the buttons on the TV set to change the volume or channel. What might be wrong? _____

e. You are allowed to watch television from 7:00 to 8:00 every night. One night there are several specials on and you can't find a program you like. What do you do? _____

Answers, Part I:
  a. cable is out
  b. volume control is turned down
  c. TV may be unplugged
  d. remote has batteries that may need replacing
  e. see process questions

Hint List—
- check the plug
- check the batteries in the remote control
- check the volume control
- check to see if the cable is working

Process Questions:

1. What else do you like to do besides watch television?

2. What special skills does a TV repairer need to do their job?

Part II

Background:

Extend this activity by discussing how television has changed the way people live.

Procedure:

1. Imagine that an electrical storm blew out all the televisions in your neighborhood. Only one TV repairer is available to fix all the televisions. The neighbors must decide whose TV gets fixed first and everyone must find other things to do while their televisions are broken.

2. Write a short story that explains why you need to have your TV fixed first. Your arguments must be convincing.

3. Share your story with the class and discuss the many different reasons that were given.

Process Questions:

1. How much television do you watch in one day? What type of programs do you watch?

2. Have you had a television repairer come to your house? Explain.

Educational Media Corporation®, Box 21311, Minneapolis, MN 55421-0311   25

Career Development Activities for the Elementary Grades

Automobile Assembler

Automobile assemblers work in large manufacturing plants that make cars. They are part of a team of people who install the engines, seats, lights, doors and even the windshield wipers of cars. They work on an assembly line. Every assembler depends on the other assemblers to do good jobs on their parts of the car. If one assembler does a poor job, the other assemblers work is affected too. For example, the assembler who installs the license plate holders on the fenders depends on the fender installer to do a good job so that the fender will hold the license plate securely.

Activity 11

Parts of a Puzzle

Subject Area: Reading
Materials: Chart paper, glue, magazines, scissors, small boxes
Time: 30 to 60 minutes

Part I

Background:
You will need a large number of magazines for this to be an interesting and challenging activity.

Procedure:
1. Using magazines, cut out pictures of cars.
2. Cut the cars into separate parts, for example, cut off the wheels, then the hood, doors, fenders, windshields and car bodies.
3. Place the parts in the boxes at the front of the room matched with the name of the part.
4. After everyone has placed their parts in boxes, take parts out of each box to remake a car.
5. Lay out your new parts on a piece of paper.
6. Look around at other students' cars. How do they look?

Process Questions:
1. What other parts of the car have to be assembled in addition to the car body?
2. How is assembling an automobile like putting a puzzle together?

Part II

Background:
You can enhance this activity by visiting the school parking lot and looking at a car inside and out. Have your students see how many different parts they can identify.

Process:
1. From the car parts cut out in Part I, begin to assemble a car that looks correct.
2. You may have to spread the parts out on a table, or trade with another student to find the parts that fit well together.
3. After you have assembled an attractive car, glue it on your paper.
4. Display your car to the class.

Process Questions:
1. What would happen if the automobile assembler got the parts from two different kinds of car mixed up?
2. What would happen if one member of the assembly line team failed to show up for work?

Chapter I

Stagehand

Stagehands work in theaters. They move the scenery that surrounds the stage and the props like furniture and plants, set up lights and assist in whatever ways are necessary to prepare the theater for a performance. During the performance, stagehands stand by to change scenery and props between acts or at intermission. In small theaters, stagehands may also build and paint the scenery, help with costumes or take tickets. Young actors sometimes work as stagehands in hopes of getting opportunities to act in the theater.

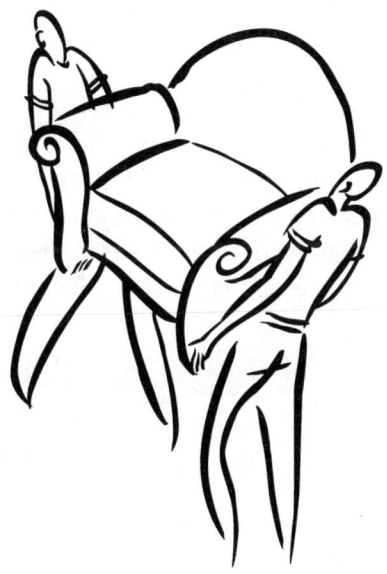

Activity 12

On Stage

Subject Area: Reading, Art
Materials: Art materials, books of plays
Time: 60 minutes

Part I

Background:
- To enhance this activity you may wish to show a video of a play, or explore a theater with the class.
- This activity is a good lead-in to reading plays and looking at drama as a form of communication.

Procedure:
1. Think of a story you read this year and really enjoyed. What were the different settings (where the story takes place) in the story? In the story of Goldilocks and the Three Bears, for example, the settings are the forest and the Bears house. In each setting there are props. In the bears' house there would be bowls of porridge, beds and chairs.
2. List the props from one setting in the story you chose.
3. Draw a picture of the scene placing the props as if on a stage.
4. Share your pictures with the class.

Process Questions:
1. Why are props important to a play?
2. What would have happened if the stagehands forgot to put out the bowls of porridge?

Part II

Background:
You may choose to use one play and have all the groups draw the props.

Procedure:
1. Visit the library with your small group, and choose a play for the group to read.
2. In your small group, take turns reading the play aloud.
3. Identify the settings (where the play takes place) in the play.
4. Identify all the props that would be needed for this play.
5. On different pieces of paper draw all the props that would be used in each scene.
6. Share your pictures with the other groups.

Process Questions:
1. Discuss what would happen if props broke or fell down in the middle of a play? What could the stagehand do?
2. Have you had a funny experience with props or scenery during a play? Relate it to the group.

Career Development Activities for the Elementary Grades

Maintenance Mechanic

Maintenance mechanics repair machines that are broken or not working properly. Many maintenance mechanics work in factories, repairing the large machines used to make products. Some maintenance mechanics work in hospitals or other places where people depend on small machines to help them with their work. The mechanics have to figure out why machines are not working before they can fix them.

Activity 13

Mr. Fix-it

Subject Area: Reading
Materials: Handout, pens or pencils
Time: 45 minutes

Part I

Background:
- If your students are keeping portfolios or journals, they can write the answers to the questions rather than answering them orally.
- If you have access to tools, you may want to bring some in for the students to handle.

Procedure:
1. Some of the tools the maintenance mechanic uses to repair machines are listed on the handout. See how many you can find and circle them.
2. Answer the following questions with your class.

   How many maintenance mechanics' tools did you find in the list?

   How does the maintenance mechanic use each of those tools?

   What other careers are represented by the tools on this list?

   Name any tools that are used in more than one job.

Process Questions:
1. Why is it important for maintenance mechanics to keep their tools in good repair?
2. Why is it equally important for families to keep home tools in good repair?

Part II

Procedure:
1. Working on your own, solve the mechanical mysteries.
2. When you think you have solved the mysteries, write your solutions.
3. In your small group, share your solutions to the mysteries. Did anyone have a different solution to the problem?

Answers to the mysteries:
1. Susan will have to use the 1 1/4" screw to repair the machine. A 1/2" long screw would not be long enough to hold two parts together that had been held previously by a 1" long screw.
2. A fan blade is probably hitting the table and making the thunking sound. When Mike picks up the machine, the fan is no longer hitting the table and the thunking stops.
3. The cleaning crew unplugged the copy machine so that they could plug in the vacuum.
4. The light bulbs may have been loosened during the truck ride. They need tightening.

Process Questions:
1. Discuss some ways that the job of maintenance mechanic is like that of a detective.
2. Why is patience a characteristic that is needed to be an effective maintenance mechanic?

Miriam McLaughlin and Sandra Peyser

Chapter I

Language Arts Activities

Handout—Activity 13

Mr Fix-it

Part I

1. Some of the tools the maintenance mechanic uses to repair machines are listed below. See how many you can find and circle them.

lawn mower	electric knife
monkey wrench	thermometer
hedge clipper	mixer
pliers	sander
stethoscope	spatula
shovel	pizza cutter
screw driver	weed whacker
pot holder	syringe
food processor	scale
rake	drill
wire cutters	measuring cup
microscope	hoe
spoon	flashlight
blood pressure cuff	bulldozer
crow bar	

2. Answer the following questions:

   How many maintenance mechanics tools did you find in the list?

   How does the maintenance mechanic use each of those tools?

   What other careers are represented by the tools on this list?

   Name any tools that are used in more than one job.

Part II

Solve the following mechanical mysteries on your own and write you answers on a separate sheet of paper.

Susan was checking a machine that had stopped working. She discovered that a 1" long screw was missing from the machine. Susan did not have any 1" long screws. She had a 1/2" long screw and a 1 1/4" long screw. The screw is supposed to go through two metal parts and hold them together. Which screw can she use to hold the parts together until she can get the right one?

Mike was looking at a small machine sitting on a table. It was making a thunking sound every few seconds. The front of the machine had a switch and two large lights. The back of the machine was covered with a fanlike device that had three blades that constantly turned. When Mike picked up the machine, the thunking stopped. What may be the cause of the thunking noise?

Jennifer's copy machine was working fine on Monday. When she came in on Tuesday and turned it on, nothing happened. The only people who had been in her office after work had been the cleaning crew. What may be wrong with Jennifer's copy machine?

Brett was a maintenance mechanic for a large poultry production company. They had purchased a machine for checking eggs. The top of the machine had strong light bulbs and automatically lifted trays of eggs to the lights so that workers could check them. A truck delivered the machine ready to go. All the workers had to do was start it up. When the motor started, the trays moved, but the lights did not go on. Can you guess what might have happened to the machine during the truck ride?

Clergy

Clergy are leaders and teachers of religion. They study their religion, talk to and teach others about it, and are the leaders of the worship and rituals of the religion. Clergy are usually the head of a group of people who practice their religion. They offer support and comfort to these people as well as leadership.

Activity 14

I Do

Subject Area: *Reading, Social Studies*
Materials: *Paper, pens or pencils*
Time: *30 to 45 minutes*

Part I

Background:
- This activity offers a wonderful opportunity to examine the topic of diversity.
- You can enhance this activity by listing questions students have about different rituals and having them research the answers.

Procedure:
1. Rituals are an important part of our lives. They are ceremonies we perform that help to renew our beliefs and to share them with others. Some of these ceremonies are religious and some are not.

2. With your small group, make a list of rituals we perform in this county, both religious and non religious. Because each member of your group is from a different family and may be of a different religion, the members' ideas about rituals will be different. Be sure to put all ideas on the list.

3. Discuss with your group which ceremonies are religious and which are not. Put one check mark beside those rituals that are sometimes religious, two check marks beside those ceremonies that are always religious and no checkmarks beside those that are never religious. **For example:** beside wedding ceremony you would put one check mark because sometimes people get married in a religious ceremony and sometimes they do not.

4. Taking turns with other group members, choose one of the rituals on the list that you know about. It may be an experience you have had with that ritual or something you have seen. Explain the ritual to the rest of the group, telling why the ritual is performed and what happens. If it is a religious ritual, explain how the clergy is involved.

5. Choose a reporter from your group to tell the rest of the class what rituals your group discussed.

6. Volunteer to share with the class anything new you learned about a ritual.

7. Families have rituals too. Some families do the same activity on every holiday. Others may celebrate the last day of school with ice cream, or always have pancakes on Sunday morning. Think of a ritual your family has and write a short paragraph describing it.

Process Questions:
1. Discuss particular rituals in your family. How are they alike or different from other class members?
2. Why is it important to honor and respect different rituals?

Chapter I

Part II

Background:
- Invite members or clergy of different religions to serve on a panel to answer student questions.
- Enhance this activity by making the symbols or drawing them.

Procedure:
1. Symbols are a part of many religions and rituals. They are used to remind us of an event or to represent something to us.
2. Read the list of symbols below.
3. Write beside each symbol, what it represents and the event or holiday with which it is usually associated. Look up the symbols that are not familiar to you.

    A. Costumes _____
    B. Flying the flag at half mast _____
    C. Cap and Gown _____
    D. Rings _____
    E. Turkey _____
    F. Black clothing _____
    G. Heart _____
    H. Shamrock _____
    I. Cake with candles _____

4. Take turns in your small group sharing what you learned.
5. With your small group, make a list of religious symbols. You may need to research the religions you don't know about.
6. Write the meaning of the religious symbols and the religious ritual associated with it beside it on the list.
7. Share your list with the class.

Process Questions:
1. Discuss the idea that countries go to war, even today, over religious differences.
2. Name some ways students can begin to change the stereotypical ideas that people have of each other.

Answers to the symbols:
A. Halloween
B. Death
C. Graduation
D. Marriage
E. Thanksgiving
F. Funeral
G. Valentine's Day
H. St. Patrick's Day
I. Birthday

Career Development Activities for the Elementary Grades

Child Care Worker

Child care workers take care of young children in day care centers and nursery schools. They watch after the children to be sure they are safe and keep them clean and fed. Some of the workers teach children skills like tying their shoes or buttoning their clothing. They often play simple games or do activities to entertain the children.

Activity 15

Playtime

Subject Area: Writing, Art
Materials: Paper plates, scraps for decoration
Time: Two 45 minute periods

Part I

Background:

Encourage children to be creative and brief. Small children do not have long attention spans.

Procedure:

1. Working on your own, fill in the games on the worksheet.
2. Share what you wrote about your game with the class.
3. With your class choose a game that a student shared to play at recess. The game you choose should be easy to learn and need very little special equipment.

Process Questions:

1. Why do small children change activities so often?
2. Why do you need to go slowly when trying to teach small children a new activity?

Part II

Background:

- If you have a pre-K or kindergarten class at your school, arrange for your students to present their puppet shows to them.
- This may also be a good activity to perform on parent or family night.

Procedure:

1. With your class, talk about the kinds of things small children need to know. Perhaps there are things you remember your mother teaching you. For example: you may have been taught not to talk to strangers or to share your toys with your friends.
2. Working with your small group, write a short play or song that teaches one of the ideas you thought of with your class. You will be making puppets to perform your play or song. Decide in your group which part each person's puppet will play. Everyone should have a part.
3. Make your puppet according to the directions below.
   a. Staple the edges of two paper plates together, rounded sides of the plates out. There will be a hollow pocket between the plates.
   b. Cut away the lower edge of one plate, making an opening large enough to slide your hand through. The plate will be worn like a mitten on your hand.
   c. On the back of the plate that is not cut, draw a face. Color the face and add yarn, scraps of paper, or other materials to represent hair, nose, eyes, etc. If you drew an animal face you can use a small cup for a nose and yarn or pipe cleaners for whiskers.
   d. Practice your play or song two or three times.
   e. Perform with your puppets for an audience of families or small children.

Process Questions:

1. What do child care workers need to know about young children in order to work at a day care center?
2. Discuss any memories you have of being in a day care situation.

Miriam McLaughlin and Sandra Peyser

Chapter I Language Arts Activities

Worksheet—Activity 15

Playtime

1. Name an indoor or outdoor game you like to play _____
   _____ .

2. Think of three pieces of information you need to know to play the game. For example: if you chose baseball you would need to know how to hold a bat, catch a ball and throw a ball. _____

   _____

   _____

   _____

3. List the equipment you need to play the game. For example: do you need a game board, cards, a bat?

   _____

   _____

   _____

4. If you were a child care worker, would you be able to teach this game to very young children? _____

   _____

   Why or why not? _____

   _____

   _____

   _____

Educational Media Corporation®, Box 21311, Minneapolis, MN 55421-0311

Career Development Activities for the Elementary Grades

Motorcycle Repairer

Motorcycle repairers fix motorcycles. They have to understand how motorcycle engines work and what each part of the motorcycle does. If the motorcycle won't start, for example, the repairer must know what parts start the engine. Motorcycle repairers are often people who enjoy riding motorcycles themselves.

Activity 16

Zoom!

Subject Area: Reading, Writing
Materials: None
Time: 30 to 45 minutes

Part I

Background:
- Ask each group to report on their ideas about what could go wrong and what might be done to fix it in the following manner:

    Group #1 reports on a hand drawn cart

    Group #2 reports on the horse

    Group #3 reports on the bicycle and so forth.

- List all ideas on the board and ask the other groups if they have anything to add to the lists.
- Continue in this manner through the entire list of modes of transportation. This reporting activity saves time and avoids repetition.

Procedure:
1. Working with your small group, read the list below. Decide what kinds of repairs would be necessary to keep each kind of transportation working.

    hand drawn cart
    horse
    bicycle
    sailboat
    glider
    steam locomotive
    motorcycle

2. Decide with your group what makes each form of transportation move and what could go wrong that would keep it from moving the way it is supposed to. (Remember, something does not have to stop working completely to be broken.) Discuss what a repair person might do to fix the problem.

3. Following your teacher's instructions, share your group's ideas with the class.

Process Questions:
1. What jobs use a motorcycle as a mode of transportation?
2. What are two safety rules pertaining to motorcycles?

Part II

Background:
- Invite your students to TELL the stories they have written to the class.

Procedure:
1. Think of a time when you were riding on some form of transportation and it broke down. Write a short story, telling about your experience. If that has never happened to you, write about another person's experience or about what you imagine might happen. Be sure to answer these questions in your story.

    What happened?

    What did you do?

    If a repair person came to fix the problem, what did they do?

    How did your experience end? Were you able to continue on your way or find some other means of transportation?

Process Questions:
1. What other repair people are important in our lives?
2. What would happen to our transportation systems if all the repair people called in sick?

Chapter 1

Actor

Actors perform in plays, movies and on television. They make stories came to life with their words and actions. Actors are able to convey the thoughts and feelings of the characters they play through the way they say their parts and their facial expressions and body movements. A few actors are paid very well for their work, but many others have to do other work to support themselves between acting jobs.

Activity 17

On With the Show

Subject Area: *Reading*
Materials: *Short plays and stories*
Time: *Several 30 to 45 minute periods*

Part I

Background:
- You may wish to choose the readings and assign them to the students.
- Remind your students to show respect for the performers by paying attention and not laughing inappropriately.

Procedure:
1. Working with a partner, choose a nursery rhyme or short fairy tale to read aloud.
2. Decide what parts each of you will read.
3. Read through your nursery rhyme or fairy tale, with your partner and decide what feelings the characters experience in the story and how they act towards each other. For example, if you read Little Red Riding Hood, one feeling Little Red Riding Hood probably experiences is fear when she meets the wolf. Also, the wolf would probably act fierce or mean towards Little Red Riding Hood.
4. With your partner, practice reading your parts in ways that show the feelings and actions of the characters.
5. Take turns with the other student partners performing your nursery rhyme or fairy tale for the class.
6. Applaud all efforts.

Language Arts Activities

Process Questions:
1. How did you feel having to perform in front of your class?
2. What other situations have you been in that are like this one?

Part II

Background:
- You may want to select the plays for the students and assign them to small groups.
- Observe each small group during their rehearsals. Suggest ways for them to improve their performances.
- During the performances, stand to the side and cue students who forget their lines.
- You may want to invite parents to see the students perform.

Procedure:
1. Working with your small group, choose a short play that has enough parts for each group member to participate.
2. Rehearse the play with your group. Read through the play two-three times, with each group member saying their lines. Discuss the different parts as a group, deciding how different characters are feeling and how they should act. Read through the play again, this time using the tones of voice and facial expressions to convey the feelings of the characters. Begin memorizing your part as you do the readings. Find a place where you can practice your play as if you were on a stage. Rehearse the play including the movements of the different characters. Continue to rehearse and to memorize your part.
3. Take turns with the other groups performing your play.
4. Applaud all efforts.

Process Questions:
1. During a play, what do actors do if they forget their lines?
2. What can you do in the middle of a play if a prop you need is missing?

Career Development Activities for the Elementary Grades

Seismologist

Seismologists study the movement of the earth's crust. They use machines that are able to find cracks in the earth which might lead to earthquakes. The machines bounce sound waves off rocks in the earth to locate the cracks. Seismologists are able to predict where earthquakes are most likely to occur and how serious they will be. Seismologists also provide us with information after an earthquake has occurred.

Activity 18

Move the Dishes

Subject Area: Reading, Writing
Materials: Paper, pens or pencils
Time: 45 to 60 minutes

Part I

Background:
- Explain to your students that a natural disaster is one that occurs in nature and over which human beings have no control.
- Read an account of an earthquake that has occurred in the world in recent years aloud to the class. If you have access to pictures, show them to students. Discuss what happens to everyday life after an earthquake has occurred.
- If you are in an area where there are earthquakes, review the safety precautions with students.

Procedure:
1. Find a book or article to read that explains what happens during an earthquake.
2. Draw a picture that shows what happens during an earthquake.
3. Share with your class any experience you have had in an earthquake or have read about.

Process Questions:
1. What other natural disasters occur in the world?
2. How is a hurricane different from an earthquake?

Part II

Background:
- This activity can be enhanced by providing students with books on home construction so that they can become familiar with the materials and techniques used to build houses.

Procedure:
1. *Using information gained in Part I, design a house that would be resistant to an earthquake. Do a line drawing, using a ruler to make sure the walls, doors and windows are symmetrical.*
2. *In your design, include the material the walls are made from or reinforced with; the way you will reduce the problems of flying and falling furniture, dishes and other objects, breaking glass; and any procedures a family living in the house should follow to protect themselves.*
3. *Share your design with your class, explain the special features that will help to protect anyone living in the house.*

Process Questions:
1. Where is the safest place to be in a natural disaster?
2. How do people usually react after a natural disaster?

---

36   Miriam McLaughlin and Sandra Peyser

Chapter 1   Language Arts Activities

Electrical Engineer

Electrical engineers design, test and oversee the manufacture of every kind of electronic device. Some electrical engineers may work on electronic equipment like computers and others may design and test the electrical wiring for buildings. The design of the electrical appliances, televisions, VCRs, tape and CD players, and electric lights all involve the expertise of electrical engineers.

Activity 19

Lights Out

Subject Area: Reading, Writing
Materials: Paper, pens or pencils
Time: 45 to 60 minutes

Part I

Background:
- You may wish to send a note home asking for parent's participation in this activity.

Procedure:
1. Make a survey of your home. Write down everything in your house that operates on electricity. Put electric lights down as one item.
2. Ask your family to assist you with the following experiment.

    Look at your family's most recent electric bill. Look at the dates that tell when each billing period begins and ends.

    Ask your family if you all can agree to stop using or cut back on using one or more of the electrical appliances in your home for one month, beginning on the date when the next electric bill starts. Be sure the whole family agrees which appliances to stop or cut back on using before starting this experiment.

3. At the end of the billing period compare the electric bills. Did your family save money? Was it difficult to give up some electric appliances?
4. Work in your small groups, using the lists you made at the beginning of this activity. Share with your group what your family gave up. Decide what other appliances on your list may not be necessary.
5. Report your group's findings to the class.

Process Questions:
1. Think of ways that electricity personally affects your life.
2. Talk about times that the electricity has gone off for an extended period of time. What did you do?

Part II

Background:
- Provide students with opportunities to visit the media center in order to do research on this report.
- This activity is just one component of a study of the effects of electricity on life in America.

Procedure:
1. Choose four electric appliances your family uses. They can be small appliances like hair dryers and vacuum cleaners or large appliances like refrigerators or washing machines.
2. Write a report on how each of these appliances has changed family life over the last one hundred years. The report should contain at least four paragraphs. Be sure to include the following information in your report:

    How has the appliance affected leisure time?

    How has the appliance changed people's expectations of how people should look or how their homes should appear?

    How has the appliance changed people's behavior, habits or customs?

    In what other way has the appliance affected the way people live?

    Note: You may have to research information on how people functioned before the electric appliance was invented.

Process Questions:
1. Name some fun activities that do not rely on electricity.
2. How did the pioneers do their everyday chores without electricity?

Educational Media Corporation®, Box 21311, Minneapolis, MN 55421-0311   37

Career Development Activities for the Elementary Grades

Aerospace Engineer

Aerospace engineers design spaceships, planes, rockets, missiles, and helicopters. They use math and science skills along with their computers, to make their designs. Aerospace engineers have designed better and faster airplanes that take people all over the world and spacecraft that can travel long distances and hold large numbers of people. They have helped Americans become leaders in space exploration and in air transportation.

Activity 20

Up, Up and Away

Subject Area: Reading, Writing
Materials: Paper, pens or pencils
Time: 45 to 60 minutes

Part I

Background:
- Remind your students that if their family chose to take a vacation on the planet, it should be a friendly place.
- Encourage them to include what they know about space travel in the story.

Procedure:
1. Imagine that your family took a vacation trip to another planet.
2. Write a story describing your vacation. Include the following information:

    Which planet did you visit?

    How did you get there?

    What were the inhabitants of the planet like?

    Where did you stay?

    What did you do there? What sights did you see?

    What did you eat?

    How did you get around?

3. Read your story aloud to your class.

Process Questions:
1. Name some of the early attempts at space travel.
2. Why do you think that most people are fascinated by the thought of space travel.

Part II

Background:
- Encourage your students to review what they know about travel in space before beginning their designs. You may want to do this review in the form of a class discussion.
- They can put their stories and designs in a book about vacations in outer space, or display them on a wall outside the classroom.

Procedure:
1. After completing the activity in Part I, design the spaceship your family traveled in to get to the planet they visited. The space ship can be a personal one, like the family car, or one that carries large numbers of people like a cruise ship. The design should be very detailed, showing where the family slept and ate and any special equipment on the space ship.
2. The design should take into account the things you know about space travel; the lack of gravity for example.
3. Share your design with the class.

Process Questions:
1. What breakthrough happened in 1969? (moon landing)
2. What was said when man stood on the moon for the first time that is still quoted today? (one small step for man, one giant step for mankind).

Miriam McLaughlin and Sandra Peyser

Chapter I

Crane Operator

Crane operators operate large pieces of machinery designed to lift and move heavy objects. Most crane operators work at construction sites moving the huge steel beams used in buildings. Cranes are used outdoors and have driver's seats that are covered over to protect the operators from the weather.

Activity 21

On the Job

Subject Area: *Reading*
Materials: *Worksheet*
Time: *30 to 45 minutes*

Part I

Background:
- This activity is designed for a class discussion. To keep students focused, you may want to record their ideas on the board. Encourage students to identify the different choices they have in each situation before making their decisions.
- Enhance this activity by asking students to identify the consequences of each choice.

Procedure:
1. With your class, discuss how you would handle the following job problems.

   You work every day from 6:00 a.m. to 1:00 p.m. The crane operator who is supposed to take over for you at 1:00 never shows up on time. Yesterday she was one hour late. What should you do?

   Your boss gives you instructions that you are not sure you understand. What should you do?

   Your alarm didn't go off and you are going to be late for work. What should you do?

   When you receive your paycheck it is short $15.00. What should you do?

   When you receive your paycheck, you notice that it is $20.00 more than it should be. What should you do?

Process Questions:
1. Have you ever received too much change in a store? What did you do?
2. Why do people not always do the "right" thing?

Part II

Background:
- Use this activity to explore the characteristics of a good worker.
- Responsibility is a major theme of this activity. You can expand on this theme by talking about what responsible behavior is for students.
- The situations described on the work sheet may have more than one acceptable answer.

Procedure:
1. Working with your small group, discuss each of the situations described on the work sheet and the consequence of each choice. Decide on the best action. Record your answers on the work sheet.
2. With your group, share your choices with the class.

Process Questions:
1. Share experiences that you have had that are similar to that of the crane operator.
2. Why is there not always one right answer to these situations?

Career Development Activities for the Elementary Grades

Worksheet—Activity 21

On the Job

You work as the only crane operator on a big construction job. One morning you wake up with the flu.

A. You go to work sick.
   Consequence _____

B. You forget about work and go back to sleep.
   Consequence _____

C. You call the boss and tell him you have the flu and won't be in.
   Consequence _____

Best choice _____
Why? _____

While you are working, an old friend spots you on the crane and comes over to talk.

A. You stop work and visit with your friend for awhile.
   Consequence _____

B. You make a date to meet your friend after work.
   Consequence _____

C. You ignore your friend and keep working.
   Consequence _____

Best choice _____
Why? _____

The beam you are supposed to move for the new building is the wrong size.

A. You talk to your supervisor and ask what you should do.
   Consequence _____

B. You stop working and wait for someone to tell you what to do.
   Consequence _____

C. You yell at the person who delivered the beam.
   Consequence _____

Best choice _____
Why? _____

Wearing a safety helmet is a strict rule on the construction job. It is very dangerous to be on the site without a helmet and you see a co-worker walking around without one.

A. You ignore the problem because it is none of your business.
   Consequence _____

B. You tell the boss about the co-worker.
   Consequence _____

C. You speak to the co-worker.
   Consequence _____

Best choice _____
Why? _____

Your boss asks you to work late. You have a family birthday party to attend.

A. You agree to work late, but walk away angry.
   Consequence _____

B. You talk to the boss and explain about the birthday party.
   Consequence _____

C. You call your family and tell them you will be late.
   Consequence _____

Best choice _____
Why? _____

Miriam McLaughlin and Sandra Peyser

Chapter I Language Arts Activities

Janitor

Janitors clean buildings. Some janitors also make repairs and paint when necessary. They work in hospitals, schools, offices, apartment complexes and other places that house large groups of people. Janitors are often called on in emergencies, to clean up spills and breakage that might cause injuries. They keep our buildings attractive, healthy, and safe.

Activity 22

Clean as a Whistle

Subject Area: Reading, Writing
Materials: None
Time: 45 to 60 minutes

Part I

Background:
- You may have to help students to identify the less obvious tools.
- You may have each student write a thank you note and put these in a book or combine the ideas into one letter.

Procedure:
1. Working with your small group, make a list of the ways janitors help keep our schools safe, for example they mop up spilled water or paint.
2. Then make a second list of the ways janitors keep our schools clean and attractive, for example they wax the floors.
3. Have one person from each group read the lists aloud and cross off the ones that are repeated.
4. Using the lists, write a thank you note to the school janitor for doing so many nice jobs for the school.

Process Questions:
1. Why is the job of janitor so important to a school?
2. Who would do the work if there were no janitor?

Part II

Background:
- Students may have to use the library for this activity, or interview the school's janitor.

Procedure:
1. Using the lists from Part I, brainstorm with your class the tools and supplies that a janitor needs in order to keep a school clean and safe.
2. Find or draw pictures of these tools and supplies. Make a collage.
3. Display your collage in the classroom.

Process Questions:
1. What other jobs may use these same tools?
2. What are some ways that a janitor takes care of these tools?

Educational Media Corporation®, Box 21311, Minneapolis, MN 55421-0311

Career Development Activities for the Elementary Grades

Hospital Administrator

Hospital administrators manage hospitals. They make sure that hospitals run smoothly and that the needs of the people who come to the hospitals for help are met. Doctors, nursing staff, pharmacists, food service people, and cleaning and repair people all come under the supervision of hospital administrators. Hospital administrators are also responsible for the hospital's budget.

Activity 23

Decisions, Decisions, Decisions

Subject Area: Reading
Materials: Paper, pens or pencils
Time: 30 to 45 minutes

Part I

Background:
- During the sharing part of this activity, you may want to write on the board the steps students take during the decision making process. There should be similarities among the answers.
- Enhance this activity by talking about the decisions students will be making when they are teenagers, young adults and parents.

Procedure:
1. Answer the questions on the worksheet about making decisions.
2. Share your answers with your class.

Process Questions:
1. What are some of the most important decisions you have to make at this stage of your life? Include family, friends, pets, and so forth..
2. What was one of the hardest decisions you ever had to make?

Part II

Background:
- During the sharing part of this activity, ask students which professional must make the most difficult decisions and why.
- Ask your students what might happen if an automobile mechanic makes the wrong decision? What might happen if a pilot makes the wrong decision?
- Enhance this activity by having them write a brief profile of a profession and the role of decision-making in the profession.

Procedure:
1. Decision making is important in every job. Think of two decisions people make for each one of these jobs?

   Example: A teacher must decide on books the class will read during the year and how to help a student who is having difficulty.

   Doctor

   Park ranger

   Automobile mechanic

2. Share your answers with the class.

Process Questions:
1. In today's society, what are some difficult decisions facing teenagers?
2. To whom can teenagers turn to help make these decisions?

Chapter 1 — Language Arts Activities

Handout—Activity 23

Decisions, Decisions, Decisions

Part I

Answer the following questions about making decisions.

a. Do you decide what you will wear to school? _____

Name two considerations you should think about before making that decision.
_____
_____

b. Do you help decide what your family will do on the weekend?

Name two things everyone in the family should think about before deciding what to do. _____
_____
_____

c. Do you decide when to do your homework

Name two ideas that you should think about before making that decision. _____
_____
_____

Hospital administrators have to make sure the hospital has the medical supplies needed to take care of the patients. They must decide how much money from the budget to allot for supplies.

d. Name two considerations the hospital administrator thinks about when making these decisions. _____
_____
_____

Part II

Decision making is important in every job. Can you think of two decisions people make for each one of these jobs?

Example: *A teacher must decide on books the class will read during the year and how to help a student who is having difficulty.*

1. A doctor must decide

   a. _____

   b. _____

2. A park ranger must decide

   a. _____

   b. _____

3. An automobile mechanic must decide

   a. _____

   b. _____

Educational Media Corporation®, Box 21311, Minneapolis, MN 55421-0311

Career Development Activities for the Elementary Grades

Service Station Attendant

Service station attendants pump gas, check the oil and clean the windows of their customers' cars. They also check the air in the tires and the water level in the radiator. Many service station attendants operate cash registers and sell cold drinks and snacks.

Activity 24

Out of Gas

Subject Area: Writing
Materials: Check sheet
Time: 30 to 45 minutes

Part I

Background:
- You may want to brainstorm with the class a list of cars.

Procedure:
1. Choose a partner. Role play the gas station attendant and a car owner. The owner drives his car to the station to be serviced. The gas station attendant uses the sheet below to see what work needs to be done on the car.
2. Reverse roles and do the same role play again. The new attendant will be filling out the sheet, but for a different car.

Process Questions:
1. How are self-service gas stations different from full service gas stations?
2. How has self-service affected the jobs of gas station attendants?

Part II

Background:
1. Ask your students what is important to include in an adventure story.
2. Read the story lines to the students aloud and with feeling.
3. Ask your students if there were similarities in the stories that were read aloud.

Procedure:
1. Choose one of the story starters below. Write an adventure story of what happened next.

   I was just opening the Quick Stop Gas Station after a long weekend when a sleek new Rolls Royce pulled in. It looked fit for royalty. When I approached the car....

   An old station wagon pulled up to the gas pumps. I walked around to the drivers side of the car, and said "Can I help you?" The driver turned to look at me. I couldn't believe my eyes. The driver was....

   A caravan of 10 great big trucks pulled to the side of the road near my gas station. The drivers all got out and walked over to buy drinks from my machine. "What's in the trucks?" I asked.

   " I'll show you," said one of the drivers. We walked to his truck and he opened the huge back doors. I saw....

Process Questions:
1. What other services do gas station attendants provide to customers besides working on their cars?
2. Why is the job of gas station attendant sometimes dangerous?

Chapter I   **Language Arts Activities**

Handout—Activity 24

Automobile Check Sheet

Customer's Name _____ Date _____

Make of Car _____ Year _____

Check if service needed:

____ radiator

____ tires

____ engine

____ belts

____ fan belt

Check if needed

____ gas

____ oil

____ power steering fluid

____ antifreeze

Career Development Activities for the Elementary Grades

Electrician

Electricians install the wires that carry electricity into new homes. They also repair the wires, and the appliances and other equipment run by electricity. Electricians must know how to make electrical outlets safe for people to use. They must be able to respond in emergencies to restore electricity to homes and buildings. Our society is very dependent on the electrician's skills to keep lights on, machines working and transportation operating.

Activity 25

Lights On!

Subject Area: Reading
Materials: Poster paper, magazines
Time: Two 45 minute periods

Part I

Background:
- Student's collages should be displayed and viewed by other students.

Procedure:
1. Cut at least twenty pictures from magazines of things that use electricity.
2. Write the title "Home" on the top of one piece of construction paper, the title "School" on another piece and the title "Hospital" on a third piece of paper.
3. Choose pictures of things used in the home and glue them in a collage, on the paper titled "Home".
4. Make collages on the papers titled "School" and "Hospital" as well.
5. Display your collages on the walls of the room.

Process Questions:
1. What are some of the most common electrical items in the collages?
2. Do schools, hospitals and homes use similar electrical items?

Part II

Background:
- Invite a spokesperson from your local power company to the school to answer students questions. They will get the most thorough and accurate information in this manner.

Procedure:
1. With your class, research the source of electricity in your community. Your teacher may have to call a local power company to get this information.
2. Find out where the power source is located and how the electricity travels from the power source to homes and other buildings.
3. Working on your own, draw a map showing the route the electricity might take to get to your school.

Process Questions:
1. Have you ever lost electricity at your house? Under what circumstances?
2. What was it like at home without electricity?

Chapter 1 Language Arts Activities

Veterinarian

Veterinarians are doctors for animals. They treat animals for illness and also give shots and treatments the animals need to stay well. Some veterinarians work only with small animals like dogs and cats. They usually have hospitals as part of their offices where they operate on the animals when it is necessary. There are also veterinarians that treat only large animals like horses and cows. They often travel to the farms and stables where the animals live to treat them. Large animals are only transported to the veterinarian when they have serious problems that must be treated with special equipment.

Activity 26

Going to the Dogs

Subject Area: Reading
Materials: None
Time: 20 to 30 minutes

Part I

Background:

1. You may want students to make a chart, noting the treatments given to each animal.

    Fluffy—1/2 small tablet

    Buster—1 large tablet

    King—1 1/2 large tablets

    Lucie—1 small tablet

    Bozo—2 small tablets

    Chester—3 1/2 small tablets

2. To enhance this activity, have students draw a dog and label its body parts.

3. Invite a veterinarian to bring a dog to the class to discuss animals and what a veterinarian has to know about dogs.

Procedure:

1. *Veterinarians prescribe medication for dogs that prevents the animals from getting roundworms. Roundworms can make dogs very sick and even kill them, if they are not treated. Veterinarians prescribe the medication according to the weight of the dog. Based on the information below, prescribe the correct amount of medication for each dog.*

    Worming Medication

    One small tablet for each 10 lbs. of weight

    One large tablet for each 50 lbs. of weight

2. *Prescribe the correct number of tablets for the following animals. You may have to prescribe 1/2 tablets in some cases.*

    Prescription

    Fluffy weighs 5 lbs   _____

    Buster weighs 50 lbs   _____

    King weighs 75 lbs   _____

    Bozo weighs 20 lbs.   _____

    Lucie weighs 11 lbs   _____

    Chester weighs 35 lbs   _____

3. *Both cats and dogs need to be vaccinated to be protected from certain diseases. Veterinarians give the animals their shots at specific times in their lives.*

Educational Media Corporation®, Box 21311, Minneapolis, MN 55421-0311

Career Development Activities for the Elementary Grades

Age	Vaccinations
8 weeks	distemper, hepatitis, kennel cough, parvo-virus, corona virus
12 weeks	distemper, hepatitis, kennel cough, parvo-virus, corona virus
16 weeks	parvo-virus, corona virus, rabies

Every six months: parvo-virus, corona virus, once a year: distemper, hepatitis, kennel cough.

* Fluffy is 3 months old and up to date with all her shots. What shots is she due to receive? _____

* Buster is five years old and is at the veterinarian for his yearly checkup. What shots is he due to receive? _____

* King was a stray dog until a family found and adopted him. The veterinarian thinks King is about two years old. No one knows if he has ever had any of his shots. What do you think the vet will recommend? _____

* Lucie is a new puppy making her eight week visit to the vet. What shots will she receive? _____

* Bozo is 4 months old. What shots will he be due to receive when he visits the vet? _____

* Chester is aged ten. What shots does the vet give Chester when he visits? _____

Process Questions:

1. What experiences have you had taking a pet to the vet?
2. If you do not have a pet, what would be your choice of pet to have?

Answers:

Fluffy receives: distemper, hepatitis, kennel cough, parvo-virus, corona virus.

Buster receives : distemper, hepatitis, kennel cough

Students will use critical thinking skills to decide what shots King should receive. It is likely the vet will start King on a series of shots as if he were a puppy. The vet and the adopted family will decide if the series is necessary.

Lucie will receive her first round of vaccinations for distemper, hepatitis, kennel cough, parvo virus, corona virus.

Bozo will receive parvo virus, corona virus and rabies shots.

Chester will receive distemper, hepatitis, kennel cough.

Miriam McLaughlin and Sandra Peyser

Chapter I

Language Arts Activities

Part II

Procedure:

1. *Veterinarians must know the body parts of the dogs and other animals that are their patients. See if you can fill in the blanks from the sentences about dogs. Use the list below to find the words that fit.*

   __are the name given to the ends of the dog's feet. Dogs walk on their __ which are attached to their __ all of which are part of their legs. The whole lower area of the face is called the __. High on the face is an area called the __. Dogs have __ above their legs just like humans. The back end of the dog is called the__. The top part of the dog's leg, where it is the widest is called the __. The __is between the back and the head.

   * Dogs have thighs at the top of their legs, just like people.
   * Part of the dog's neck and upper back is called the withers.
   * Dogs toes are called digits.
   * Humans sit on their buttocks or bottoms. Dogs sit on their rumps.
   * There is an area just above the dog's eyebrow called the stop.
   * The part of the dog that includes the nose and mouth is called the muzzle.
   * The area around the ankle of a dog is called the carpus and is part of the dog's leg.
   * Dogs walk on paws which are their feet.
   * People and dogs have hips which are above the legs.

2. *Share your answers with the class.*

Process Questions:

1. What are some good ways to care for a dog?
2. Why is equally important to take an animal for a checkup as it is a human?

Answers:

- (Digits) are the names given to the end of the dog's feet.
- Dogs walk on their (paws) which are attached to their (carpus).
- The whole lower part of the face is called a (muzzle).
- High on the face is an area called the (stop).
- Dogs have (hips) above their legs just like humans.
- The back end of a dog is called a (rump).
- The top part of a dog's leg where it is the widest is called the (thigh).
- The (withers) is between the back and the head.

Educational Media Corporation®, Box 21311, Minneapolis, MN 55421-0311

Career Development Activities for the Elementary Grades

Sound Engineer

Sound engineers mix the sounds and music for television, radio, movies and recording studios. They work with highly technical equipment that includes tape tracks, special speakers and electronic devices to add the sound effects we hear when we watch movies. Sound engineers who work with film makers may add the music and sound effects after the movie is complete. They watch the film with the director and script writers to decide what music and sounds to use and where to place them in the movie. Music and sound effects make television and movies more interesting and exciting.

Activity 27

Noisemakers

Subject Area: Reading
Materials: Childrens stories, radio tapes, props
Time: Several 30 minute periods

Part I

Background:
- You can use excerpts from literature, poetry or plays in place of the stories listed in the activity. Make sure that the text you use has action to which sound effects can be applied.
- Stress the importance of using sound effects to make the story more interesting or exciting.

Procedure:
1. Working with your small group, choose a story from the list below to read together.

   Three Little Pigs, Little Red Riding Hood, Goldilocks and the Three Bears, Hansel and Gretel

2. Read through the story with your group. Decide where you could add sound effects to make the story more exciting.

3. Decide what sound effects you will add to the story and then divide the responsibilities for sound effects among group members. For example, if you choose a story about a wolf, one sound effect you may want to use is a growl. In that case, you would decide who in the group will be the growler. One group member will read the story while other group members provide the sound effects. It is important for all group members to participate.

4. Practice your story using sound effects.

5. Perform the story for the class. Applaud all efforts.

Process Questions:
1. Can you name some interesting sound effects you have heard on T.V. or in a movie?
2. How do you think they were made?

Chapter I — Language Arts Activities

Part II

Background:
- To enhance this activity, bring in a tape of an old radio show and have the class listen to the sound effects.
- You may wish to provide some tools or props for making the sounds.
- To be really effective, performing students should be out of sight of the rest of the class.

Procedure:
1. Before television, radio performers read plays aloud and depended on sound effects to suggest action. For example, radio programs about cowboys had the sound of horses hooves, and because cowboys were often outdoors, listeners heard the sounds of wind or storms. When they were indoors, listeners heard doors open and shut, people's footsteps and chairs sliding on the floor. Working with your small group, brainstorm ideas for a short play to read aloud as if you were on the radio. The play should have plenty of action that calls for sound effects. Two or more people should have parts in the play.
2. Write the play. Using a colored pen or pencil, write in the sound effects where they belong. Each group member should have a copy of the play.
3. Decide who will read the parts of the play and who will provide sound effects. Decide how each sound effect will be created. Practice different methods of creating the sounds you want. For example, you may be able to create the sound of someone walking, by taking steps or by slapping hands on a table. Closing a book may sound like closing a door.
4. Practice the play and the sound effects.
5. Stand behind a screen or in the back of the room to perform the play for your class. The audience should listen to the play without being able to see you.

Process Questions:
1. How does a hearing impaired person enjoy a show when they cannot hear the sound effects?
2. How does a sight impaired person depend on the sound and sound effects to enjoy a show?

Career Development Activities for the Elementary Grades

Clothing Salesperson

Clothing salespeople assist their customers in choosing and buying clothes. They make suggestions for gifts, handle returns and exchanges, answer customer's questions and complaints and help them locate the clothing they want. Clothing salespeople record the sales on a computer or cash register and take customers payments. They are also responsible for the shelves and racks of clothing they sell. They must keep the clothing neat and tidy and put out new clothing as it is delivered.

Activity 28

Listen Up

Subject Area: Reading
Materials: Paper, pens and pencils
Time: 20 to 45 minutes

Part I

Background:
- You can enhance this activity by visiting a store in your community that sells clothing, or inviting a clothing salesperson to visit the class.

Procedure:
1. Down one side of a piece of paper list different kinds of clothing.
2. Next to each item on the list, write how many of the item people need. For example, people need more than one pair of socks.
3. Next to that number, write how much each item might cost. (Costs vary, so you can write what you think they may cost).
4. With your class, discuss what items of clothing are most important for people to own. For example, if you live in a cold climate, a coat would be important to own.
5. Discuss where different clothing items can be purchased.

Process Questions:
1. What do you think are the clothing items most often purchased? The ones that are least often purchased?
2. What different types of stores sell clothing?

Chapter I

Part II

Background:
- You may want to have students put price tags on clothing items and then figure the cost of their purchases.

Procedure:
1. Make a list of the clothing you would buy from a clothing salesperson to go on a camping trip.

   _____
   _____
   _____
   _____

2. List the clothing you would buy from a clothing salesperson to go to your sister's graduation.

   _____
   _____
   _____
   _____

3. List the clothing you would buy from a clothing salesperson to attend a friend's birthday party.

   _____
   _____
   _____
   _____

4. Think of an event you would like to attend or a place you would like to go. What would you buy from a clothing salesperson to wear?

   _____
   _____
   _____
   _____

Language Arts Activities

Process Questions:
1. Is some of the clothing you wear to different events the same? Give examples.
2. What are some other places you can get clothing besides a store?

Career Development Activities for the Elementary Grades

Dental Lab Technician

Dental lab technicians make false teeth and caps for people who have lost or damaged their teeth from injury or poor care. They make the teeth by following the prescriptions and molds the dentists send them. Dental lab technicians use porcelain and plastic to make the teeth. They must follow the directions sent by the dentists exactly in order to make teeth that will fit the patients' mouths.

Activity 29

Following Directions

Subject Area: Reading
Materials: Handout
Time: 20 to 30 minutes

Part I

Background:
- The first part of this activity serves to remind students to read directions carefully.
- The second part of this activity should produce a snowman.

Procedure:
1. Prescriptions are like directions that the dental lab technicians must follow very carefully. Read the directions on the handout and follow them carefully.
2. With your class, discuss what happened during this activity. How many class members did not read the directions all the way through before beginning the activity?
3. Read the next set of directions. Follow the directions carefully.

Process Questions:
1. What would happen if the dental lab technician didn't read the prescriptions carefully?
2. Do you know people who have false teeth or bridges? What are some of their experiences?

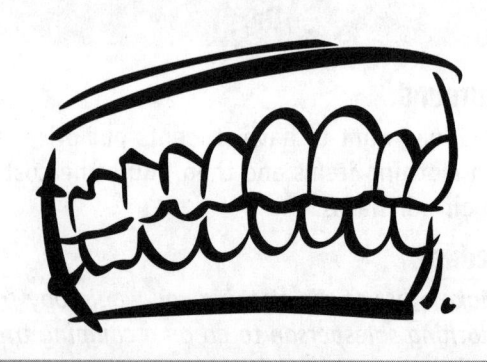

Part II

Background:
- During the discussion, be sure students include recipes, maps, the instructions that come inside and on the packages of different products, traffic signs and signals, clothing labels and so forth.
- If students have difficulty thinking of simple drawings suggest the following:

    Pepperoni pizza, house, tree, stick figure, basketball, bicycle, cat

Procedure:
1. With your class, discuss the different forms of directions, in addition to prescriptions, that people provide to others.
2. Working on your own, write the directions for making a simple drawing, without revealing what the drawing is or what the parts are. Follow the style of the second activity in Part I.
3. When you have completed your directions for the drawing, swap directions with a classmate.
4. Follow your classmate's directions to make a drawing.
5. Share the drawing with your classmate.
6. As a class, discuss what directions are easy or difficult to follow.

Process Questions:
1. Dentists make molds of a person's mouth to send to the dental technician. Share an experience you or someone you know has had, with having a mold made.
2. Why do dentists make a mold of your mouth before and after you have braces?

Chapter I   **Language Arts Activities**

Handout—Activity 29A

Following Directions

Directions:

- Read all of the following statements carefully before you do anything.
- Write your name in the upper right-hand corner of a plain piece of paper
- Circle your last name
- Draw five circles in the upper left-hand corner of your paper.
- Draw a square around each circle
- Put an "X" in the center of each circle.
- Draw a triangle in the lower left-hand corner of your paper.
- In the center of the paper multiply 4x10 and write the answer.
- Say your name out loud when you read this statement.
- Count out loud from 1 to 10.
- Now that you have finished reading the directions carefully, do only the first two statements on the list.

Handout—Activity 29A

Following Directions

Directions:

- Using a pencil, draw a large circle on the bottom half of a piece of plain white paper.
- Draw a smaller circle above the larger circle. The smaller circle's edge should rest on the larger circle's edge.
- Put a vertical row of 3 dots down the center of the smaller circle.
- Draw an even smaller circle directly on top of the 2 circles. The smallest circle's edge should rest on the edge of the next smallest circle.
- Make a dot in the center of the smallest circle.
- Add one dot just above the center dot to the left of the center.
- Add another dot just above the center dot to the right.
- Draw a short line across the outside top of the smallest circle. The line should extend just a little beyond each side of the circle.
- Draw a small half circle on top of the line with the open end of the half-circle resting on the line.

Career Development Activities for the Elementary Grades

Mail Carrier

Mail carriers work for the US Postal Service. They deliver letters, bills, and packages to businesses and homes. Some mail carriers work in cities and walk to make their deliveries. In rural areas, mail carriers drive from mailbox to mailbox. They sell stamps and collect letters people want mailed.

Activity 30

Lots of Letters

Subject Area: *Writing*
Materials: *Paper, envelopes*
Time: *Two 30 minute periods*

Part I

Background:
- Review letter writing form and envelope addressing with students.
- Demonstrate how to fold a letter. Use an envelope to show students why folding the letter properly is important.
- You may enhance this activity by having students check each other's spelling. Discuss why it is important to use good penmanship when writing a letter.
- Write the name and address of the school on the board.

Procedure:
1. With your class, review the proper form for writing a letter.
2. Working on your own, write a letter using the form you reviewed. The letter should begin "Dear Friend."
3. In the body of the letter write three facts about yourself and ask three questions of your "Friend." For example, you may tell about a favorite book and why you like it and ask what the "Friend's" favorite book is and why it is a favorite. Be sure to sign your name to the letter.
4. Fold the letter as instructed by your teacher. On the outside of the letter, draw a stamp and postmark. Address the letter to "A Friend," Mr./Ms. (name of teacher) classroom, name of school, and school's address.
5. To mail the letter, place it in a box at the front of the class.
6. Ask for volunteers to serve as mail carriers and deliver the letters, one per student. (Be sure you do not get your own letter back.)
7. Read the letter, and thank the person who sent it to you.

Process Questions:
1. If you were writing a letter to apply for a job, how would you want the letter to look? Why?
2. Should your letter to a friend look as good as a job application letter? Why or why not?

Chapter I

Part II

Background:
- This activity should follow the part I activity.
- You can enhance this activity with a discussion of zip codes and why they are necessary. Borrow a zip code book from the school office or the post office so students can see how the codes work.

Procedure:
1. Using the letter you received in part I, write a thank you note for the letter and include a response to the questions the sender asked.
2. Use the proper letter form for your response. You can begin this letter using the person's name. Sign your name to the letter.
3. Fold the letter and write the address on the outside. Use the person's name, your teacher's classroom, and the name and address of your school. Draw a stamp and postmark on the letter.
4. Mail the letter by placing it in the box at the front of the room. Ask the mail carriers to deliver the letters to the students to whom they are addressed.
5. Read your letter and thank the student who wrote it.

Process Questions:
1. Discuss how E-mail on the computer and the telephone have impacted letter writing.
2. How can letters be considered a part of history? Name some important historical letters.

Career Development Activities for the Elementary Grades

Librarian

Librarians make information available to people. They organize and manage libraries and help people find information. They keep records of the books that are checked in and out of the library and may keep files of documents and other information. Librarians use catalogues and publishers information to choose the books they will carry in their libraries.

Activity 31

A Visit to the Library

Subject Area: Reading
Materials: None
Time: Several 30 minute periods

Part I

Background:
- Divide a list of Caldecott and Newbury books among the small groups.
- Explain to students how fiction and non-fiction books are located in libraries.
- Allow time during the library visit for students to look around. If the library has computers, have the class try to look up some of their books on the computer.
- If you are able to arrange the visit ahead of time, ask the librarians to explain their duties to students.

Procedure:
1. Plan a visit to the library with your class. Discuss with your class how to find the books you are looking for in the library.
2. Work with your teacher to divide a list of books among the small groups. The list will contain award winning Caldecott and Newbury books.
3. When you get to the library, work with your small group to see how many of the books on your part of the list you can locate. Check off a book, when you find it, but do not remove it from the shelf.
4. Working with your list, choose a book to check out and read. It should be a different book than the ones other group members choose.
5. After you read your book, tell your group about the book and why you liked or did not like it.

Process Questions:
1. What are some other job duties of the librarian?
2. Discuss the best book you have read recently.

Part II

Background:
- Work with the whole class to identify the way books are catalogued. Explore the library to find the different number series that correspond to the catalogued numbers.
- To enhance this activity, visit the section of the library that has reference books. Have small groups choose reference books to look through and report back to the class on the information the books provide. Note that reference books include a variety of directories for locating people and organizations.

Procedure:
1. With your class, explore how the Dewey Decimal System works as a way of cataloguing non-fiction books in libraries.
2. Visit a library in your community. Find out what the main subject is in each number series in the Dewey Decimal System. For example, what is the main subject in the 100s, the 200s, and so forth.

Chapter I Language Arts Activities

3. *Choose a topic that interests you from the list below and make a list of the books available on the subject. You may choose a topic not on the list.*

Volcanoes	Earthquakes
Dog Training	Florida
Chinese cooking	Sailboats
Dinosaurs	Sewing
Antiques	Soccer
Monaco	Boston, MA.
Babies	Plants
Gardening	Mississippi River
Baseball	Painting
Diet	German cooking
Camping	Hockey
Photography	Flying
Wood working	Movies
Tahiti	Martin Luther King
Swimming	Biking

4. *Using the books available in the library as resources, write a brief report on your topic.*
5. *Share your report with the class.*

Process Questions:

1. *Why are some libraries called media centers?*
2. *How has the computer enhanced the flow of information?*

Career Development Activities for the Elementary Grades

Computer Repairer

Computer repairers install computer equipment, correct problems and maintain computers. They work on word processing systems and make cable and wiring connections. Some computer repair people work for one company or organization, taking care of the computers and assisting the workers using the computers. Others have their own businesses and go to different locations each day or have customers bring their computers into their shops. Now that we can shop, receive and send mail, do our banking and other business by computer, we are very dependent on computer repair people to help us keep our computer connections.

Activity 32

On Line

Subject Area: Reading, Writing
Materials: Worksheet
Time: 20 to 30 minutes

Part I

Background:
- Use a computer to demonstrate the answers. For example, show how a keyboard talks to a computer.

Procedure:
1. With your class, talk about how computers work and the ways people use them.
2. On the worksheet are two lists. The first list is the parts of a computer. The second list describes what the different parts do. The lists are mixed up. Draw a line between each part and what the part does.
3. As a class, review your answers.

Process Questions:
1. How many parts of the computer can you see just by looking at it?
2. Why do many "business" people use a laptop computer?

Part II

Background:
- If you are living in an area where many businesses are not computerized, you may want to choose one business for all the students to research. If you have a local business that is familiar to your students, invite a representative to talk to the class.

Procedure:
1. Many businesses now depend on computers and need computer repairers to keep their computers running properly. Choose one of the businesses listed below and find out how they use computers. You may need to call the business or do research for the information.

    BANK, GROCERY STORE, DRY CLEANERS, CAR DEALERSHIP, RESTAURANT, GAS STATION, DEPARTMENT STORE

2. Write two paragraphs describing how the business uses computers and what would happen if the computer broke down.
3. Share the information with your class.

Process Questions:
1. What do computer repairers need to know to fix computers?
2. Why is a knowledge of math important to computer repairers?

Miriam McLaughlin and Sandra Peyser

Chapter 1 — **Language Arts Activities**

Handout—Activity 32

On Line

Below are two lists. The first list is the parts of a computer. The second list describes what the different parts do. The lists are mixed up. Draw a line between each part and what the part does.

computer chip	powers the computer
key board	used to talk to the computer
modem	used to give computer directions
disc drive	hooks to phone line
mouse	the brain of the computer
hard drive	used to add or store information from computer
plug	where information is stored
monitor	shows what is going on in computer

Press Operator

Press operators prepare and maintain presses that print newspapers, magazines, books and other publications. Offset printing is the most common kind of printing and is used in producing newspapers. The press operators check the paper and ink, keep the paper feeders stocked, and make sure the printed pages stack properly. They also repair the presses and fix paper jams.

Activity 33

Going to Press

Subject Area: Writing
Materials: Samples of printed material
Time: Two 30 minute periods

Part I

Background:
- You may want to provide some types of publications, so that students will have a variety of examples.

Procedure:

You will be comparing the different types of printed matter that come off a printing press.

1. Bring samples of newspapers, books, magazines, brochures, reports and any other publications you may have at home, to class.
2. For each type of publication, answer the following questions:
   a. what color ink was used?
   b. what kind of paper was used?
   c. what size paper was used?
   d. how was the publication held together (staples, spiral, folded)?
   e. what distinguishes one publication from another (size of print, pictures, drawings, designs on the cover)?

Process Questions:

1. What have you learned about different kinds of publications?
2. What makes magazines different from newspapers?

Part II

Background:
- You can enhance this activity by having the students actually write a short story to go with their book cover.

Procedure:

You will be designing a book cover.

1. Decide what the book will be about.
2. Collect a variety of papers and samples of print styles from magazines.
3. Choose the paper and print style you think best for the cover of the book you chose.
4. Design the cover. You may draw or glue a picture on the cover if you wish.
5. Share your book cover with the class. Explain why you chose the paper, print style and picture.

Process Questions:

1. How does the subject of the book impact on the design of the cover?
2. What types are easiest to read?

Chapter I

Automobile Mechanic

Automobile mechanics repair cars. They understand how the different parts of cars work and are able to identify problems when people have trouble with their cars. The more complicated cars become, the more automobile mechanics must know to repair them. Most Americans travel by car and they depend on automobile mechanics to keep their cars in good condition.

Activity 34

Car Parts

Subject Area: Reading
Materials: Handout
Time: 45 to 60 minutes

Part I

Background:
You can enhance this activity by inviting a person who is knowledgeable about cars to lift the hood of a car in the school parking lot, point out the parts underneath and explain what each part does.

Procedure:
1. Make a list of all the different parts of a car. Be sure to include small parts like the lock buttons on the doors.
2. Put an x beside the parts that need an electric battery to operate.
3. Some parts operate differently in different kinds of cars. For example, in some cars the door locks operate by battery. In others, doors are locked by using a key. Put an o by those parts of a car that may be operated either way.
4. With your class, discuss the parts on your list. Talk about what happens if the part does not work.

Process Questions:
1. How can people get to school and work if their cars are being repaired?
2. How would your family function for a week without a car?

Language Arts Activities

Part II

Background:
Enhance this activity by having students draw their favorite cars. They should include all the parts on their comparison sheets in their drawing.

Procedure:
1. With your class, visit the school parking lot. Choose three cars in the lot that are different in size, shape and make.
2. Compare the cars and write the differences among them on the chart.

Process Questions:
1. Why aren't cars all made the same?
2. How does an auto mechanic get trained for the job?

Car Parts

	CAR I	CAR II	CAR III
MAKE	_____	_____	_____
COLOR	_____	_____	_____
STYLE	_____	_____	_____
# OF DOORS	_____	_____	_____
SIZE	_____	_____	_____
SIZE/SHAPE OF FENDERS	_____	_____	_____
DECORATION	_____	_____	_____
TIRES	_____	_____	_____
SEATS	_____	_____	_____
STEERING WHEEL	_____	_____	_____
OTHER	_____	_____	_____

Chapter II

Mathematics Activities

Career Development Activities for the Elementary Grades

Restaurant Manager

Restaurant managers are in charge of the overall operation of the restaurant. They may own the restaurant, work for a large company that owns many restaurants or work directly for the person who is the owner.

In a small restaurant, managers plan the menu, buy the food and supplies, hire the workers and even assist with the cooking and serving. In large restaurants, managers have people working for them to do these things. Restaurant managers must follow many laws and rules to protect the health and safety of the people who work and eat in the restaurant.

Activity 35

Food for Sale

Subject areas: Math
Materials: Handout
Time: 30 to 45 minutes

Part I

Background:
Explain to your students that restaurant managers have a variety of duties which require many different skills. Instruct them to read the description of a restaurant manager and to do the Part I activity.

Procedure:
Imagine that you are the owner and manager of a new fast food restaurant. Complete the worksheet.

Process Questions:
1. How did you decide on the name for your restaurant?
2. Why did you choose the people you named to work in your restaurant?
3. Which of the rules you wrote down do you think is most important? (Make students aware of any rules they mention that may be laws in your state.)

Part II

Background:
- Instruct your students to complete Part II.
- Ask for volunteers to share their answers with the class.
- Remind your students that they must pay their expenses out of the money the restaurant brings in each week. Brainstorm the kinds of expenses a restaurant would have. (Food, salaries, telephone etc.)

Procedure:
1. Write the amount of money you will charge for each of the three items you are planning to sell beside that item on your list (#4, Part I).
2. One hundred people a day will buy one of each of these items. How much money will the restaurant take in each week?

Process Questions:
1. What math skills did you use to figure out how much money your restaurant would bring in during a week?
2. What interests would a person have who might become a restaurant manager?

Miriam McLaughlin and Sandra Peyser

Chapter II

Mathematics Activities

Handout—Activity 35

Food for Sale

Imagine that you are the owner and manager of a new fast food restaurant. Complete the items on this worksheet.

1. Name your restaurant _____.

2. Name three people you want to hire to work in your restaurant.

   _____
   _____
   _____

3. List three rules you think are important to have in your restaurant to protect the health and safety of your customers and workers.

   _____
   _____
   _____

4. Decide on three items to sell in your restaurant.

   _____
   _____
   _____

5. You expect to serve 100 people these items every day, 7 days a week. How many of each item will you need to order for a week?

   _____
   _____
   _____

Educational Media Corporation®, Box 21311, Minneapolis, MN 55421-0311

Career Development Activities for the Elementary Grades

Architect

Architects design buildings and draw the plans needed to build them. The drawings show exactly how a building should be built, from the inside out. A builder can look at architects' plans and know exactly where to put a wall or a window. Electricians, plumbers and other construction workers also use architects' plans to guide them.

Activity 36

A House for Little People

Subject area: Math and Language Arts
Materials: Handout, paper, pencils, rulers, crayons or markers
Architect's house plans
Time: 45 to 50 minutes

Part I

Background:
- Explain to your students that an architect's plans are like maps. They show the workers who are constructing the building exactly where to go to do their work.
- Show a sample of an architect's drawings. Point out the variety of information available on the plans.
- Have your students follow the directions given on the activity sheet. Stress the importance of being precise in their measurements.
- Ask them what other areas in the house need to be measured.
- Teachers may want to have the class write a story about the people who live in the little house.

Procedure:
Follow the directions on the worksheet to draw a plan for the front of your little house. Remember that someone may want to use your plan to build a house for dolls, or even for a teeny tiny person, so be exact.

Process Questions:
1. Why was it important for you to measure carefully?
2. Share with the class who will live in the house you designed.

Part II

Background:
- Brainstorm with the class ways to get the information needed to answer the questions.
- As an alternate activity, ask students to find the square feet in the rectangle, door, windows and roof.

Procedure:
1. On a separate piece of paper, draw a rectangle the same size as the one above. This rectangle will represent the inside of your little house.
2. Decide which side of the rectangle will be the front of the house and which will be the back. Put a mark where the front and back doors are located.
3. Ask yourself these questions:
   Where do I want to put the kitchen?
   Should my house have a dining room?
   How many bedrooms should I put in my house?
   Where should the bathroom be located?
   What other rooms do I want in my house?
4. Draw lines in the rectangle to represent the walls of the rooms in your house and write the names of each room inside the room space.
5. Measure each room and write the measurements inside the room space.
6. Share your work with your class.

Process Questions:
1. What information helped you make these decisions?
2. Where did you go to get the information?
   For example: How did you decide how many bedrooms the house needed?

A House for Little People

Follow the directions on this worksheet to draw a plan for the front of your little house. Remember that someone may want to use your plan to build a house for dolls, or even for a teeny tiny person, so be exact.

1. Imagine that the rectangle below is the front of your little house.
2. Measure the sides of the rectangle and write the measurements along each side.
3. Draw a door in the center of the rectangle.
4. Measure the door and write the measurements in the door space.
5. Draw a window on each side of the door. The windows should be square, so that all sides of the windows measure the same.
6. Write the window measurements in the window space.
7. Add a roof. The roof can be any style you want.
8. Measure the roof and include the measurements in the roof space.
9. Now decorate the outside of your house, being careful to leave the measurements visible. Be creative. What can you see through the window curtains or a lamp? Is your house brick or wood? Does it have a chimney? What color is your little house?
10. When you are finished, take an opportunity to see what others have done.

Career Development Activities for the Elementary Grades

Truck Driver

Truck drivers spend their days and many of their nights driving. They transport food, building materials, products of every kind and even animals in their trucks from one part of the country to another.

To do this work truck drivers must know all the rules of safe driving and must be able to read maps well, to find the best route to their destinations. Driving a large truck is very different from driving a car and truck drivers must be trained to handle the large rigs.

Activity 37

On the Road

Subject Area: Math, Social Studies
Materials: State maps (one per small group), rulers
Time: 30 to 60 minutes

Part I

Background:
- Instruct your students to give everyone in their group an opportunity to measure the mileage scale.
- Explain that the 200 mile distance to the city they chose will be approximate, because the roads curve more than a ruler can.
- Point out the chart that lists distances between cities if your maps have one.
- Invite the groups to share and compare their findings with the rest of the class.

Procedure:
1. Working with your small group, find the mileage scale on your state map.
2. Using a ruler, measure the mileage scale. The scale measures miles by the inch. How many miles equal 1/2 inch on the scale? How many miles equal one inch?
3. Next, locate the capital city of your state on the map.
4. Once you know how many miles equal one inch on the map, locate a city that is about 200 miles north or south from the capital city (it can be in another state).
5. Look for a road or roads that lead from the capital city to the city that you picked.
6. List the cities you would pass through on those roads.
7. Share the information you found with the rest of your class.

Did any of the groups find other routes to get to the city you chose? Were the routes shorter or longer?

Process Questions:
1. What happens if the truck driver reads the map incorrectly?
2. What are you learning in school that truck drivers need to know to do their job?

Part II

Background:
- Your students can do this problem themselves, and then work in their small groups to be sure everyone has the answer.
- Ask them to identify a lake, a park, an airport, and an historical site on their maps.
- It is important that they see the interrelationship between careers.

Procedure:
1. If the truck is traveling 50 miles per hour, how long will it take for the truck to get from the capital city to the city you have located 200 miles away?
2. What kind of roads will the truck travel on? How can you tell from the map what kind of roads they are?
3. Discuss with the class how the job of weather person impacts on the truck driver's job.

Process Questions:
1. What other occupations use maps?
2. How do truck drivers make our lives better or easier?

Chapter II   Mathematics Activities

Shipping and Receiving Clerk

Shipping and receiving clerks keep records of all products shipped from one place to another. The shipping clerk makes sure orders are filled correctly, and addressed properly. In small companies, shipping clerks keep track of how much of a product is shipped and how much is still in stock.

Receiving clerks check the products that come into a company. They make sure they receive the right products in the correct amounts, and check for damage. Their records show when the product is received, how much is received and where in the company it will be sent.

Activity 38

Fill the Order

Subject Area: Mathematics
Materials: Paper, pens or pencils
Time: 20 to 30 minutes

Part I

Background:

You may want to list a number of examples on the board.

Procedure:

1. In small groups think of a product and where you would ship it, for example books could be shipped to schools or dresses to department stores.
2. Look in the telephone book and find all the schools, department stores or other places where your product shipment will go.
3. Make address labels to put on each package of product. Be sure to include the zip code of the receiver.

Process Questions:

1. Why is it important for the shippers to get the correct addresses?
2. Why should the receivers let the shippers know that the product has arrived safely?

Part II

Procedure:

1. You will be shipping boxes of books all over the country. The charge will depend on how heavy the box is and how far it must travel.
2. Using the chart below, determine the cost of sending each box.

   a. 15 pounds   246 miles
   b. 45 pounds   612 miles
   c. 4 pounds   17 miles
   d. 98 pounds   869 miles

Shipping Chart

   0 - 35   pounds $2.00
   36 - 65   pounds $4.00
   66 - 100   pounds $10.00

   100-300 miles   add $5.00
   to the cost of shipping

   301-600 miles   add $7.00
   to the cost of shipping

   601-900 miles   add $10.00
   to the cost of shipping

Process Questions:

1. Why would it cost more to mail a heavy package than a lighter one?
2. Why do shippers have to be good in math?

Answers:

   a. $7.00   b. $14.00
   c. $7.00   d. $20.00

Career Development Activities for the Elementary Grades

Travel Agent

Travel agents help people plan trips. They know about the costs of different kinds of transportation, hotels and resorts and can arrange for tickets and reservations. Whether people want to take cruises, tour foreign countries or visit friends in other states, travel agents have the information people need to make their plans.

Activity 39

Lets Go!

Subject Area: Math, Social Studies
Materials: None
Time: 30 to 45 minutes

Part I

Background:
- The trip will cost $257.
- Have your students plan the trip to a real city in your state and find out some interesting facts about it.

Procedure:
1. You will be planning a trip to a city at the other end of your state.
2. You will be driving and the cost will be $106 for gas.
3. You will be staying at a hotel at $37.50 per night for 2 nights.
4. The budget allows you $28 per day for food.
5. You will take $10 per day for extras and souvenirs.
6. How much will this trip cost?

Process Questions:
1. Why do we do so much planning before a trip?
2. What are some things that happen on a trip no matter how much you plan?

Part II

Background:
- This activity builds consensus. It allows everyone in the class to have a voice in the decision.
- Ask questions of the class if their choices are not reasonable. For example: If they chose a distant state, the airline tickets will cost more than $500 per student and a bus trip would take more than a week.
- Share the class activity with a travel agent and invite the agent to visit the class. The agent will come prepared to work with the class on their plan or suggest reasonable alternatives.

Procedure:
1. Imagine that someone gave each member of your class $500 to use for a class trip. The trip can last from one day to one week.
2. Write on a slip of paper where you would like the class to go. The slips will be collected and the top 10 choices put on the board.
3. Decide which of those 10 choices you like best and second best. Write your initials beside the two choices.
4. With your class, plan a trip to the place you all have chosen. Remember, the $500 per student is all you have to spend. With that money you must pay for transportation, a place to stay, and meals. You may also have to buy admission tickets.
5. Once you have a plan, invite a travel agent to your class to discuss the plan.
6. The travel agent will tell you if your plan is affordable and if not will make suggestions for other plans.

Process Questions:
1. Why did we give everyone a vote as to where the class would go on a trip?
2. What are some other activities people vote for?

Chapter II   Mathematics Activities

Newspaper Carrier

Newspaper carriers deliver newspapers to people's homes. In areas where houses are close together, the carriers can ride bicycles to deliver the papers. These carriers are often students who deliver papers before and after school. In the country, papers are delivered by car. Some newspaper carriers are responsible for collecting payments from their customers for the papers. They must also keep track of the money they collect, and the customers who have and have not paid for their papers.

Activity 40

Money Makers

Subject Area: Math
Materials: Handout
Time: 20 to 45 minutes

Part I

Procedure:
Help Michelle spend the money she made delivering papers by solving the problems on the handout.

Process Questions:
1. *How does having a paper route help prepare you for the business world?*
2. *Why does a newspaper carrier need interpersonal skills?*

Answers:
Michelle has $10.35 left after buying the flashlight and batteries.

Michell needs $27.60.

Michelle earns $15.00 per week delivering newspapers.

She cannot buy the tape player sooner, because she needs more than the $17.50 she would get adding a customer and only gets paid at the end of the week.

Part II

Background:
You can add to this activity by asking students to think of one thing they would like to buy and how much it costs. Ask them how long it would take to earn the money to buy it, if they were working in Michelle's job. Ask them how long it would take if they added the extra street of customers to their paper route.

Procedure:
Marcus collects from his customers every two weeks. Each customer must pay him $2.75 a week to receive the paper. Help Marcus with his collections by solving the problems on part II of the worksheet.

Process Questions:
1. *Think of some other jobs that require math skills.*
2. *What are some machines that have taken the place of adding and subtracting on paper?*

Answers:
Marcus gives Ms. Quade $2.00 in change.

The Lawsons pay $5.50.

The Richards pay $16.50.

The Donaldsons owe 0.

The McLaughlins pay $8.25.

Mr. Person pays $6.50.

The total for the apartment building is $36.75.

The Serwin family paid two months ago.

Marcus will turn in $56.25.

Marcus will be paid $14.06.

Educational Media Corporation®, Box 21311, Minneapolis, MN 55421-0311

Career Development Activities for the Elementary Grades

Handout—Activity 40

Money Makers

Part I

Help Michelle spend the money she made delivering papers, by solving the following problems

Michelle has earned $22.00. She bought a flashlight for $1.65 and batteries for $10. How much does she have left?_____

Michelle wants a tape player that costs $37.95. How much more money will she have to earn to afford the tape player. (Remember, she has already bought a flashlight and batteries.)_____

Michelle figures she will have to save two weeks pay to have enough to buy the tape player. Can you guess about how much Michelle earns delivering papers every week?_____

She can add another street to her paper route and earn $2.50 more each week. She gets paid at the end of each week she works. If she takes on those new customers will she be able to buy the tape player sooner?_____

Part II

Marcus collects from his customers every two weeks. Each customer must pay him $2.75 a week to receive the paper. Help Marcus with his collections by solving the problems below.

Ms. Quade is seldom home when Marcus collects and she owes Marcus for 1 and 1/2 months of the paper. She gives him a twenty dollar bill and tells him to keep an extra $1.50 as a tip. How much change should Marcus give Ms. Quade?_____

Marcus also delivers papers to Maplewood Apartments. All five families who live there get the paper. The families give Mr. Person, who lives on the first floor, the money for the papers. He then pays Marcus.

Marcus keeps a list of the families that live in the apartments. The Lawson family is up to date. They always give Mr. Person the money for the paper. How much will they give Mr. Person?_____

The Richards family is one month behind. If they make their regular payment and catch up the one month, how much will they give Mr. Person to pay Marcus?_____

Mrs. Donaldson paid two weeks ahead the last time Marcus collected. How much does she owe at this time?_____

The McLaughlins were short of money last time and only paid for one week of the paper. How much money should they give to Mr. Person so they will be caught up?_____

Mr. Person always pays on time and adds a dollar to tip Marcus. How much will he pay this time?_____

The Serwin family is the last one on the block. They owe $22.00. When was the last time they paid?_____

Marcus deducts the amount of money he receives as tips and turns the rest into the newspaper company. How much will he turn in?_____

Marcus receives 25% of the money he collects as pay. How much will he be paid?_____

Chapter II   Mathematics Activities

Cosmetologist

Cosmetologists cut and style hair. They may also color hair, manicure fingernails and toenails and give their customers facials and other skin treatments. They need to know what products work best on different kinds of hair and what hairstyles work best for different people. Some cosmetologists have their own shops. They must have the knowledge and skills to manage their business.

Activity 41

Cuts and Curls

Subject Area: Math
Materials: Handout
Time: 30 to 45 minutes

Part I

Background:
- You may want to bring samples of hair care products to class so that students can practice reading the labels.
- Ask your students to share what they learned about hair care products. Do not require them to share the numbers of products, the kind or the amount of money spent on products in their homes.

Procedure:
1. Using the data on the handout, survey your home to find out about the hair care products your family uses.
2. With the class, share what you learned about the hair care products in your home.

Process Questions:
1. Name some of the unusual ingredients found in hair care products.
2. Discuss any unusual experience you may have had with a cosmetologist or shampooing your hair at home.

Part II

Procedure:
Answer the questions on the handout.

Process Questions:
1. Discuss the gradual change from beauty salons for women and barber shops for men to one salon where both can get the services of a cosmetologist.
2. What kind of training does it take to become a cosmetologist?

Answers to math problems:
1. 288 shampoos month
2. 4 1/2 bottles a month
3. $40.50
4. $.14
5. $1.68
6. $2.86

Educational Media Corporation®, Box 21311, Minneapolis, MN 55421-0311

75

Career Development Activities for the Elementary Grades

Handout—Activity 41

Cuts and Curls

Part I

Read the bottle or jar of each hair care product your family uses and answer the following questions.

1. Name of the product. _____

2. What is the product used for? _____

3. How many ounces of the product does the bottle or jar contain? _____

4. If there is more than one hair care product in your home, compare the labels to see if any of the ingredients in them are the same.
   If so, list the ingredient and the products in which it is found. _____

5. If each hair care product in your home cost $1.50, how much has your family most recently spent for hair care products . _____

Part II

Answer the following questions:

1. You are a cosmetologist who gives 12 shampoos a day, 6 days a week. How many shampoos do you give each month? _____

2. You use one fluid ounce of shampoo each time you wash a customer's hair. You buy shampoo in bottles containing 64 fluid ounces. How many bottles will you use up each month? _____

3. If each 64 fluid oz. bottle of shampoo costs $9.00, how much do you spend on shampoo each month?
   _____

4. How much is one ounce of the shampoo? _____

5. How much do you spend on shampoo each day? _____

6. If you charge $3.00 to shampoo a customer's hair, how much profit do you make on one shampoo?
   _____

Chapter II

Mathematics Activities

Waitperson

Waitpeople serve food in restaurants. They also take the orders for food from customers, clear the tables when the customers are through eating, and bring the customers their bills and change. Some waitpeople also add up the cost of the food their customers order and make change, while others give the bill to a cashier who has that responsibility. Waitpeople are on their feet for most of their work hours and lift and carry heavy trays of food and dishes.

Activity 42

Let's Eat Out

Subject Area: Math
Materials: Handout
Time: 30 to 45 minutes

Part I

Answer the questions on the handout.

Process Questions:
1. Why do waitpeople need good math skills?
2. What other skills should waitpeople have?

Answers:
1. $12.63
2. None
3. $4.91

Part II

Procedure:
1. Use the following steps for figuring and rounding off tips:
   a. To figure 10%, move the decimal point in the price of the item one place to the left, $1.50 item gives you a $.15 tip
   b. To figure 20%, move the decimal point in the price of the item one place to the left and multiply (x) by 2, $1.50 item is $.15 x 2 = $.30 tip.
   c. To figure 15%, move the decimal point one place to the left, divide that answer by 2 and add the two answers together; $1.50 item is $.15 divided by 2 = $.075. $.15 + $.075 = $.225 rounded off to $.23 for a tip.
2. Working from the menu in part I, figure out how much money you will get for a tip (round to the nearest even number) in each of the cases on the handout.

Process Questions:
1. If the waitperson provided poor service, how would you handle the tip?
2. Who should you tell about poor service or food?

Answers:
1. 15% tip for the purchase of a fried chicken dinner is $1.57.

   20% tip for the steak dinner and an extra ice cream is $2.98.

   3 pizzas= $19.50. 15% tip is $2.92.

2. $.28 tip for an order of french fries

   $1.30 tip for an order of pizza

   $.74 tip for spaghetti and meatballs

Educational Media Corporation®, Box 21311, Minneapolis, MN 55421-0311

77

Career Development Activities for the Elementary Grades

Handout—Activity 42

Let's Eat Out

Part I

Answer the following questions:

1. You are a waitperson. Your customer's bill is $7.37. She gives you $20.00. How much change do you give her? _____

2. Your customer had a piece of pie for $1.75 and coffee for $.45. He gives you a one dollar bill, 3 quarters, 3 dimes, 2 nickels and five pennies. How much change does he get back? _____

3. Three friends named Nancy, Harold and Juan have finished lunch. Nancy spent $5.47 and pays you $7.00. Harold spent $7.96 and gives you a ten dollar bill. Juan only spent $3.66 and gives you a five dollar bill. All three customers tell you to keep the change as your tip. How much is you total tip from those three customers? _____

4. The restaurant where you work has the following menu:

A LA CARTE

Spaghetti and Meatballs	$4.95
Pizza	$6.50
Fried Chicken	$7.95
Steak	$8.95
Salad	$3.50
French Fries	$2.75
Baked Potatoes	$1.60
Green Beans	$ .75
Ice cream	$1.40

DINNERS

Fried chicken, french fries, green beans, ice cream	$10.50
Steak, baked potato, salad, ice cream	$13.50
Spaghetti, salad, ice cream	$ 7.95

All meals are served with free water, iced tea, or coffee

Answer the following questions.

How much would each special dinner cost if all the items in the dinner were ordered separately? _____

How much money is a customer saving by ordering each special dinner? _____

Which special dinner saves the customer the most money? _____

If you were a customer in this restaurant and had $10.00 to spend on food what would you order? _____

How much change would you get back? _____

Part II

1. Working from the menu in part I, figure out how much money you will get for a tip (round to the nearest even number) in each if a customer:

   - buys the fried chicken dinner and leaves a 15% tip
   - buys the steak dinner and orders an extra dish of ice cream and leaves a 20% tip
   - orders 3 pizzas for the family and leaves a 15% tip.

2. Try to figure these tips in your head. Then round them off.

   a 10% tip for an order of french fries

   a 20% tip for a pizza

   a 15 % tip for spaghetti & meatballs.

Chapter II   Mathematics Activities

Floral Designer

Floral designers use flowers and greenery to create designs and arrangements. They usually work in flower shops that sell their designs. People purchase flower arrangements for decorations, gifts and remembrances and for every kind of special occasion from weddings to funerals. In America, sending flowers is a way people let others know they are thinking of them.

Activity 43

Rose Petals

Subject Area: Math
Materials: Handout
Time: 20 to 45 minutes

Part I

Procedure:

You are a floral designer. Someone orders the arrangements listed on the handout. How much should you charge?

Process Questions:

1. What is your favorite flower?
2. Have you ever sent or received flowers? What was the occasion?

Part II

Procedure:

When floral designers order flowers, they expect that a small percentage of them will be unusable because of breaking or wilting. Answer the questions in part II on the handout.

Process Questions:

1. Why does the price of flowers vary so much?
2. Why are flowers different prices at different times of the year?

Answers:

1. $6.00 for roses
   $2.00 for daises
   $2.00 for mums
   $10.00 for one hour of designer work
   Total cost= $20.00
2. $35.00
3. $75.00
4. $47.00

Answers:

1. 120 roses are left in good condition
   230 carnations
   69 tulips
2. 68 roses, 40 carnations, 42 gardenias, 109 stems of baby's breath
3. 2 roses must be replaced,
4. 5% of the carnations must be replaced
5. 14%

Career Development Activities for the Elementary Grades

Handout—Activity 43

Rose Petals

Part I

Answer the following questions:

1. You are a floral designer. Someone orders an arrangement of six roses, eight white daisies, and five yellow mums.

   Roses cost $1.50 each

   Daises cost $.25 each

   Mums cost $.40 each

   It takes you one hour to do the arrangement and you charge $10.00 for one hour of your work.

   How much should you charge the customer for the arrangement? _____

2. Someone else orders the same arrangement only twice as large.

   It takes you 1 1/2 hrs. to make this arrangement. How much will this arrangement cost the customer? _____

3. In one day you make three of the arrangements described in #1. Each arrangement goes to a different place. You charge $5.00 for delivery of each arrangement. What is the total amount you will charge for the three arrangements including delivery charges? _____

4. A bride comes to you to make her bouquet. It will take one dozen pink sweetheart roses which cost $3.50 each and a small amount of greenery which you will add for free. You estimate it will take you 30 minutes to make the bouquet. How much will the bride's bouquet cost? _____

Part II

Procedure:

1. When floral designers order flowers, they expect that a small percentage of them will be unusable because of breaking or wilting.

   If a designer orders:

   125 roses and 4% of them are not usable, how many will be left that are in good condition? _____

   250 carnations and 8% are not usable, how many will be left that are in good condition? _____

   75 tulips and 8% are not usable, how many will be left that are in good condition? _____

2. The floral designer must make eight bouquets for a large wedding and three flower arrangements for the wedding decorations. The designer must decide what flowers are needed to make the bouquets and arrangements and how many of each flower to order from the growers.

   The designer decides to put 4 roses, 2 carnations, 3 gardenias and eight stems of baby's breath in each bouquet. She decides to use one dozen roses, 8 carnations, 6 gardenias and 15 stems of baby's breath in each arrangement. How many of each flower must the designer order from the grower? _____

3. When the designer gets the order, she discovers that 3% of the roses are not usable. How many roses must the grower replace? _____

4. Two carnations are not usable and must be replaced. What percentage of the total order of carnations must be replaced? _____

5. Six gardenias must be replaced. What percentage of the total order of gardenias must be replaced? _____

6. Three percent of the baby's breath have broken stems. How many stems must be replaced? _____

Chapter II

Interior Designer

Interior designers plan, decorate and arrange the rooms in homes and buildings. They choose colors and fabrics to use for the curtains and furniture, the kinds of furniture and rugs to use in the rooms and sometimes even the pictures, plants and other room accessories. They usually design the interiors of homes based on what their customers like. Interior designers know what colors go well together, the best kind of furniture to use in different rooms and about different kinds of fabric. They make suggestions to their customers and help their customers make choices.

Activity 44

Best Room in the House

Subject Area: Math, Art
Materials: Magazines, paper, pencils
Time: 30 to 60 minutes

Part I

Background:
Encourage your students to be very creative with their room designs.

Procedure:
1. Working on your own, design a room you would like to have in your house, using the piece of paper I have given you. Decide if your room will be a bedroom, living room, or other room in your house.
2. Decide where you would put a window in the room and draw it in, using a ruler to make sure the parallel sides of the window are the same measurements.
3. Use pictures of furniture, lamps and rugs cut from magazines to design your room. If you cannot find the colors or styles you like in magazines, draw the furniture in with colored pencils, markers or crayons.
4. Be sure to add any pictures, plants or other accessories you would like to have in this room.
5. Share your room design with your class. Explain why you chose the colors and styles of furniture you used in your room.

Process Questions:
1. How do designers decide how to arrange a room? Is there a right or wrong way?
2. Discuss what you have on the walls of your room. Did you have any input on the decisions?

Part II

Procedure:
1. The window in your room measures 2' wide and 4' long. You must order fabric that is 2 1/2 times the width of the window to make the drapes. You must order the fabric in yards. How much fabric should you order?
2. Your room measures 12' wide by 14' long. You want a rug that is 10" away from the wall all the way around. What size rug will you need for this room?
3. Another room in your house is 12' wide by 12' long. You want to put a table and chairs in the room and use it for a dining room. You are considering a rectangular table that is 10' wide and 11 1/2 feet long, a round table that is 4' across and a square table that is 8' on all sides. Which table would you choose and why?

Process Questions:
1. Besides hiring an interior designer, how do families decide how to decorate their homes?
2. Ask if anyone has furniture or accessories passed on to them from ancestors.

Answers:
1. 1.6 yards.
2. Convert the feet to inches. The room is 144" wide by 168" long. Subtract 20" from the width and 20" from the length for an inch measurement of 124" by 148". Convert the inches back to feet. The rug should be 10.3' wide by 12.3' long.
3. This activity encourages students to picture the furniture in the room and visualize what table would work best. If students are not able to visualize, work the problem as a class. The square table would fit best and leave room (4' all the way around for the chairs). The rectangular table is too large for the room. The round table would fit but would be very small for the room. Students could argue that they could put other pieces of furniture in the room if they use the round table.

Career Development Activities for the Elementary Grades

Petroleum Field Worker

Petroleum field workers work on oil rigs. The rigs are located all over the world. Some of them are even out in the ocean. The rigs pump oil out of the earth and send it through pipes to huge collection tanks. From the tanks, the oil is trucked or shipped to people who use it to make fuel and products. The petroleum field workers run the rigs, keeping them operating safely and making needed repairs.

Activity 45

Looking for Oil

Subject Area: Math, Social Studies
Materials: None
Time: 30 to 45 minutes

Part I

Background:
Encourage your students to get as much detail as possible about the different products made from oil.

Procedure:
1. Working with your small group, do research to find the different ways we use oil. Make sure you learn what products use most of the world's oil.
2. Once you have learned what products are made from oil, make a chart listing the steps required to produce the product.

    For example: rubber is made from oil and tires are made from rubber. This information should be recorded in chart form as follows:

    Petroleum Products

    Oil = Rubber = Tires

3. Compare your findings with other small groups.

Process Questions:
1. What are the most common uses for oil worldwide?
2. What happens when there is a shortage of oil?

Part II

Background:
This activity ties very well to a discussion of the problems in other parts of the world that affect Americans.

Procedure:
1. Working on your own, research the path oil takes from the ground to the gas station. Be sure to include the oil rig, pipes to the oil tank and how it gets to the gas station.
2. Work with your class to make a mural showing the steps from the oil rig to the gas station.

Process Questions:
1. What major role does the petroleum field worker play in getting the oil out of the ground?
2. Fuel is one of the primary uses for oil. Explore with the class how oil shortages can affect lifestyles.

Chapter II   Mathematics Activities

Elevator Mechanic

Elevator mechanics fix elevators. Because of elevators, people are able to live and work in very tall buildings. The elevator mechanics make sure the elevators are operating safely. They must be prepared at all hours of the day and night to answer emergency calls when elevators get stuck.

Activity 46

A Little Lift

Subject Area: Math
Materials: Handout, pencils
Time: 30 to 45 minutes

Part I

Background:

You may want to work through the first problem with your students.

Procedure:

Read the information on the handout and answer the questions. Keep in mind that elevators usually return to the first floor after delivering the passengers. Also, people who take an elevator to leave the building must also use the elevator to return.

Process Questions:

1. Discuss ways that senior citizens could cope with the elevator being broken in their building.
2. How do people call for help if they are stuck in an elevator?

Answers:

1. Eight times a week. The elevator must go to the tenth floor to pick up Mr. and Mrs. Gomez and then go up again to take them back to their apartment. Ms. Cohen must take the elevator to the tenth floor and call for it again to pick her up.
2. 2 times a week
3. 0 times a week
4. 8 times a week
5. 2 times a week
6. 0 times a week
7. 4 times a week
8. 16 times a week

Part II

Procedure:

Answer the elevator brainteasers on part II of the handout.

Process Questions:

1. Discuss what people can do to relieve the stress of being stuck in an elevator.
2. Why do some people use the stairs instead of the elevator?

Answers:

1. Only if the building was 22 floors high. If it was higher than 22 floors, the elevator stopped before it got to the ground.
2. One of the females was expecting a baby. She delivered a baby boy on the elevator. The relationship is mother and son.
3. Sharon is very short. The button for the 15th floor is the highest one she can reach.
4. The building is all on one level and has no steps.

Educational Media Corporation®, Box 21311, Minneapolis, MN 55421-0311

Career Development Activities for the Elementary Grades

Handout—Activity 46

A Little Lift

Part I

Read the information below and answer the questions. Keep in mind that elevators usually return to the first floor after delivering the passengers. Also, people who take an elevator to leave the building must also use the elevator to return.

Sunshine Towers is an apartment complex for senior citizens. It has ten floors.

1. Mr. and Mrs. Gomez live on the tenth floor. They take the elevator three times a week to the first floor and then walk to the grocery store. Their only visitor is Ms. Cohen, who comes once a week. How many times a week does the elevator go to the tenth floor? _____

2. Mr. Lee lives on the ninth floor. Every Sunday he takes the elevator to the first floor and then takes the bus to visit his grandchildren. How many times a week does the elevator go to the ninth floor? _____

The apartments on the sixth, seventh and eighth floors are empty.

3. The Pollards live on the first floor. John and Maria Pollard go out every day to take walks and do errands. They are new residents and do not know anyone else in the building. How many times a week do they use the elevator? _____

4. The Freys live on the fourth floor. Mrs. Frey takes the elevator to the first floor and then takes a cab to the beauty shop every Friday. Mr. Frey stays home. He has a visiting nurse that comes twice a week to check on him. The Freys' daughter visits them once a week. How many times a week does the elevator stop at the fourth floor? _____

5. Ms. Cohen lives on the third floor. She rides the elevator to visit her friend Mrs. Gomez every Tuesday. How many times a week does the elevator stop at the third floor? _____

6. Mr. Davidson lives on the second floor. He goes out every day, but he never rides the elevator. He never has visitors. How many times a week does the elevator stop at the second floor? _____

7. Ms. Speers lives on the fifth floor. She takes the elevator to visit Mrs. Frey every Tuesday and Mrs. Pollard every Wednesday. She doesn't have visitors. How many times a week does the elevator stop at the fifth floor? _____

8. How many times a week does the elevator go past the second floor? _____

Part II

Answer the following elevator brainteasers.

1. An elevator was at the top of a high rise building when a cable came loose. The elevator fell 22 floors before stopping. Did it stop by crashing into the ground?

2. Three people, 1 male and 2 females got on an elevator. They were stuck on the elevator for several hours. Four people, 2 females and 2 males got off the elevator when it finally started working. Two of those people were related to each other. What is the relationship?

3. Sharon is always the first one to arrive at her office. She works on the 34th floor of a high rise building. She always takes the elevator to the fifteenth floor and takes the stairs the rest of the way. Her co-worker Jim is always the next person to arrive at the office. He always takes the same elevator all the way to the 34th floor. Why does Sharon get off at the fifteenth floor?

4. A large building houses 75 senior citizens. Many of them use canes or wheelchairs, yet the building does not have an elevator. How do the senior citizens manage to get around and in and out of the building?

Chapter II

Buyer

Buyers select and purchase the goods that stores sell. Clothing buyers attend fashion shows and visit clothing design houses and clothing manufacturers to see the latest styles. They decide which styles will sell best in their stores and place orders to purchase the clothing they choose. Buyers also may work for furniture and appliance stores, electronic and computer stores, and even grocery stores. They must know what the customers at their stores like and what they will buy.

Activity 47

Fashions to Buy

Subject Area: Math
Materials: None
Time: 45 to 60 minutes

Part I

Background:
You may have to discuss the idea of specialty shops with the students.

Procedure:
1. Think about the stores where your family shops for clothing. What types of clothing do they buy in each store?
2. What are your favorite types of clothing and which are your favorite stores?
3. Pretend that you are a store buyer going on a trip to pick out the spring clothing for your store.
a. Name the kind of store you will buy for.
b. Name 10 items of clothing you will buy for spring.
4. Share your list with the rest of the class.

Process Questions:
1. How does someone get interested in being a store buyer?
2. What does it mean if someone has an "eye for color?" Why would that be important to being a buyer?

Mathematics Activities

Part II

Procedure:
You are trying to find the best buys for your store so you are comparing prices from people trying to sell you their products. Decide which is the best buy.

1a. 10 pairs of socks for $6.00.
 b. 25 pairs of socks for $18.00.
2a. 15 pairs of shorts for $60.00.
 b. 12 pairs of shorts for $42.00.
3a. 5 pairs of athletic shoes for $175.00.
 b. 22 pairs of athletic shoes for $814.
4a. 30 tee shirts for $45.00
 b. 40 tee shirts for $51.20

Process Questions:
1. How do buyers decide what to purchase?
2. Discuss some of the current trends in clothing.

Answers:
1a. 10 pairs of socks for $6.00 = 60 cents a pair.
 b. 25 pairs of socks for $18.00 = 72 cents a pair.
   (a is the best buy)
2a. 15 pairs of shorts for $60.00 = $4.00 a pair.
 b. 12 pairs of shorts for $42.00 = $3.50 a pair.
   (b is the best buy)
3a. 5 pairs of athletic shoes for $175.00 = $35.00 a pair.
 b. 22 pairs of athletic shoes for $814.00 = 37.00 a pair.
   (a is the best buy)
4a. 30 tee shirts for $45.00 = $1.50 per shirt.
 b. 40 tee shirts for $51.20 = $1.28 per shirt.
   (b is the best buy)

5. To enhance the activity, ask the following questions.
  a. If the buyer buys socks at 60 cents a piece, how much would the store have to sell the socks for to earn 12 cents a pair?
   (72 cents)
  b. If the buyer buys tee shirts for the store at $1.28, how much will the store have to charge to make $2.25 on each shirt?
   ($3.53)

Career Development Activities for the Elementary Grades

Bricklayer

Bricklayers build walls, chimneys, buildings and walkways out of brick. They use a cement-like material called mortar to stick the bricks together. Bricklayers follow blue prints to know where they should lay the brick. They often work with the carpenters, plumbers, electricians and other trades people at construction sites.

Activity 48

Brick by Brick

Subject Area: Math, reading
Materials: Handout, pencils
Time: 30 to 45 minutes

Part I

Procedure:

Working on your own, read the story of Betsy the Brick Layer. Fill in the blanks with the correct words from the list below.

The story reads as follows:

Betsy the Bricklayer works outside in the hot sun of summer and the cold winds of winter. She builds chimneys for new houses. Sometimes she builds brick walls around the yards of the new houses. First she mixes a cement-like material called mortar. She applies the mixture with a tool called a trowel, smoothing it carefully over the brick. Then she looks at a blueprint so that she will know exactly where to place the bricks. She makes a pattern as she lays the bricks to make the chimney or wall strong. Laying bricks is hard, physical work.

Process Questions:

1. Why would a bricklayer sometimes be called an artist?
2. Discuss the fact that bricklayers used to be only men and now many women have that job.

Part II

Procedure:

1. You are a brick layer who must build a wall that is 6 feet high by 30 feet long. The bricks you are using are 2" high and 6" long.
2. To figure how many bricks you will need, convert the feet in the wall to inches.

   The wall is ___ inches high and ___ inches long.

3. Next you must figure out how many bricks you will use in one row across and one row up.

   You will use ___ bricks in one row going the length of the wall.

   You will use ___ bricks in one row going the height of the wall.

4. Now figure how many total bricks you will need for the wall.

   You will need ___ bricks to build the wall.

   Note: You will actually have more than enough bricks, because the mortar takes up some of the space.

5. Your next job is to lay a brick patio behind the house. The patio should be 14' wide by 14' long. The bricks you will be using are 3" wide and 6" long. How many bricks will you need to build the patio.

Process Questions:

1. Why do bricklayer have to cooperate with all the other construction workers on a job?
2. In what parts of the United States do you find more houses made of brick?

Answers:

1. The wall converted to inches is 72" by 360". The number of bricks in one row across is 60 and the number for one row up is 36. The total number of bricks needed to build the wall is 2160.
2. You will need 784 bricks to build the patio.
3. To make these problems more complex, have the students factor in a 1/4 inch of mortar surrounding each brick.

Chapter 11   Mathematics Activities

Handout—Activity 48

Brick by Brick

Part I

Working on your own, read the story of Betsy the Brick Layer. Fill in the blanks with the correct words from the list below.

Betsy the Brick Layer works _____ in the hot sun of _____ and the cold winds of _____. She builds _____ for new houses. Sometimes she builds brick _____ around the yards of the new houses. First she mixes a cement-like material called _____. She applies the mixture with a tool called a _____, smoothing it carefully over the brick. Then she looks at a _____ so that she will know exactly where to place the bricks. She makes a _____ as she lays the bricks, to make sure the chimney or wall is strong. Laying bricks is hard, _____ work.

| Winter, | mortar, | blueprint, | outside, | walls, |
| summer, | pattern, | physical, | chimneys, | trowel |

Part II

1. You are a brick layer who must build a wall that is 6 feet high by 30 feet long. The bricks you are using are 2" high and 6" long.

2. To figure how many bricks you will need, convert the feet in the wall to inches.

    The wall is _____ inches high and _____ inches long.

3. Next you must figure out how many bricks you will use in one row across and one row up.

    You will use _____ bricks in one row going the length of the wall.

    You will use _____ bricks in one row going the height of the wall.

4. Now figure how many total bricks you will need for the wall.

    You will need _____ bricks to build the wall.

    Note: You will actually have more than enough bricks, because the mortar takes up some of the space.

5. Your next job is to lay a brick patio behind the house. The patio should be 14' wide by 14' long. The bricks you will be using are 3" wide and 6" long. How many bricks will you need to build the patio.

Career Development Activities for the Elementary Grades

Accountant

Accountants keep track of money for organizations and individuals. They know the tax laws and help people to figure out what they must pay in taxes. Accountants may set up record keeping systems to help companies keep track of money, keep records themselves for companies and organizations of the money earned and money spent, and prepare financial reports. They often work independently, charging companies or individuals fees for the work they do.

Activity 49

Dollars and Cents

Subject Area: Math
Materials: Handout, Monopoly game
Time: 20 to 60 minutes

Part I

Background:
- You may want to draw a sample ledger on the board to demonstrate how your students should fill out their ledgers.
- Your students can use calculators for this activity.

Procedure:
1. A debit is money spent. Credit is money received. The balance is the money you have after an amount has been received or spent. With that knowledge, fill out the Ledger Sheet using the information on the handout.
2. You want to go to the movies with a friend on July 6th. A ticket costs $4.00. Do you have enough money left? If so, what will you have left to spend until you receive your next allowance?
3. What would be your decision about the movies?

Process Questions:
1. How does a ledger sheet help you keep up with your money?
2. Many people figure out their own taxes. How do they do that?

Answers:
Ledger balances:
Beginning balance is 26.30
Less 6.25
Balance is 20.05
Less 7.50
Balance is 12.55
Plus 5.00
Balance is 17.55
Plus 12.50
Balance is 30.05
Less 14.95
Balance is 15.10
Less 6.95
Balance is 8.15

Part II

Background:
Use the enclosed ledger sheet and a board game such as Monopoly®.

Procedure:
1. Play a board game that uses play money with your small groups.
2. Keep a ledger of every transaction you make throughout the game. For example, you start with a balance of $1500 dollars. If you buy something during the game, write the amount you paid in the debit column of the ledger. If you collect money during the game, that amount would go in the credit column. Keep a running balance as you play.
3. At the end of the game, count your remaining money to see if it checks with the balance in your ledger.

Account balance (the amount with which you begin game)$ _____

(for example, Monopoly starts with $1500)

Process Questions:
1. Do most households keep a ledger sheet for their debits and credits? Why or why not?
2. Would such a system help people who are constantly in debt? Why or why not?

Chapter II   Mathematics Activities

Handout—Activity 49

Dollars and Cents

Part I

A debit, is money spent. Credit is money received. The balance is the money you have after an amount has been received or spent. Fill out the Ledger Sheet using the following information.

Note: be sure to record your balance after each transaction.

It is July 1st and you have $1.30 left from last week's allowance.

You receive $25 dollars for you birthday on July 2nd.

You spent $6.25 for a hamburger, soft drink, french fries and ice cream at the mall on July 2nd.

On July 3rd you spent $7.50 for the movies.

You received $5.00 allowance July 5th.

You received $12.50 for mowing the neighbor's lawn on July 5th.

You spent $14.95 on a tee shirt on July 5th.

You spent $6.95 for a plant for your mother on July 5.

Ledger Sheet

Date	Credit	Debit	Balance

Career Development Activities for the Elementary Grades

Drywall Worker

Drywall workers put up the walls in houses and other buildings. They measure and cut the drywall and attach it to the frame of the building. Once they have installed the drywall, they must fill in the gaps between pieces with material called joint compound. Drywall workers have to wait for plumbers to install pipes and electricians to install wires before they can put up the walls.

Activity 50

Dollhouses

Subject Area: Math, Art
Materials: Cardboard, scissors, rulers
Time: 45 to 60 minutes

Part I

Background:
- You may need to work with your students as they measure the cardboard and draw lines where they will be cutting.
- To enhance this activity, have them draw the window and door openings according to measurements, windows, 1" on all sides and doors, 5 1/2 inches wide and 3 inches high.

Procedure:
1. You are a drywall worker cutting walls for a doll house. Using cardboard and scissors, cut walls with the following measurements.
    a. The front wall of the doll house is 4 inches wide and 5 inches tall.
    b. The back wall has the same measurements as the front.
    c. Walls on the sides of the house are 3 inches wide and 5 inches tall.
2. Draw doorways and window openings on the walls you have cut, like a drywall worker would do inside a house.

Process Questions:
1. What might happen if the drywall measurements were not accurate?
2. What sometimes happens to drywall during a hurricane or flood?

Part II

Procedure:

Doll House Costs:
1. Drywall costs $.10 per inch and is measured by the width of the piece. Working from the information on drywall in Part I, how much would the drywall cost for the doll house?
2. How much would the drywall cost for 20 doll houses just like the first one?

Process Questions:
1. How is drywall on a house frame like skin over bones?
2. How do individual home owners make their drywalls more interesting?

Answers:
1. Drywall for one doll house is $1.40.
   Drywall for 20 doll houses is $28.00.
2. To enhance this activity, tell students that the drywall worker will get 6% discount on large amounts of drywall. If that is true, how much money can the drywall worker save by buying enough drywall for 20 doll houses? ($1.68)

Chapter II

Bulldozer Operator

Bulldozer operators work with large pieces of machinery that are used to move earth, rocks, and other heavy objects. They often work on building sites, moving large quantities of earth around with their machines. Bulldozer operators must know how to operate their machines safely to avoid roll overs, collisions and other accidents.

Activity 51

Out of My Way

Subject Area: Math
Materials: Handout, pencils
Time: 30 to 45 minutes

Part I

Background:
You may wish to have your students work these problems as a class, depending on their level of ability.

Procedure:
Work on your own to solve the problems on the worksheet.

Process Questions:
1. What are the positive aspects of being a bulldozer operator?
2. What are the drawbacks?

Part II

Background:
Your students must work the problems in part I in order to do the part II problems.

Procedure:
Use the information from 1b. in part I for the problem on the worksheet.

Process Questions:
1. If you were a bulldozer operator in a small town and there was no work, what could you do?
2. Why is bulldozer operator a job that requires a cooperative attitude?

Answers:

a. Joanne earned $336 that week.

b. Mike earns $12.35 per hour.

c. The job will pay $8000 for two months work. The room expense will be $800 and the airline ticket will be $1200. The bulldozer operator would take home $6000.

d. The bulldozer operator makes $440 per week. The steam shovel operator makes $500 per week. The supervisor makes $550 per week, making their pay the highest per week.

Answers:

a. Mike's overtime pay is $15.35 per hour.

b. Mike earned a total of $908.90.

c. The first month he earns $168.85
The fourth month he earns $107.45.
After 4 months he had put $276.30 in his account.

d. The final amount after four months is $279.34

Career Development Activities for the Elementary Grades

Handout—Activity 51

Out of My Way

Part I

Work on your own to solve these problems:

a. Joanne operates a bulldozer. She gets paid $12 for each hour she works in a week. On Monday Joanne worked eight hours. Tuesday she worked just three hours in the morning because a heavy rain stopped the work. Wednesday Joanne went to work at noon, when the ground had a chance to dry. That day she worked until 5:00. Thursday Joanne worked eight hours and Friday she worked from 7:00 a.m. to 11:00 a.m. How much money did Joanne earn that week.

b. Mike also operates a bulldozer. He earns $494 for working a 40 hour week. How much does Mike earn in one hour.

c. There is a job for a bulldozer operator on the Alaska pipeline. The job will last two months and will pay $1,000 per week. The bulldozer operator must pay for a plane ticket to and from Alaska and a room. Meals will be provided. The airline ticket will cost $1200 round trip. The room charge is $400 per month. How much money will the bulldozer operator take home at the end of two months after paying for a room and airline ticket.

d. At one construction site, the bulldozer operator makes $11 per hour for a 40 hour week, the steam shovel operator makes $500 per 40 hour week and the supervisor makes $2200 a month. Who has the highest weekly pay?

Part II

Use the information from 1b. in part I for this problem.

a. Mike earns $3.00 more than his hourly pay for overtime. What is his overtime pay per hour?

b. One week Mike worked 40 hours and 14 hours overtime. How much did Mike earn that week?

c. Mike decided to open a savings account for just his overtime pay. The first month he earned 11 hours of overtime. The second and third months he did not earn any over time. The fourth month he earned 7 hours of overtime. How much had Mike put in his savings account after 4 months?

d. The bank paid $11.04 interest into Mike's account for that 4 month period. They also charged a $2.00 service fee each month which they deduct from his account. What is the final amount of Mike's savings account?

Chapter II
Cashier

Cashiers take money and make change in supermarkets, department stores, restaurants, gas stations and many other businesses. They put the cost of each item into a cash register or record it on a computer, total the amount of all the items, and deduct coupons or special offers from the total. Cashiers also take money from customers and give them change. Many cashiers receive checks or credit cards from their customers and must know how to process these forms of payment.

Activity 52

Making Change

Subject Area: Math
Materials: Calculators, paper, pencils, handout
Time: 30 to 45 minutes

Part I

Background:
To enhance this activity, instruct your students to write a problem that is similar to the one on the handout. They should write the answers to their problem on a separate sheet of paper and put the paper aside. Students can swap problems, solve them and return them for checking.

The second set of problems may require discussion. If you wish, have your students work on these problems as a class or in small groups.

Procedure:
Using a calculator, work the problems on the worksheet.

Process Questions:
1. *How have bar codes on foods made cashiering faster and easier?*
2. *What foods cannot be bar coded?*

Answers:
1a. Total of Ms. Bower-Lane's purchase is $17.23.
    Total less the coupon is $16.73.
    Change from a $20 bill is $3.27.
 b. Mr. Polaski's total is $18.80.
    The total less $1.10 in coupons is $16.73
    The change from $20 is $3.27

2a. Pink pretties are the best buy. They are $.05 cheaper.
 b. The large box of cereal is the best buy. They are $.88 cheaper.
 c. Students can discuss which kind of lettuce to buy. They should decide if the cost difference is worth the waste of some of the lettuce.
 d. The large size detergent is a great savings of $4.40.
 e. The best buy in dog food is the special boxes which total 6 pounds for $5.00.
 f. Have a discussion about cookies.

Part II

Background:
Depending on the amount of time you have for this activity, have your students repeat totaling different customers orders.

Procedure:
Imagine that you are the cashier at a grocery store. Check the clock before you begin. Use a calculator to total each customer's order.

Process Questions:
1. *How has the computer made cashiering easier?*
2. *How does someone bagging the groceries make the cashiers job easier?*

Answers:
Customer	
# 1	$13.27
# 2	$14.28
# 3	$25.64

Career Development Activities for the Elementary Grades

Handout—Activity 52

Making Change

Part I

Using a calculator, work the following problems:

a. Ms. Bower-Lane purchased a box of rice for $1.95, frozen pizza for $2.75, 1/2 gallon of milk for $1.65, a head of lettuce for $.99, 3 bags of potato chips at $.87 each, cookies for $1.89, and one box of PopNpuff cereal at $2.39. Ms. Bower-Lane also had a $.50 off coupon for the cereal. Ms. Bower-Lane gave the cashier a $20 bill. How much change did she receive? _____

b. Mr. Polaski bought 1 quart of orange juice for $1.19, 2 pounds of apples at $.65 per pound, 2 pounds of ground beef at $2.00 per pound, 2 boxes of cookies at 2 for $2.39, one frozen blueberry pie for $3.50, 3 pounds of potatoes at $.49 per pound, l box of Crispy Wispy cereal for $2.65 and 2 boxes of sugar at $1.15 per box. He also has a coupon for $.50 off the cereal and another for $.60 off the blueberry pie. What is the total amount Mr. Polaski must pay for his groceries. If he pays with a $20 bill, how much change will he receive? _____

2. Have you ever done the grocery shopping for your family? Michael O'Brian did the shopping for his mother. She instructed him to look for the lowest prices for the items on the shopping list. The list is as follows:

2 pounds of peaches, one box of cereal, a head of lettuce, a bottle of laundry detergent (large), one large bag of dry dog food, cookies

a. Michael found two kinds of peaches. Golden glows were $1.37 a pound. The pink pretties were 2 pounds for $2.69. Which kind of peach is the best buy? _____

b. Michael found the cereal his family liked. One small box of the cereal was $2.19. This box contained 16 ounces of cereal. The large box was $3.50 and contained 32 ounces of cereal. Which size box was the best buy? _____

c. Michael looked at the lettuce. All the heads were the same size. One group of lettuce heads was older and some of the leaves were brown. This group was $.20 less than the fresh lettuce heads. Which would you choose and why? _____

d. Michael found laundry detergent in two sizes. The small one contained one quart of detergent and cost $3.10. The large one contained a gallon of detergent and cost $8.00. Which was the best buy? _____

e. Michael found dog food in small boxes as well as large bags. There was a special on the boxes at 3 for $5.00. Each box contained 2 pounds of dog food. The large bag of dog food contained 5 pounds of dog food and cost $8.00. Which was the best buy? _____

f. Michael saw his favorite chocolate marshmallow cookies. They cost $2.89. Graham crackers were only $1.10. Which would you buy? _____

Chapter II   Mathematics Activities

Handout—Activity 52 (cont.)

Making Change

Part II

Imagine that you are the cashier at a grocery store. The store is running the following specials:

   Peaches at $1.09 per pound

   2 cans of Willow green beans for $.99

   1 dozen large eggs for $1.25

   2 cans Super soup for the price of one $.89

   Woof dog food for $.75 off the regular price of $3.50

   2 boxes spaghetti for $1.19

   Shine soap powder-extra large only $5.75 (regular size is $4.50)

   2 rolls Star paper towels for the price of one (one is $.65)

   Uncle John's toothpaste $2.19

   Head of lettuce $.89. Additional $.25 off with coupon

1. *I will say 'Go' when you can start. Check the clock before you begin. Use a calculator to total your first customer's order as follows:*

   1 bag Woof dog food

   1 regular size Shine soap powder

   2 Uncle John's toothpaste

   2 cans Willow green beans

   2 rolls Star paper towels

   Compare your totals with other students. How long did it take for you to total this order?

2. *Time yourself again for the same order. Were you faster? Did you remember the cost of some items?*

3. *Follow the same procedure for the second customer. Use a calculator to total this customer's order as follows:*

   2 pounds peaches

   4 cans Super soup

   1 head lettuce (no coupon)

   1 extra large Shine soap powder

   4 boxes spaghetti

   6 rolls paper towels

4. *Follow the same procedure for the third customer. Use a calculator to total this customer's order as follows:*

   1 head lettuce (with coupon)

   6 pounds peaches

   1 roll Star paper towels

   8 cans Willow green beans

   4 cans Super soup

   3 Uncle John's toothpaste

   2 bags Woof dog food

Career Development Activities for the Elementary Grades

Drafter

Drafters work for architects and other designers. They take the ideas of the designers and turn them into blueprints. The blueprints are the instructions for building the design. Drafters who work for architects design blueprints that builders, plumbers, electricians and carpenters all use to tell them how the house should be built. Drafters use sketch pads or computers to make the blueprints. They must include every detail of the design and precise measurements for each part.

Activity 53

First Draft

Subject Area: Math
Materials: Handout
Time: 30 to 45 minute

Part I

Background:
- You may want to read the instructions aloud, one at a time.
- Ask for volunteers to share their pictures. The pictures should resemble flowers.
- Ask your students if the activity would have been easier if they had known ahead of time that they were building a flower and why?

Procedure:
1. Read and follow the instructions below, as if you were a builder reading blueprints, and see what you build.
2. Color and decorate your picture to make it more attractive.

Instructions
- Draw a small circle in the center of a piece of paper.
- Draw a line straight down from the bottom edge of the circle. The line should be at least 3 inches long.
- Halfway down the line make a long oval shape beside the line on the left side. One end of the oval shape should touch the line on the left side.
- Halfway between the small circle and the oval shape, draw another oval shape on the right side of the line, with one end of the oval shape touching the line on the right side.
- Draw half circles around the small circle in the center of the paper.

Process Questions:
1. Why do drafters have to like detailed work?
2. How are drafters different from architects?

Part II

Background:
- You may want to copy the instructions on separate sheets of paper so that students will not read ahead to the second set of instructions.
- Discuss with your students why there are differences in the drawing from the first set of instructions.
- Ask them why drawings from the second set of instructions are more similar.
- On the second set of drawings, the small square in the center of the larger square may be located in different parts of the space in different drawings. Ask your students why that happened.

Procedure:
1. Follow the instructions in set I. If the instructions are not clear to you, do the best you can. You may not ask any questions.
2. Compare your pictures with your classmates. Notice the differences in your drawings.
3. Follow the instructions below. If the instructions are not clear, do the best you can. You may not ask questions.
4. Compare your drawing with those of other class members. Discuss with your class what parts of your drawings are most alike. Is there one part of your drawing that is different from other students?

Compare the drawings the class did with the first set of instructions to those done using the second set of instructions.

Process Questions:
1. Why do blueprints need to be detailed?
2. Is this a good job for an outdoor person? Why or why not?

First Draft

Instructions—Set I

- *Draw triangles in the four corners of a piece of paper*
- *Draw a large square in the middle of the paper.*
- *Draw a smaller square inside the large square.*
- *Under the square, draw a rectangle.*
- *Draw another rectangle above the square.*
- *Draw a circle under each triangle.*

Instructions—Set II

- Using a piece of 8 1/2x11 piece of plain white paper, draw one triangle in each corner of the paper. The top of each triangle should point to the corner of the paper. All sides of the triangles should be 1".
- Measure 3 1/2 inches down from the top of the paper and mark it. Measure 3 1/2 inches up from the bottom of the paper and mark it. Now measure 2 inches in from each side of the paper. Draw a four inch square in the center of your paper using the marks as guides.
- Draw a 2 inch square inside the 4 inch square. The 2 inch square does not need to be centered.
- 1 inch below the four inch square draw a rectangle that is 4 inches long and 2 inches high.
- 1 inch above the 4 inch square draw another rectangle with exactly the same measurements.
- Draw a circle right against the bottom edge of each of the four triangles. Use a penny to trace the circle.

Career Development Activities for the Elementary Grades

Carpenter

Carpenters work with wood. They build houses and other buildings. They also make and install cabinets and shelves for the inside of buildings. Carpenters must be able to measure accurately, use hand tools like hammers and electrical tools like saws and drills. People who want to become carpenters usually work with experienced carpenters to learn how to do the job.

Activity 54

Hammer and Nails

Subject Area: Math, Health & Safety
Materials: Wood, nails, hammer
Time: 30 to 45 minutes

Part I

Background:
- This activity should probably take place outdoors. You will need to ask the parents or a local construction company to loan hammers. Any building company in your area will have scraps of wood and nails they can contribute to the class.
- Before beginning this activity, discuss with your students how to start hammering the nail slowly and gently, to set it in the wood and to avoid hurt fingers.
- Stress that they can only take ten tries in each round.
- If there is a carpenter willing to demonstrate hammering to the class, invite him or her to participate in this activity.
- Students who hammer their nails all the way in on the first or second try have completed the activity and should continue to assist their partners.

Procedure:
1. Work with a partner to do this activity.
2. Each of you should receive a piece of wood and one large nail. Share the hammer with a partner.
3. Your partner will watch closely while you try to hammer the nail into the wood. You will have ten tries. Your partner will keep a record of each time you hit the nail on the head.
4. Keep score while your partner takes ten tries at hammering the nail.
5. Repeat this activity. You try another ten times to hit the nail on the head and your partner tries ten times. Each of you keeps track of the other's score.
6. Compare your first and second scores. Did you improve?
7. Do this activity one more time. Compare your three scores. Which is the best score?
8. With your class, discuss what you learned about hammering nails during this activity. Was it harder or easier than you thought it would be?

Process Questions:
1. Why does a carpenter have to have good hand-eye coordination?
2. How can changing your hand position on the hammer change how hard you hit the nail?

Chapter II　　　　　　　　　　　　　　　　　　　Mathematics Activities

Part II

1. You are a carpenter who has been hired to build shelves for a hardware store.
2. The store owner has given you a list of the shelves she wants.

    4 shelves that are 3 feet long and one foot wide

    2 shelves that are 5 feet long and two feet wide

    1 shelf that is 4 feet long and 2 feet wide

3. The wood you will buy to make the shelves comes in pieces 6 feet long by 1 foot wide. Figure out how much wood will be left over.

Process Questions:

1. What else would the carpenter need to buy in addition to the wood, to make the shelves?
2. Why is math important to a carpenter?

Answer:

8 pieces

4 shelves that are 3 feet long and 1 foot wide require 2 pieces of wood cut in half. There would be no left over wood.

2 shelves that are 5 feet long and two feet wide require two pieces of wood per shelf to get the 2 feet of width or 4 total pieces. 4 one foot pieces of wood would be left over.

1 shelf 4 feet long and two feet wide would require two pieces of wood. Two 2 foot long pieces of wood would be left over.

Career Development Activities for the Elementary Grades

Bus Driver

Bus drivers transport people between different places in communities and between cities and states. They take tickets, check the bus for cleanliness and safety, and announce different stops. Bus drivers have special routes they follow to pick up people and let them off. They must keep to time schedules on their routes, because people count on the buses to get them to school and work on time.

Activity 55

Ride the Bus

Subject Area: Math, Safety
Materials: None
Time: 20 to 45 minutes

Part I

Background:
You may want to have samples of timetables for your students to see or write a sample time table on the board.

Procedure:
1. Working with your small group, make a time table for Mr. Fritter's bus, using the information below. Time tables list each place the bus stops and the time the bus stops at that place.

   Mr. Fritter's bus leaves the Atlantic Avenue station at 7:10 a.m.

   The first stop is Elm Street. Elm Street is 12 minutes away from the Atlantic Avenue station.

   The second stop is Little Road. Little Road is 8 minutes away from Elm Street.

   The third stop is Peachtree Plaza. Peachtree Plaza is 11 minutes away from Little Road.

   The fourth stop is Midway Station. Midway Station is 45 minutes away from Atlantic Avenue, counting all the stops along the way.

   The fifth stop is Johnson Corners. Johnson Corners is 6 minutes away from Midway Station.

   The sixth stop is Bencher Street. Bencher Street is 16 minutes way from Johnson Corners.

   The seventh stop is First Avenue. First Avenue is 14 minutes from Bencher Street.

   The eighth stop is Atlantic Avenue station. Atlantic Avenue station is 48 minutes from Midway Station.

2. Compare your answers as a class.

Process Questions:
1. What would happen to the traffic in big cities if more people decided to take the bus to work?
2. Why don't more people take the bus to work?

Answers:
The bus arrives at Elm Street at 7:22.
The bus arrives at Little Road at 7:30.
The bus arrives at Peachtree Plaza at 7:41.
The bus arrives at Midway Station at 7:55.
The bus arrives at Johnson Corners at 8:01.
The bus arrives at Bencher street at 8:17.
The bus arrives at first Avenue at 8:31.
The bus arrives back at Atlantic Avenue station at 8:43.

Part II

Background:
- You can enhance this activity by inviting a bus driver to class to answer the questions of your students.
- Ask them what some of the existing rules are for riding the school bus.

Part II

Procedure:
1. Working with your small group, brainstorm a list of some of the problems school bus drivers have with students at bus stops and on the bus.
2. Working from your brainstorm list, write rules for the bus that would help to control the problems.
3. Taking turns with other groups, set chairs up in the style of a bus and role play one problem and one rule that could solve the problem. Applaud all efforts.

Process Questions:
1. What needs to be done to see that students follow bus rules?
2. Why are school bus rules very important?

Chapter III
Social Studies Activities

Real Estate Salesperson

Real estate salespeople help with the buying and selling of homes, buildings of every kind, and land. To do this work, they must know the value of property, the different ways people can purchase property and the laws that have to do with the purchase and sale of buildings and land.

It is also important for real estate salespeople to know many facts about the community and state in which they work. Real estate salespeople are often the first people a family meets when they are preparing to move to a new community. They will have many questions about their new home that the salespeople must be prepared to answer.

Activity 56

New Family in Town

Subject area: Social Studies, Writing
Materials: Paper and pencil
Time: 30 to 60 minutes

Part I

Background:
- Instruct your students to work alone to answer the questions. Review possible sources for answers.
- Discuss the answers as a class. Have them explain how they found their answers.
- Ask for volunteers to tell one new thing they learned about their community.

Procedure:
1. Read the following story and answer the questions the family asks. Discuss the different places you will have to look to find answers to these questions.

   John and Tanya Williams and their children Kim, age 8, and Chad, age 11, are moving from another state to your community. Their old home is in a large city. The children take the city bus to school and Mr. Williams rides the subway to work. Mrs. Williams walks to her job, and to the grocery store. Chad plays ball with his friends at a park across the street from their home. The street they live on is always busy with trucks, buses, cars and taxis. Kim cannot cross the street to the park alone, but must wait for a family member to take her.

   Mr. Williams asks you:

   "What do people here do for work?

   Are there farms here or factories?"

   He also likes to go fishing. He asks:

   "Is your community near the ocean, lakes or rivers?

   How far are these bodies of water from here?"

   Mrs. Williams asks:

   "How is this community different from our old home?

   How is it the same?"

   She also wants to know:

   "Does your community have museums?

   How many and what kind are they?"

   Chad likes to play baseball. He asks:

   "Is there a team I can join here?"

   Kim wants to know:

   "What is this town famous for?"

2. After you have answered the questions, share your answers with your class.

Process Questions:
1. Chad and Kim may be sad about leaving their old home. What can the real estate salesperson do to help them feel better?
2. Why do people care whether or not there are museums in a community?

Chapter III   Social Studies Activities

Part II

Procedure:

1. Write a letter to the Williams family about your state. In the letter try to convince them to move to your state.

2. Be sure to include the following information in your letter:

3. After your students have written their letters, direct them to trade letters with a partner. Give them time to read the partner's letter and then ask for volunteers to share some of the most convincing statements they read in their partner's letter.

Suggestions:

- The weather; tell the Williams why it is enjoyable to live in this climate.
- The geography; tell the family what people enjoy doing in the different regions of the state.
- The cultures and ethnic groups; tell the Williams why these different groups help make the state a good place to live.
- The history; tell the family some of the highlights of the history of your state.

Process Questions:

1. What personal qualities would a real estate salesperson need to have to be successful in the job?

2. Name some other situations where making a good first impression is important.

Camp Counselor

Camp Counselors are leaders of recreational activities for young people. Because camps are usually held during the summer, camp counselors know how to swim and play outdoor sports. They often have special skills they teach to the children and youth who attend the camp. Camp counselors are also responsible for supervising the young people in their charge and keeping them safe.

Activity 57

Summer Fun

Subject Area: Social Studies
Materials: Drawing paper
Time: 30 to 60 minute

Part I

Background:
Some of the children may never have attended camp and will need some discussion first.

Procedure:
1. Think of an overnight camp you have attended or imagine one you would like to attend. Working with a large piece of paper, write the name of your camp at the top.
2. Draw the sleeping cabins on the paper.
3. Draw in buildings for the kitchen and dining area and another for the bathhouse.
4. This camp has a lake for boating and swimming. Draw the lake, the dock and the boats.
5. There is an area behind the lake for hiking. Draw in the trails.

Process Questions:
1. How is a camp counselor like a teacher?
2. What training would a camp counselor need?

Part II

Background:
This can be a small group activity.

Procedure:
1. Using the map from Part I, plan an activity using each of the facilities.
2. There will be a counselor led activity at the lake for swimming, one for boating and another activity for hiking in the woods.
3. You may plan other activities for your camp, like crafts or a marshmallow roast over a campfire.

Process Questions:
1. How does going to camp help students learn about other people?
2. Why does a camp counselor need water safety skills?

Chapter III   Social Studies Activities

Law Enforcement Officer

Law enforcement officers are responsible for keeping our communities safe. Controlling traffic, answering emergency calls, preventing crimes and helping to solve crimes that occur are among their many responsibilities. Laws are made to protect people and their communities and police officers enforce those laws.

Activity 58

Keeping Safe

Subject Area: Social Studies
Materials: Drawing paper, handout
Time: 30 to 60 minute

Part I

Background:
This activity offers a good opportunity to review your school's student handbook.

Procedure:
1. With your class, think of some of the laws a law enforcement officer enforces to keep people and communities safe.

2. Rules in school are also made to protect the students, teachers and the school. With your class, brainstorm some of the school rules.

3. With your class, choose a day when you will look for evidence that a school rule has been broken. Each time you find a rule being broken, write it up on your ticket sheet.

    For example: if your school has a rule that states, 'No Gum Chewing", and you see gum on a chair in the cafeteria, that would be evidence that a school rule was broken. It is important that you do not use names on your tickets.

4. Bring your ticket sheet back to the class and share the evidence you saw that school rules were broken.

5. When people break the law, law enforcement officers may arrest them or give them tickets that require them to pay an amount of money. These are the consequences of breaking the law.

6. With your class, discuss some of the consequences for breaking school rules. What would be a fair consequence for each of the school rules you saw broken. Write your idea for a fair consequence at the bottom of each ticket on your ticket sheet.

7. Share your ideas for consequences with the class.

Process Questions:
1. What would happen if the school had no rules?

2. Who should be involved in making school rules?

Part II

Background:
Students are often fascinated with crime and the consequences. This activity offers a good opportunity for exploring the effect law breaking has on other law abiding people and the reason laws are made.

Procedure:
1. Read each of the scenes described on the handout. Decide if a law in your community was broken. Name the law that was broken and the consequence for breaking that law, if you know it. Decide why you think the community has that law. Write your answers below each description.

2. Discuss your decisions about each of the scenes on the handout with your class.

3. If there are some consequences the class is not sure of, have a student call the police station and ask for the information.

4. Brainstorm other laws of your community with the class.

Process Questions:
1. If people disagree with the law enforcement officer, what is the process open to them to discuss their disagreement?

2. Discuss whether consequences always fit the crime.

Career Development Activities for the Elementary Grades

Handout—Activity 58

Keeping Safe

Read each of the scenes described below. Decide if a law in your community was broken. Name the law that was broken and the consequence for breaking that law, if you know it. Decide why you think the community has that law. Write your answers below each description.

- When he was through eating, John threw his hamburger wrapper and drink cup into the street.

- The school bus was stopped and it's lights were flashing as Wanda's mother passed it in her car.

- Tyrone's father kept driving even though the light had turned red.

- Mary took a pack of gum from the drug store because she knew they wouldn't miss it.

- William's go cart got out of control and ran into Mr. Hanson's fence, knocked it down and ran over his flower bed. The fence was badly damaged and the flower bed was ruined. William got out of there in a hurry so that Mr. Hanson wouldn't know what he had done.

- Joe never wears a helmet when he rides his bike.

Chapter III — Social Studies Activities

Tourist Information Specialist

Tourist Information Specialists provide information to visitors who come to their community or state. Information Specialists know about the history of the area, where visitors can stay and eat, places they might want to see while they are in the area and the special events that are occurring. They make tourists feel welcome and give them directions and advice. In some historic areas, Tourist Information Specialists dress in costumes and give short talks about the history of the area. Wherever they work, they must be friendly, patient and present a good appearance.

Activity 59

The Good Old Days

Subject Area: Social Studies
Materials: Plain paper, markers
Time: 30 to 45 minutes

Part I

Background:
You may want to brainstorm tourist attractions in your state with the class.

Procedure:
1. Draw an outline of your state. Put a star where the capital is located.
2. Put a large dot where your town or city is located.
3. List 3 places of interest to see in your city.
4. List 3 places to eat in your city.
5. List 3 places to stay over night in your city.
6. If there are major tourist attractions in your state, put small dots on the map to show where they are located.

Process Questions:
1. What makes your town or city interesting to tourists?
2. What could your town or city do to attract more tourists?

Part II

Background:
This part may require sensitivity to the feelings of some students.

Procedure:
1. Answer the following questions with your class.
   - Who lives in your community today? What ethnic groups and cultures are represented in your community?
   - What do people do for work today? What are some of the major occupations? How have occupations changed?
   - In what kind of homes do people live in your community?
   - How do people get from one place to another today?
   - What do people wear today?
2. Think of some reasons that people might want to visit your community.

Process Questions:
1. What new information did you learn about your community?
2. What would you tell students your age to see in your community?

Career Development Activities for the Elementary Grades

Commercial Fisher

Commercial fishers make their living catching fish. They work on oceans, rivers, and bays, in large boats rigged with heavy nets. Most of the fish they catch are sold to stores, factories, and restaurants. Some countries use fish to make other products. Fish is an important food and to protect this resource, every nation that borders an ocean has protected waters where no other country can fish.

Activity 60

Gone Fishin'

Subject Area: *Social Studies, Spelling*
Materials: *Map of the continents, handout, pencils*
Time: *20 to 45 minutes*

Part I

Background:
- You may wish to expand this activity into a discussion of how the economy is affected by the commercial fishing industry, particularly if you live in a community affected by the industry of fishing.
- This activity may also be expanded with a discussion of the fish that live in the lakes and rivers of your state.

Procedure:
1. Fish are hiding in the word scramble on the handout. Find the fish listed and circle them in the scramble. There are some extra fish in the list.
2. People eat many more kinds of fish than are on the list. How many others can you name?
3. One of the fish listed is a relative of the octopus. Which one is it?
4. Can you find the shellfish in this list?
5. Some shellfish have claws. Do you know which ones they are?
6. What kind of fish sandwich is a favorite with many Americans?

Process Questions:
1. Fishers may be gone from home for long periods of time to do their job. How do they cope with loneliness?
2. If you are going to be away from your family for a week, how do you cope with missing them?

Part II

Background:
You may wish to enhance this activity by researching the amount of fish different countries consume and the dependence of some nations on the fish they catch in their waters.

Procedure:
1. On a map of the world, label all the continents and oceans.
2. Research where in the world commercial fishers catch the fish listed below.
- Write the name of the fish on the correct location on your map.
- Answer the following questions:

   Name three oceans where sardines are caught.

   Name five fish that are caught off the coast of the United States.

   Are cod a warm or cold water fish?

   Where on the coast of North America are most lobsters caught?

Process Questions:
1. Why are fish such an important resource to some countries?
2. Try to find out about the health of people who eat mainly fish.

Chapter III

Social Studies Activities

Handout—Activity 60

Gone Fishin'

Part I

Fish are hiding in this word scramble. Find the fish listed below, and circle them in the scramble. There are some extra fish in the list.

Word Scramble

```
F M T U N A S A R B I U
L U U N A T Q N S O N S
O A N C H O V I E S U V
U G B O D L W S K H F C
N I T D P U L H C R A B
D M U S S E L S R I X I
E A D G O S P O M S J T
R C A P E L I N M P Y L
S K Q U A C R P E P L P
H E R R I N G I S S O N
A R I H U E L N A L C L
D A S A L M O N R L R T
D L Q D K A B I D A O S
O P U O N R S Q I C A C
C S I M A K T A N K K R
K O Y S T E R S S T R N
```

COD, TUNA, SALMON, LOBSTER, MACKEREL, FLOUNDER, SARDINES, HADDOCK, SHRIMP, HERRING, ANCHOVIES, OYSTERS, CROAKER, MUSSELS, HAKE, POLLOCK, SQUID, CAPELIN, CRAB.

Part II

There is information about commercial fishing sites in the encyclopedia. The following information is from that resource and can be used to complete this activity.

cod	North Atlantic
salmon	North Pacific
tuna	North Pacific, South Pacific, Indian
lobster	North Atlantic, South Pacific
mackerel	North Pacific, North & South Atlantic
flounder	North Pacific, North Atlantic
sardines	North & South Pacific, North & South Atlantic, Indian
haddock	South Pacific, North & South Atlantic
shrimp	North Atlantic, Indian, North & South Pacific
herring	North Pacific, North Atlantic
anchovies	South Pacific, South Atlantic
oysters	North Atlantic
croaker	South Atlantic
mussels	North Atlantic
hake	South Pacific, North & South Atlantic
pollock	North Pacific
squid	North Pacific
capelin	North Atlantic
crab	North Pacific

Educational Media Corporation®, Box 21311, Minneapolis, MN 55421-0311

Career Development Activities for the Elementary Grades

Telephone Installer and Repairer

Telephone repair people maintain the telephone lines that connect us to the outside world. They fix or replace damaged wires and install and repair telephones. Our country is very dependent on telephones. We connect to the Internet on our computers through telephone lines and fax documents all over the world using telephone technology. Telephones can be tied into cameras so that people can see as well as talk to others. All these activities depend on telephone installers and repairers keeping the lines in good working order.

Activity 61

On the Line

Subject Area: Social Studies, Writing
Materials: Paper, markers, crayons
Time: 20 to 45 minutes

Part I

Background:

Encourage your students to make the picture look like the houses and neighborhood where they live.

Procedure:

1. Telephone wires reach from the telephone in a room of your house to the main walls of the house. From the house they reach to the telephone pole and from there to other poles until they get to the main telephone company.
2. Draw a picture showing how the telephone line is connected from your house to the telephone company. Put a circle on spots a repairer or installer would look at if there was a problem.

Process Questions:

1. Why is the job of repairer more difficult after a major storm?
2. Why do repairers need to be in good physical shape and not be afraid of heights?

Part II

Background:

- You may wish to hold a class discussion around this theme, prior to having your students write their stories.
- You may wish to ask for volunteers to share their stories with the class rather than having students share in small groups.
- Another theme for this activity is "What Telecommunications will be like in the 21st century." What will we be able to do that we cannot do now?

Procedure:

1. Imagine what it would be like if all the telephone lines were down all over the world and all the telephone installers and repairers were on strike. Write a story about what a day in American life would be like without the telephone.
2. After you have written your story, tell it to your small group.
3. After everyone has had a chance to tell their story, choose one of the group's stories to share with the class.

Process Questions:

1. Name some ways that life is easier because of the telephone.
2. Name some ways that life has become more complicated because of the telephone.

Chapter III   Social Studies Activities

Mayor

Mayors are the elected leaders of cities and towns. They are in charge of all the departments that serve their communities. They make decisions about budgets and may decide who to hire to supervise the different departments. They also represent their communities at special events and meetings. Mayors make speeches and announcements, hold meetings with other community officials, and sometimes appear on television and in newspapers.

Activity 62

Key to the City

Subject Area: Social Studies, Art
Materials: Paper, paint, crayons, or markers
Time: Two-three, forty-five minute periods

Part I

Background:
- Some examples of city government departments might include;
   a. fire/police/rescue   d. parks/recreation
   b. artsinformation   e. dog catcher
   c. water department   f. garbage collection
- To enhance this activity, take a field trip to the government offices in your community.
- You may want to spread the mural activity over several days.

Procedure:
1. With your small group, draw a slip of paper from the box the teacher passes around. The slip will name a department in your city that you will be studying.
2. Using this information, make a mural of the different departments that shows them serving the community.
3. With your class, plan the mural. It should show your community and the workers from the different departments doing their jobs. For example, if your department is law enforcement, talk with the class about where law enforcement officers might be drawn and what they could be doing in the mural.
4. Use pencil to draw on the mural. Decide as a class how you want to color the mural once the pencil drawings are completed.
5. After the mural is colored, display it in the hall outside your classroom or in the media center.

Process Questions:
1. Is the mayor an elected or appointed official in your town?
2. Is mayor a full time job in your town?

Part II

Background:
Have students present their problems to the class as if they were the mayor and the class was the city council. You may have the class prioritize the problems.

Procedure:
1. Using the departments from part I, pretend you are the mayor.
2. Think of a problem that might develop at your school that would require the help of one of the city departments, such as too much trash on the playground or a fire in the building.
3. Outline the problem to that department and what the mayor would like to have done to correct the problem.
4. Present the problems and discuss them with the class as the mayor would in a city council meeting.

Process Questions:
1. How did it feel to be in charge of making decisions for a city?
2. Was it easy or harder to lead the whole class in the discussion of the problem?

Career Development Activities for the Elementary Grades

Farm Worker

Farm workers help with the planting, raising and harvesting of crops or the care and feeding of animals being raised for food. They may need to know how to use machinery like milking machines and tractors and how to tell when fruits and vegetables are ready for picking. Some farm workers have been replaced by machines that plant and harvest certain crops. However, there are still many fruits and vegetables that are picked by these workers. They play an important role in getting food to our tables.

Activity 63

On the Farm

Subject Area: Social Studies
Materials: Paper, pencil
Time: 30 to 45 minutes

Part I

Background:

This activity is a demonstration of how workers must depend on others to do their jobs. It is also an opportunity to discuss the important role of agriculture in all our lives.

Procedure:

1. With your class, divide into groups of six. If one of your groups has fewer than six, one of the people will play two parts.
2. Each group member should be assigned a part to play from the list below.
   - Gather the hay
   - Feed the cows
   - Do the milking
   - Pasteurize the milk
   - Fill the milk cartons
   - Deliver the milk to the grocery store.
3. Practice the actions that will show what your part does. For example, if you are the pasteurizer, you put the milk into large vats and heat and stir the milk to blend it and kill any germs. You could make purring and stirring actions to imitate a pasteurizer.
4. Form a line with your group so that the hay gatherer is at the head of the line and the delivery person is last.
5. Beginning with the hay gatherer, act out your parts one at a time.
6. Ask all the hay gatherers to go back to their seats. With the class, talk about what would happen to the milk, if the hay gatherers did not do their parts. Bring all the hay gatherers back to the lines and ask the carton fillers to sit down. Again, discuss with your class what happens to the milk if the carton fillers do not do their parts.
7. Try doing your parts again, this time without the milker. What happens to the milk this time?

Process Questions:

1. What happened to the other jobs when the hay gatherer was not there? What jobs were affected when no one was milking the cows?
2. Why do we need to cooperate and be responsible in our own work?

Part II

Background:

This is an opportunity for your students to see how dairy farming has changed over the years.

Procedure:

1. From the list below make a flow chart of the different levels of milk production before it gets to your table.

   Cow
   grocery store
   creamery/pasteurizing
   hay/grain
   farm
   distributor/deliverer

2. Beside each level of the flow chart, write the names of jobs people might have at that level that would help get the milk to your table. For example, beside hay/grain you might write harvester, feed store owner.
3. With your class, add the number of different jobs you thought of for each level of milk production.

Process Questions:

1. How has machinery changed the work of the dairy farmer?
2. How has farming in general changed over the years?

112   Miriam McLaughlin and Sandra Peyser

Chapter III

Ship's Crew Member

Ship's crew members work on large ships. They move and organize the ship's cargo, make repairs and keep the ship clean. They spend many months on the ship as it travels from port to port, delivering and picking up cargo.

Activity 64

Ship Ahoy

Subject Area: *Social Studies*
Materials: *Relief map materials, map of the East Coast of the US*
Time: *Two 45 minute periods*

Part I

Background:
- The cities your students should identify include Boston, New York City, Baltimore, Savannah, and Miami.
- This activity ties well with a study of the earliest settlements in our country.
- Your students will need access to reference material on the different states and a map of the east coast.

Procedure:
1. You are a crew member on a cargo ship. The ship is leaving from the port city of Portland, Maine. It is stopping at ports along the east coast of the United States. The ship will be stopping in: Massachusetts, New York, Maryland, Georgia, and South Florida. Do research to find out what the port cities are in each of these states.

   Massachusetts _____
   New York _____
   Maryland _____
   Georgia _____
   South Florida _____

2. You will have time to visit one famous landmark in each city. Do research to find out which landmark in each city you would most like to visit?

3. During your short visit, you learn one historical fact about each port city. What is that fact?

4. If you had time to go back and visit one of these port cities for a longer time, which one would you choose? Why?

Process Questions:
1. Ask if any of your students have visited or lived in any of the port cities identified in this activity.
2. Which city sounds like the most fun to visit and why?

Part II

Background:
You may wish to tie this activity to a study of the products of different states. For example, what might a ship that picked up cargo in Portland, Maine, be carrying (logs, timber).

Procedure:
1. Using the information you obtained in Part I, make a three dimensional map of the east coast of the United States, including coastal characteristics such as islands and waterways. You can use plaster, papier mache, clay or any other materials that will create the three dimensional effect.
2. Mark the port cities you researched in Part I. You may put a small flag or label for each city.
3. Do research to identify the other port cities on the east coast. Mark those ports on your map.
4. Using a marker or small pins, trace the route of the cargo ship as it is described in Part I. You will not know the exact route, but remember that large ships avoid inland waterways and islands.
5. Display your map in the classroom.

Process Questions:
1. Why do you think most of these cities became so important to their states?
2. How are port cities different from inland cities?

Career Development Activities for the Elementary Grades

Surveyor

Surveyors measure and map the earth's surface. Surveyors establish the boundaries around land, water and even air space. They write descriptions of the areas they have measured that become part of landowners deeds to their properties. When surveyors write descriptions of land, they include all the important features on the land and around the boundaries of the land, which help to identify the property.

Activity 65

Over the Meadow and through the Woods

Subject Area: Social Studies
Materials   Paper, pencil
Time: Two 45-minute periods

Part I

Background:
- You will want to walk the boundary of the school prior to this activity. If the boundary is not marked, request a copy of the surveyors map that accompanies the deed to the property. Mark the boundary before students walk it.

Procedure:
1. With your class, walk the lot line around your school. Notice and take notes of all the physical features of the land, including hills and streams, and be sure to note any buildings that border the school property. Note which boundary is north, south, east and west of the school.
2. Write a description of the land on which the school sits. The description should include the physical features of the land, where the boundaries are located and where the school sits on the land. Be sure to include all the buildings that sit on the land.
3. Share what you learned about the land your school is on with the class.

Process Questions:
1. What kind of land do you think is best for building a school?
2. Were there any trees left on the land when your school was built or were there any planted after it was built?

Part II

Background:
- This activity is much more effective if you are able to have a surveyor visit the school and help your students take actual measurements of the school property. If they have that opportunity, their map should include the exact measurements of the school property.
- Be sure to give them an opportunity to work with surveyors maps before instructing them to make their own.

Procedure:
1. Study a surveyors map. Notice the way different physical features are portrayed on the map.
2. Using the information you gathered in Part I, draw a facsimile of a surveyor's map. You will not have measurements, which are the most important part of the map. However, you can draw the shape of the lot line and the physical features of the property and those that border the property.

   Estimate the approximate placement of the school within the property by walking off the distance from each border to the building. To walk off a distance, walk in measured steps from a starting to an ending point. You will be able to determine which are the closest borders to the school and which are the farthest away.
3. Draw the shape of the school and it's approximate location on the property on your map. Draw any other buildings that are on the school property as well.

Process Questions:
1. Would you buy a piece of property that had not been surveyed? Why?
2. Why is measurement such an important part of surveying?

Chapter III   Social Studies Activities

Taxi Driver

Taxi drivers drive cars that take people from one place to another in a community or city. They pick people up from their homes, and from airports, train stations, hotels, restaurants and even street corners. Many of the people the taxi drivers transport are visitors to an area. They do not know how to get around the city or community and depend on the taxi drivers to help them. Taxi drivers need to know a great deal about the city or community in which they work.

Activity 66

Finding Your Way Around

Subject Area: Social Studies
Materials: Telephone book, map of your city
Time: 45 to 60 minutes

Part I

Background:

Some children have never ridden in a taxi before. Some discussion may have to take place before this activity starts.

Procedure:

1. Find a partner. Decide who will be the taxi driver and who will be the rider.

2. Do the following role plays:

    a. The rider wants to go to a grocery store and calls the taxi. The taxi driver picks the rider up. They discuss where a near by grocery store is and how much the ride will cost.

    b. Change roles. The rider wants to go home from school. He or she must give the taxi driver directions and the driver needs to ask questions.

Process Questions:

1. Why must taxi drivers know their way around a city or town?

2. Discuss times that you have ridden in a taxi.

Part II

Background:

- This activity should promote your student's familiarity with the services and businesses in their community. You may extend this activity by having them research other services available in the community.

Procedure:

Use a phone book and a map to solve these problems.

a. You are a taxi driver. The first customer you pick up wants to find work in your community. Find the name and address of the place you should take him. _____

b. You pick up your second customer at home. Her house happens to be on the same street as the school. She is about to have a baby. Find the name and address of the place you should take her. _____

c. Your next customer has an appointment with the mayor. Find the name and address of the place you should take him. _____

d. You pick up a customer at the bus station who needs a room for the night. Find the name and address of a place you could take her. _____

e. A family with 11-year-old twins gets into your taxi. They want to go somewhere the twins will really like. What is the name and address of the place you suggest. _____

f. Your customer has to appear in court. Find the name and address of the place you should take her. _____

g. You have a customer that wants to buy yarn for a sweater he is knitting. Find the name and address of the place you should take him. _____

h. You have a customer who needs to pay her phone bill and her electric bill. Find the names and addresses of the places you should take her. _____

Process Questions:

1. Why do some people use a taxi to get around town instead of buying a car?

2. How is a taxi driver providing a needed service to people in a town?

Educational Media Corporation®, Box 21311, Minneapolis, MN 55421-0311

Career Development Activities for the Elementary Grades

Chauffeur

Chauffeurs work for people who do not want to drive themselves to their destinations. Many chauffeurs have jobs driving limousines for famous people like movie and television stars. Some chauffeurs work for themselves and own their own limousines. These chauffeurs are hired to drive brides to their weddings or young couples to their proms.

Activity 67

A Road to the Stars

Subject Area: Social Studies
Materials: Maps
Time: 45 to 60 minutes

Part I

Background:
- You may want your students to do this activity at home and involve their families.
- Have a few simple maps available for them to look at before they do their own maps.

Procedure:
Imagine that a famous television star is visiting your school. You invite the star to your home to meet your family. She agrees to come, but asks you to give her chauffeur a map and clear directions to your house.

1. Draw a map from your school to your house. Be sure to include each street name or route number. If you are not sure of all the streets, ask your parents to assist you.

2. At the bottom of the map, write the directions. The directions should explain the map you have drawn. Be very detailed with your directions so that the television star won't get lost.

3. Share your map with your small group. Tell your group which television star you imagine visiting your home.

Process Questions:
1. What kind of preparations would your family make before the star came for a visit?
2. Would you make these same preparations if a friend was coming for a visit?

Part II

Background:
- This activity involves map reading. In many areas, local travel and tourism bureaus are willing to donate maps of the area. Maps that are copied are harder to read.
- For number four, give an example of how to work the problem.

Procedure:
1. The same television star must leave your home and get to the nearest airport. Once again she asks you to draw a map and clear directions for getting there for her chauffeur.

2. Working from a map of your area, decide which is the shortest way to get to the airport from your house. Trace a route on the map (using a highlighter or pencil) that the chauffeur can follow to get there.

3. Read the map carefully and write down each road and each turn the chauffeur must take to get to the airport.

4. Look at the map scale. The scale will tell you how many miles are in each 1/2" or inch of road. Measure the line you traced on the map. How may miles is it from your house to the airport?

5. If the chauffeur can cover about 45 miles in an hour, how long will it take for the limousine to get to the airport?

6. With your class, discuss the following questions:

    Was the map difficult or easy to follow? Why or why not?

    Is the shortest distance always the best way to go? Why or why not?

Process Questions:
1. What kind of information does a chauffeur hear that may be confidential?
2. Discuss the fact that people who work for stars often write books about them. Is this legal or ethical?

Chapter III   Social Studies Activities

Home Health Aide

Home health aides take care of people who are very old or sick. They visit the homes of these people to help them with simple medical procedures prescribed by the doctor. They also help their patients bathe and take care of other personal needs. Some home health aides may do light housework or prepare simple meals for their patients.

Activity 68

Helping Hand

Subject Area: Social Studies
Materials: Small notebook or paper, pens, pencils
Time: Several hours

Part I

Background:
- When preparing your students for this journaling activity, encourage them to think of ways they can help their families and friends during the week.
- You may want to give them a minimum number of helping activities they should perform during the week.

Procedure:
1. With your class, share something you have done to help someone. Discuss the different kinds of helping. For example, helping very old and sick people is the home health aides job; helping around the house is part of your responsibility as a family member. Helping a neighbor find her lost dog is voluntary helping. Weeding your grandmother's garden and not even telling her what you did is perhaps the most generous helping of all.
2. For one week, keep a journal of your helping experiences. Each time you help someone, record it in the journal. Write the kind of helping you did, and what the person you helped said to you (if the person knew you helped). You can help friends, family members, neighbors or other adults. Write how you felt after you helped.
3. During the week, help someone without telling anyone what you did. Perhaps you can pick up your little sister's toys and put them away or take out the trash when no one is around. Record what you did and how you felt in your journal.
4. After your journal is complete, discuss the experience of helping with your class.

Process Questions:
1. When you helped without saying anything, why was it difficult not to tell anyone?
2. What was your favorite helping activity?

Part II

Background:
- Plan a community service activity with the class. This can be a one-time activity like singing at a senior citizen's home for a holiday or a series of visits to a daycare center. Let the parents know of your project and solicit their help.
- Enhance this activity by having your students write a story about their experience.

Procedure:
1. Doing community service means helping in the community. Your city or town depends on citizens to volunteer to help in the community. With your class, discuss a way that you can help someone outside your family or classmates.
2. Make arrangements for beginning your community service.
3. Keep a journal of the experience.
4. At the end of the experience, write in your journal about any new skills you learned and what you found out about other people and your community.

Process Questions:
1. Discuss as a class how both groups (students and those they helped) *benefit from a community service project.*
2. How is volunteering, practice for the world of work?

Social Worker

Social workers help people find the services they need to live and to make changes that will improve their lives. Some social workers work with children, making sure they have safe and have healthy places to live. Others work with prisoners, preparing them to return to the world outside of prison. They need to know about all the helping agencies in their communities and where they can go to get assistance for their clients. Many people who are in trouble or in need depend on social workers to help them.

Activity 69

Where to Go

Subject Area: Social Studies
Materials: Handout, pencils
Time: Two class periods

Part I

Procedure:

1. Working on your own, on the handout, match the people with the places you think could help them.
2. As a class review the agencies listed. Each small group should choose one agency to research and write a one page report.
3. Share the information you learned about the agency with your class.

Process Questions:

1. What are some jobs in our school systems that are like those in the public agencies?
2. How do schools help out families in need?

Answers:

- Families who have a place to live but no money for food may be able to get food from the Food Bank. Also, many religious institutions will provide food for families in an emergency.
- People who abuse substances can be referred to an Alcohol and Drug Treatment Center. In some communities this center is part of the Mental Health Center.
- Women and children who have been physically abused can find help at the Battered Woman's Shelter.
- Most communities have shelters where homeless people can stay at night. Many of these shelters serve meals.
- The Employment Security Commission helps people find work. They arrange for people who have lost their jobs to receive unemployment benefit pay.
- Students who have school problems should first be referred to a school counselor and/or school social worker.
- The Public Housing Authority arranges for families to be placed in low rent housing.
- The Public Health Department offers free and low cost health care for all ages.

Part II

Background:

- You may want to write this plan as a class.
- Be sure your students address the family's needs in order of immediacy.

Procedure:

1. Using the information gained in part I, write a plan for helping the Sanchez family.
2. When writing your plan, be sure to address the immediate needs of the family as well as their long term needs. Begin the plan with what you will do first, next and so on. The end of the plan would include the steps you will take to help the family meet their long term needs.
3. Discuss your plans as a class.

Process Questions:

1. Many people believe that our country should do away with these services. Discuss this issue.
2. Where would needy people go if we did not have public agencies?

Chapter III — Social Studies Activities

Handout–Activity 69

Where to Go

Part I

Working on your own, match the people with the places you think could help them.

People	Places
Family without food	Public Health Department
Person who abuses drugs	School Counselor/ School Social Worker
Mother and child abused by father	Public Housing Authority
Homeless man	Battered Women's Shelter
Woman needs job	Drug Treatment Center
Student skipping school	Shelter for homeless
Family evicted from home	Food Bank
Infant needs vaccinations	Employment Security Commission

Part II

Using the information gained in part I, write a plan for helping the Sanchez family.

Hernando and Theresa Sanchez and their two children have arrived in your community from Mexico. They were promised seasonal farm work. However, the weather has been bad and the farmers are not yet hiring workers. Hernando and Theresa used most of their money just to get to your community. They have no place to live and have not eaten in two days. They are using the money they have left to buy milk for the children. They are dressed in very thin clothes and have no jackets. The oldest child should be in the second grade, but, of course, is not in school. The baby has not yet had her vaccinations. At one time Theresa worked as a maid. Hernando has no experience doing anything except farm work.

Career Development Activities for the Elementary Grades

Civil Engineer

Civil engineers design and build road systems, bridges, tunnels, buildings and water supply and sewage systems. They decide where roads will go and the locations of bridges and tunnels. This profession is the oldest engineering occupation in existence. Civil engineers are at the forefront of growth in America.

Activity 70

Bridge Builders

Subject Area: Social Studies
Materials: See activity
Time: Two 45-minute class periods

Part I

Background:
- The encyclopedia is an excellent resource for information on bridges.
- If you have bridges in your community, have your students research those as well.

Procedure:
1. Working with your small group, choose a bridge to research from the list below.

Notable Bridges

Suspension
Humber	England
Golden Gate	San Francisco
Verrazano Narrows	New York

Cantilever
Jaques Cartier	Quebec
Quebec	Quebec
Forth	Scotland

Steel Arch
New River	West Virginia
Bayonne	New York
Sidney Harbor	Australia

Concrete Arch
Gladesville	Australia
Friendship	Brazil

Continuous Truss
Astoria	Washington
Tenmon	Japan

2. Prepare a report for the class. Divide the responsibilities for the report as follows:
   - Write a paragraph about the bridge telling location, age and interesting facts about the bridge.
   - Make a list on chart paper of the special features of the bridge.
   - Draw a picture of the bridge.
   - Make a presentation to the class about the bridge.
   - If there are more than four students in your group, share the responsibility for one or more of the tasks.

3. Present your report to the class. Respond to questions from students.

Process Questions:
1. How did bridges speed up colonization of the United States?
2. How did bridges change the coast of our country?

Chapter III   Social Studies Activities

Part II

Background:
- This project can be as complex as you choose. Your students can make the project to scale, which will require measuring. They can use as diverse a supply of materials as you wish to provide.
- This project can also be a home assignment for individual students.
- Allow several class periods for students to complete this project. If the project is a homework assignment, students should be given at least three weeks to complete it.

Procedure:
1. Working in your small group, design a small community using a plywood or other firm base and three dimensional material like clay or papier mache, very small items like toothpicks, paper clips, very small pieces of wood or little boxes, would all be useful in doing this project.
2. The community should have an area where people live, and a road system that allows residents to get around easily. Other features may include a water way, park, factory or other businesses, a hill or mountain or anything else the group decides to include. The community should also have a name.
3. You should work with your group to draw a design on paper, before beginning the project.
4. Write a brief explanation of your project, including the name of the community and the names of the students who built it. Display your project in the classroom.

Process Questions:
1. Discuss the many ways that neighborhoods are laid out; single homes, duplexes, townhouses, apartments.
2. What kind of buildings do you have in your neighborhood besides houses (offices, schools)?

Career Development Activities for the Elementary Grades

Construction Laborer

Construction laborers work at building sites. They unload supplies, move materials around and take tools and supplies to the other workers. Construction laborers are responsible for keeping building sites clean and free of dangerous materials. Most construction laborers work on big construction jobs where there are large numbers of workers.

Activity 71

Pick Up Sticks

Subject Area: *Social Studies*
Materials: *Handout, pencils*
Time: *45 to 60 minutes*

Part I

Background:
- You can enhance this activity by collecting materials found at a construction site for the class to identify. Besides different sizes of nails and pieces of wood, there is often tile, tar paper, pieces of electrical wire, small pieces of pipe, plastic and bits of insulation.
- You can also invite a builder to visit the class and talk about the different jobs available on construction sites.

Procedure:
1. Working with the on the handout, cross out those materials that do not belong on a construction site.
2. Beside each of the materials that are left on the list, write how they are used in building.
3. Discuss your answers with your class.

Process Questions:
1. What are some characteristics you have now that would help you become a construction worker?
2. What are some safety issues around the construction site?

Part II

Background:
To enhance this activity, arrange to visit a construction site to see how these machines work.

Procedure:
1. Constructing a building requires several large pieces of equipment. Brainstorm with your class what equipment a construction laborer might need.
2. Match the equipment with the tasks listed below:
    a. digging a foundation
    b. lifting large metal beams
    c. leveling the ground
    d. making a cement driveway
    e. taking away large amounts of dirt or very large trees.
3. Write a short paragraph telling how the tasks above may have been done before there were machines to do the work.
4. Share your ideas with your class.

Process Questions:
1. What other machines do we use to do work for us?
2. Does a constructioin worker need any training? If so, what is it?

Chapter III

Social Studies Activities

Handout—Activity 71

Pick Up Sticks

Part I

1. Working with the following list, cross out those materials that do not belong on a construction site.

nail _____

mailbox _____

hammer _____

flower pot _____

hair dryer _____

boards _____

saw _____

grocery cart _____

tire _____

drill _____

metal pipe _____

math book _____

brick _____

cement _____

blackboard _____

2. Beside each of the materials that are left on the list, write how they are used in building.

Part II

Constructing a building requires several large pieces of equipment. List the equipment that is needed for each of the following tasks:

a. digging a foundation _____

b. lifting large metal beams _____

c. leveling the ground _____

d. making a cement driveway _____

e. taking away large amounts of dirt or very large trees. _____

Roofer

Roofers work on top of buildings installing roofs. They work with shingles, sealers, tar and gravel to make the roofs. Sometimes they even build roofs out of clay. Roofers do repair work too. People who live and work in buildings depend on the roofers to repair the holes and leaks in roofs that are caused by strong winds, rain and snow.

Activity 72

Tippity Top

Subject Area: Social Studies
Materials: Handout, paper, pencils
Time: 30 to 45 minutes

Part I

Background:
- If your school is not near a street that has buildings on it, or a neighborhood, plan a field trip to a community nearby.
- Some of the reasons roofs have different shapes have to do with cost, appearance, practicality, and weather.

Procedure:
1. With your class, plan a walk through a nearby neighborhood or down a nearby street.
2. When you leave for the walk, take a pad of paper for sketching and a pencil.
3. As you walk, stop and sketch each kind of roof you see. If you see more than one of the same kind of roof, do not sketch it a second time. Be sure to include the roof of the school among your sketches.
4. When you return from your walk, share the following information with your class.
   - What was the most common shape of the roofs you sketched?
   - Are the roofs of houses different from the roofs of stores, churches, schools or other buildings? How are they different?
   - What reasons are there for having different roofs?

Process Questions:
1. Discuss the saying "having a roof over your head."
2. What kind of weather can blow the roof off a house?

Part II

Background:
- Parts I and II of this activity work well together but can be done separately.
- Enhance this activity by discussing roofs that have symbolic meaning. Have your students find pictures of religious, government and other buildings in America and other countries that have roofs that are symbolic of something.

Procedure:
Working on your own, read the information on the handout and answer the questions that follow.

Process Questions:
1. Find out what kind of roof you have on your house. Discuss with the class. See if you can find out who built the roof on your house?
2. How often does the roof on a house have to be replaced?

Answers
a. Sharp angle, dark shingles
b. Flat roof
c. Snow can not run off
d. Clay. Many Arizona houses have roofs made of clay tile.

Chapter III Social Studies Activities

Handout—Activity 72

Tippity Top

Part I

Working on your own, read the information below and answer the questions that follow.

Roofs are made in different shapes and from different materials for a variety of reasons. The angle of the roof determines how easily rain and snow run off the roof. Also, dark, shingled roofs attract heat and lighter roofs deflect the heat.

People sometimes use materials for roofs that are found near where they live. Roofs can be made of metal, clay tiles, tar paper, shingles and wood.

Flat roofs are easier to build and so are likely to be less expensive. Even flat roofs have angles that allow the rain to run off.

a. If you lived in Alaska, what would be a good roof to have on your house? What would the roof look like and what would it be made of? _____

b. If you were building a huge office building in Maryland, and were trying to control the costs, what kind of roof would you build? _____

c. What is the risk of having a flat-roofed house in the mountains of Maine where there are heavy snows?
_____

d. You are building a house in Arizona. Building is expensive there and you are watching your building costs carefully. There is a great deal of clay in the soil there. Temperatures in Arizona can rise to well over 100 degrees. What kind of roof do you think might be suitable for your Arizona house? _____
_____

e. Money is no object. You can build any kind of house any place, with any kind of roof you want. Draw a picture of your dream house. Be sure to pay attention to the style of the roof and the materials used to build it.

Career Development Activities for the Elementary Grades

Landscape Architect

Landscape architects design outdoor areas. They plan parks, gardens and the surroundings for large office buildings. Some architects work for people who are building new homes, helping them decide what kinds of trees and shrubs to plant and where to put them. Landscape architects draw designs and sketches of the areas they are landscaping. Some plants and trees do very well in hot, sunny places and others can only grow in cool, wet places, so the landscape architect must know a great deal about plants and trees and how they grow.

Activity 73

Parks and Playgrounds

Subject Area: Social Studies
Materials: Pad and pencil
Time: 30 to 60 minutes

Part I

Background:

Your students can work as a group and make one picture of a park.

Procedure:

1. With your class, walk around the outside of the school. Take a pad and pencil with you.
2. Make notes of areas around the school that would be good park areas.
3. Think of equipment, walkways, gardens, trees or benches that would look good in a park.
4. When you return to the classroom, share your ideas with your small group.
5. Decide, as a group, which ideas you could use to design a park. Decide how many of each color of flower you will plant and where they should go and how many trees you will want.
6. Decide how long the sidewalk should be. Choose the special items you will have, like bird baths, statues and benches.
7. On your own, draw a picture of the park the group has designed. Be sure to give it a name.

Process Questions:

1. Name some parks in your city or town.
2. What are some fun activities to do in a park?

Part II

Background:

Real flowers and leaves or pictures may be substituted for the names.

Procedure:

1. Draw a line down the center of the park you drew in part I.

   The right side of your park gets quite a bit of sun, the left is very shady. Find out what trees and flowers need sun and which ones can thrive in the shade.

2. On the proper side of the park, write the names of the flowers and trees.

Process Questions:

1. Why does a landscape architect need to know about sun and shade for trees and flowers?
2. What trees and flowers are most often found in your community?

Chapter III

Railroad Engineer

Railroad engineers operate trains. They run the locomotives that carry passengers or cargo over railroad tracks to all parts of the country. The railroad engineers are responsible for operating trains safely, controlling speeds, keeping track of the fuel and engine temperatures, and being sure the brakes function properly.

Activity 74

All Aboard

Subject Area: Social Studies
Materials: Handout, maps of the US
Time: 45 to 60 minutes

Part 1

Background:
- You may want to do this activity as a class, tracing the route of the train on a map.
- To enhance this activity, add additional states or have your students write clues for other students to guess.

Procedure:
You are traveling on a train all around the United States. At each stop on the handout, you must figure out what state you are in. You may have to use an encyclopedia and an Atlas to find the answers.

Process Questions:
1. Discuss any experiences you have had riding a train.
2. Discuss any time you have visited any of these states.

Answers:
- 1st stop—New York
- 2nd stop—Massachusetts
- 3rd stop—Michigan
- 4th stop—Illinois
- 5th stop—Kentucky
- 6th stop—Mississippi
- 7th stop—Texas
- 8th stop—California

Social Studies Activities

Part II

Background:
- To enhance this activity, instruct your students to draw maps of the United States.
- Have an atlas and encyclopedia available for students who are not sure where some of the places on the list are located.

Procedure:
1. Working with your small group, chart the shortest routes for you to travel by train to see the sights below.
2. Use pencils and a copy of a map of the United States to chart your train ride. It may take several tries to find the best route.
3. Be sure you start where you live now and return to the same place. Avoid back tracking when planning the route.

Sights to See

United Nations, Seattle, Yellowstone National Park, Disney World, The White House, Memphis, Mount Washington, Death Valley, Everglades, New Orleans, Las Vegas, Mount Rushmore

4. After you and your group have charted a route, look at the states and cities you pass through on your trip. Are there other sites you and your group would like to stop and see. Name those sites and where they are located.
5. Share your group's map with the class.

Process Questions:
1. If you have visited any of these sites, talk about your experience.
2. How has riding the train changed over the years? How has it remained the same?

Career Development Activities for the Elementary Grades

Handout—Activity 74

All Aboard!

You are traveling on a train all around the United States. At each stop, you must figure out what state you are in. You may have to use an encyclopedia and an Atlas to find the answers.

1st stop—Your train station is near the Empire State Building.
What state are you in? _____

2nd stop—It is just twenty miles from the station to Plymouth Rock.
What state are you in? _____

3rd stop—This state has the same name as one of the Great Lakes.
What state are you in? _____

4th stop—The train stops in one of the largest cities in the country. The city sits on another of the Great Lakes. It is often cold and windy there.
What state are you in? _____

5th stop—On the way to the next station, the train passes through farm county. Beautiful horses graze everywhere. At the station you see a sign that says 'Welcome to the Blue Grass State'.
What state are you in? _____

6th stop—This southern state has the same name as the longest river in the country. (Hint: The letter i is an important part of this state's name).
What state are you in? _____

7th stop—The train passes huge ranches where cattle graze. It pulls into a station on the southwestern border of our country. Everywhere you look you see people wearing cowboy hats and boots.
What state are you in? _____

8th stop—The train whizzes through deserts and over mountains, coming to a stop at a station near the Pacific Ocean. The conductor says "Welcome to the land of Hollywood and the Golden Gate Bridge."
What state are you in? _____

Miriam McLaughlin and Sandra Peyser

Chapter III   Social Studies Activities

Astronaut

Astronauts often start their careers in the military service. Many of them have been trained to fly fighter planes. Once they become astronauts, they must learn to use all the technical tools and equipment found in spacecraft. Astronauts go through physical training too, learning to live and move around without gravity. They also practice wearing their space suits to perform special tasks outside the space ship.

Activity 75

Off in Space

Subject Area: *Social Studies*
Materials: *Handout, pencils, paper, markers or crayons*
Time: *20 to 45 minutes*

Part I

Background:
You can enhance this activity by having your students make a diorama of the inside of a space ship.

Procedure:
1. You will be working with the handout.
2. Look up the answer to the question in each section. You may find resources in the media center or your library.
3. Draw a picture of the answer and color it.
4. Share what you have learned about the life of an astronaut in space with your class.

Process Questions:
1. How many of you think you may want to be an astronaut? Why?
2. Why do so few people become astronauts?

Part II

Background:
If you have computer access, have your students use the Internet to access information about astronauts and space exploration.

Procedure:
1. Read the biography of a famous astronaut.
2. Write a report that answers the following questions:
a. Why did the person decide to become an astronaut?
b. What kind of education did the person have—high school, college?
c. What special training do astronauts get?
d. With what mission was the astronaut involved?

Process Questions:
1. What do the different astronauts you reported on have in common?
2. Discuss being an astronaut in relation to having a fear of small, enclosed spaces (claustrophobia).

Educational Media Corporation®, Box 21311, Minneapolis, MN 55421-0311   129

Off in Space

What do astronauts eat in space?
_____

What do astronauts wear in space?
_____

How do astronauts move around in space?
_____

What animal has been in space?
_____

Chapter III

Engineering Technician

Engineering technicians assist engineers with research, the development of new products and building roads and bridges. Some engineering technicians supervise workers, solve manufacturing problems in factories or do surveys to determine where highways can be built. They also may be responsible for setting up and caring for the equipment engineers use.

Activity 76

Building Zones

Subject Area: Social Studies
Materials: See list
Time: Two 45-minute periods

Part I

Background:
- You may want to address the questions in the first part of the activity as a class.
- Encourage your students to use their imaginations when designing the new road for the front of the school.

Procedure:
1. In your small group, discuss the following questions:
   - Why do roads have to be widened?
   - Why are some roads straightened?
   - Why are there highways? What is the difference between a highway and a road in a neighborhood?
   - What kinds of roads did people travel on when the first settlers arrived in our country?

2. Working with your small group, draw a design for a road that looks different from the one that is in front of your school. You may make the road wider, or more narrow. You may put a center strip down the middle, or add trees to the middle or side of the road. Be sure you include cross walks and traffic lights in your design.

3. Share your design with your class.

Process Questions:
1. Why do the roads near schools have crosswalks and traffic lights?
2. How does the weather damage roads?

Social Studies Activities

Part II

Background:
- Once your students have done the research on the materials used in roads, you may want to have them discuss their findings as a class before starting on their models.
- To enhance this activity, have them build their models on pieces of pressed board. Instruct them to paint in grass around the road and make buildings, cars, trees, fences, animals and people for the roadside from available materials.

Procedure:
1. All communities in the United States have zoning laws. These laws are made to protect land and property from roads and buildings that might cause damage. When engineers decide to build a road the engineering technicians check the zoning laws for any restrictions on the size of the road or the materials used in the road. For example, a road being built in a low area near water may have to be raised up to avoid flooding, and may have many layers of stone under the road for drainage. Working with your small group, look up the kinds of materials found in roads. These may include tar, sand, rock and cement.

2. Build a model section of road, using paper, cardboard, stones, sand and other available materials to represent the different materials in the road layers.

3. Once you have completed the model, put labels on the layers of road, telling what materials they represent. If your road is unusual, or built especially for a particular area, write that information on a index card and include it with your model.

4. Display your model in the classroom.

Process Questions:
1. We sometimes take roads for granted. When we want to get to school or the grocery store we forget how much work went in to building the roads on which we travel. What other things do Americans take for granted?

2. From where does most of the money for roads come?

School Principal

Principals are the managers of the school. They make sure the students are studying what they are supposed to learn in their classes. They supervise the teachers, check on the curriculum that is taught in the school, and help to select the books the students use. Principals make many decisions every day. When there is an emergency or a serious problem at the school, the principal must make the decision about what to do.

Activity 77

Head of the Class

Subject Area: Social Studies
Materials: Paper, pencils
Time: 30 to 45 minutes

Part I

Background:
- You may want to talk about some of the rules that actually exist in your school. What are they? What are the consequences for breaking the rules?
- If there are any existing rules in your school that your students would like to explore, include those in this activity.

Procedure:
1. Principals deal with many issues. They often work with the school board to decide what rules and policies the school will have and what consequences will be for breaking the rules. Working with your small group, read the rules below. Pretend that these are new rules and policies at your school. In your small group decide what both the positive and negative sides are to each rule. Ask for a different volunteer from your group to record your ideas about each issue.
    - *Beginning next week, students will wear uniforms. (If you already wear uniforms at your school, you will not wear uniforms beginning next week.)*
    - *Starting today, there will be no more homework assignments.*
    - *You will have a different teacher every week from now on.*
    - *For one hour every morning the entire school will do exercises.*
2. Discuss each issue with the class. Tell the class what your group decided about the two sides, positive and negative, for each issue.

Process Questions:
1. How does it feel when a rule that affects you is made without asking you how you feel about it?
2. Why do some people see certain issues as positive and some see them as negative? Was it hard to see the negative side of the no homework rule?

Chapter III   Social Studies Activities

Part II

Background:
- If you have some issues being debated at your school, use those in place of or in addition to the ones in this activity.
- You will serve as moderator for this activity. It will help move the activity along if you time each group when they present their opinions.

Procedure:
1. Principals work with the school board, parents, teachers, students and community members to make decisions about the school. Imagine you are one of these people attending a school board meeting where decisions affecting the school will be made.

2. The class will divide into five small groups and you will be a member of one of those groups.

   Group I - Principal and school board members

   Group II - Parents

   Group III - Teachers

   Group IV - Students

   Group V - Members of the community (YMCA Director, Owner of fast food restaurant, police officer, doctor, city soft ball coach, real estate sales person.)

3. The issue before the board is Saturday classes. The students in your area miss a great deal of school every winter due to the weather. Students are required to attend 180 days of school every year. Having school on Saturday is one solution.

4. Discuss the issue in your group as if you were the people you represent. Decide how the people you represent would feel about this issue. For example, if you are the principal or a school board member, you may feel Saturday classes are a good solution to this problem or you may have another idea that could solve the problem.

5. I (the moderator) will call on each group to present it's opinions on Saturday classes.

6. Once all groups have presented their opinions, I will summarize, and identify the majority opinion.

7. The next issue before the board is the dress code. The principal feels that too many students come to class improperly dressed. The board is recommending a stricter dress code, including no tee shirts, shorts, hats, or short skirts.

8. Discuss the issue in your group as if you were the people you represent. Decide how the people you represent would feel about this issue. For example, if you are a student, you may not like the idea of a dress code, or you may have a suggestion for a different dress code.

9. I will call on each group to present it's opinions on a stricter dress code.

10. Once all groups have presented their opinions, I will summarize and identify the majority opinion.

Process Questions:
1. Why does the school have rules?
2. How does it affect the school when the rules are different in each classroom?

Aircraft Mechanic

Airplane mechanics repair and maintain airplanes. They check engines, landing gear, instrument panels, cabin pressure, brakes, and even air conditioning systems to be sure they are in good working order. Airplane mechanics are responsible for the mechanical safety of airplanes and regularly inspect the planes for signs of problems. Pilots, flight attendants and passengers depend on them to keep aircraft safe.

Activity 78

Good Working Order

Subject Area: Social Studies
Materials: Paper, pencils, markers or crayons
Time: 20 to 30 minutes

Part I

Background:

You can enhance this activity by discussing different kinds of airplanes, having students identify how the planes are different and why.

Procedure:

1. Working with the outline of a plane, draw in all the parts you know.
2. Beside the picture, list parts of the plane that are inside the plane. Draw arrows to the picture showing where they would be located in the plane.
3. Using a crayon or pen, circle the parts of the plane an aircraft mechanic might fix.

Process Questions:

1. How did people travel long distances before airplanes were invented?
2. What other forms of transportation take people long distances today?

Part II

Procedure:

You are an aircraft mechanic for an airline and are called to fix the following problems:

a. The air to ground radio in the cockpit is not working and the reading lights over four of the seats are blinking.

   Which of these parts should be fixed first? _____
   Why? _____

b. The airplane has a tire that looks like it is going flat. Also, the stewardess has reported that the snack refrigerator is not as cold as it should be.

   Which problem is more serious? _____
   Why? _____

c. The outside door to the main cabin has a loose latch. Also, a faucet in the restroom is dripping.

   Which part would the aircraft mechanic fix first?
   _____ Why? _____

Process Questions:

1. What other parts of planes may cause serious problems if they do not work properly?
2. Share an experience you or someone you know has had on an airplane.

Answers:

a. The air to ground radio is crucial to a safe flight.

b. The safe landing and take off of an airplane is dependent on all the equipment being in good working order.

c. If the door of the plane came loose during flight, it would cause a change in air pressure inside the plane.

Chapter III Social Studies Activities

Tool and Die Worker

Tool and die workers make molds and other devices for machines. The machines they make devices for usually produce products like furniture, parts for airplanes, clothing, television sets, and computers. Tool and die workers work from blue prints or instructions to measure, cut and construct the tools and dies. They must understand how machines work and how different metals react to heat and pressure.

Activity 79

Making It

Subject Area: Science
Materials: Small tools and machines, modeling clay
Time: 45 to 60 minutes

Part I

Background:
- Explore the concept of different factories producing the parts for one product. Students often think that one factory makes all the parts, when in fact, many different manufacturing plants may be involved. A good example of this concept is the pillow stuffed with feathers. The feathers are gathered and sterilized in one factory and the material for the pillows is made in another factory. A third factory may make the pillows from the material and stuff it with the feathers.
- Discuss the different jobs that may be involved in making pillows.
- Explain that tool and die workers make the parts for the machines that make the pillow material, sterilize the feathers and sew and stuff the pillows.

Procedure:
1. Working with your small group, choose a machine that you would like to construct out of modeling clay. Each group member will make one or more parts of the machine, as if each of you was a different manufacturing plant. For example, if your group wants to make a television set, one group member can make the knobs for the volume and other controls and another can make the picture tube. Be sure all group members have assignments. You may choose a machine from the list below or choose one of your own.

   Washing machine, computer, vacuum cleaner, lawn mower, microwave oven

2. Once group members have made their assigned parts of the machine, put the parts together to build your machine.

3. Share your machine with the rest of the class. Explain the different parts your group made to create the machine.

Process Questions:
1. Why do some plants specialize in making only one part?
2. What would happen to the machine if one of the plants closes down?

Educational Media Corporation®, Box 21311, Minneapolis, MN 55421-0311

Career Development Activities for the Elementary Grades

Part II

Background:
- To accomplish this activity, you must request the contribution of discarded televisions, radios, tape players and other small machines.
- Once your students have completed the work on the machines, talk about how the machines had been assembled when they were first made. Imagine, for example, that the class was a factory that made television sets. They would order the knobs from one factory, the picture tube from another factory and the remote from somewhere else in order to assemble the finished product.

Procedure:
1. Working with your small group, choose a machine to disassemble.
2. Collect the tools necessary to work on the machine. You will need at least one screw driver, wire cutters or very good scissors, and a small wrench.
3. Disassemble your machine carefully, being sure to record information on each part you remove. For example, if you remove a plastic clamp, write '1 plastic clamp' on the list. This list is your inventory of the parts in the machine. If your group cannot identify a part, draw a small sketch of the part on your list. If you cannot separate some parts that look like they are different, count them as different parts. For example, if a metal disk is stuck to two plastic wires and cannot be removed, write ' 1 metal disk' and '2 plastic wires' as separate items on your inventory.
4. Once the machine is completely apart, count the number of different parts. If the machine has 22 different sized screws they would be counted as one kind of part.
5. Share with your class how many different parts your machine contained. Discuss the idea that each part may have been made at a different manufacturing plant.

Process Questions:
1. Discuss some of the controversy about making parts in other countries. Why do American companies have parts made in other countries?
2. Discuss the conditions that some workers face everyday.

Chapter III

Social Studies Activities

Forester

Foresters manage timberland. They usually work for lumber companies that own large tracts of forest. Foresters protect the land, by telling the companies what trees they can cut and where to plant new seedlings. It is the job of the forester to see that there is always new growth to replace the trees that are cut.

Activity 80

Do you want to be a Forester?

Subject Area: *Social Studies*
Materials: *Paper, pencils*
Time: *45 minutes*

Part I

Background:
- You may use this activity as a guide for your students to research any occupation that interests them.
- This activity exposes them to the process of identifying appropriate schools, jobs, and courses that will help them reach their goals.

Procedure:
1. Go to your media center or the Internet on your computer. Find out more about what foresters do and share it with your class.

2. Working on your own, write three skills you have now that would help you be a good forester. If you believe you do not have the skills now to help you be a forester, write three skills you have and what job those skills could help you do.

3. Write what kind of environment and the amount of physical activity you like best. Do you like to be inside or outside, standing, walking or sitting? Do you like to be with other people or alone?

4. Write three interests a forester has that are similar to your interests. If you do not have interests that you think are similar to a forester's interests, what occupation might require interests similar to yours?

5. If you wanted to be a forester and there were no forests anywhere near your home, what would you do? If the only forester job was in a foreign country, would you go?

6. What other jobs could you get that would be similar to the job of forester.

7. Share and compare your answers in your small group.

8. As a class, answer the following questions:
   - Were some of the answers in your group similar? What was one noticeable difference in the answers?
   - Did the answers of other group members make you want to change your answers? Why or why not?

Process Questions:
1. Do you have to decide now what career you will be in for the rest of your life? Why or why not?

2. Which people in your life can help you make career decisions?

Career Development Activities for the Elementary Grades

Part II

Background:
- Your students can write their letters in class or as part of a home project. They should save all the information they receive from the schools they write to, for future reference.
- Obtain a course listing from your high school. The list should identify required courses, pre-college courses and electives.

Procedure:
1. Forestry is a very specialized field. According to information in the **Occupational Outlook Handbook,** there were only 55 colleges and universities in 1993 that offered degrees in forestry.
2. Using your library resource center, find out where these schools are located.
3. Write to one of the schools and ask for information on what courses are required to receive a forestry degree.
4. Once you have received a response from the school, decide what you would have to take in high school that would help you get into a forestry program in college. The teacher can provide you with information on high school courses.
5. One way people prepare for a career is to take summer jobs that are related to the field. What summers jobs could your get that would help you prepare for work as a forester?
6. Share what you have learned about becoming a forester with your class.

Process Questions:
1. Discuss the idea that people change jobs and even careers several times during their lives.
2. Why do you need to be concerned about career planning in elementary and middle school?

Chapter III   Social Studies Activities

Heating and Cooling Systems Mechanic

Heating and cooling mechanics work on cooling and heating systems. They install, repair and maintain air conditioners, furnaces and other kinds of heating units, and refrigeration systems. Heating and cooling mechanics also know about electrical wiring, plumbing and machine parts. They must respond quickly when there are breakdowns in heating or cooling systems in hospitals, blood banks and other medical facilities and anywhere where heat or cold threatens people's lives.

Activity 81

Hot and Cold

Subject Area: Social Studies, Writing
Materials: Map, atlas, local paper
Time: Two 45-minute periods

Part I

Background:
- Have your students use a map or atlas for this part of the activity.
- *USA Today* has a list of temperatures around the country. Copy that list or use one from your local paper.
- To enhance this activity, have your students identify extremes in temperatures. Ask them what city is currently the coldest spot in the United states and what city is the warmest.

Procedure:
1. In some parts of the country, heating systems are very necessary. In other parts of the country, air conditioning is very important. Working on your own, decide which is more important in each of these major cities.

   Anchorage, Alaska _____
   Chicago, Illinois _____
   Miami, Florida _____
   Honolulu, Hawaii _____
   Minneapolis, Minnesota _____
   Boston, Massachusetts _____

   Answers: AA, CI, MM, BM (Heating)
   MF, HH (Air conditioning)

2. Look in the newspaper and find a high and a low temperature for this time of year for each city.

3. Share your answers with your class. Discuss how people live in areas that can be very hot or very cold. How do they stay comfortable? What do they do for fun?

Process Questions:
1. Discuss any experiences you may have had living in extremely cold or warm climates.
2. How do people stay cool if there is no air conditioning?

Educational Media Corporation®, Box 21311, Minneapolis, MN 55421-0311   139

Career Development Activities for the Elementary Grades

Part II

Background:
- This activity will take place over several weeks. If your students do not receive prompt responses to their requests, encourage them to choose another city to research.
- To enhance this activity, have them access information on the city they chose on the Internet.

Procedure:
1. Choose a city from the list in Part I, or think of a city you are interested in, and write to the Chamber of Commerce in that city. Explain that you are a student seeking information on the climate of the area and the recreational activities in the area. Ask them to send you the information. Be sure to include your home or classroom address.
2. Once you have received the information, prepare an oral report on your city for the class. Tell what you learned about the climate and recreational activities.
3. With your class, compare the climate and recreational activities of the different cities. Does the climate have an effect on the kinds of recreation people participate in? If so, what kind of effect?
4. Working with your class, assemble the information you received in a notebook to keep in the classroom.

Process Questions:
1. Relate any experiences you may have had moving from one climate to another or vacationing in a different climate.
2. What effect does the climate in your state have on recreational activities?

Chapter IV

Science Activities

Career Development Activities for the Elementary Grades

Park Ranger

Park rangers patrol the forests and park lands looking for problems like fires or flooding, assisting park visitors and sometimes rescuing people who have become lost or injured. They are also the police for the park, enforcing the laws that protect the forests, beaches, mountains and waters that are part of state or national park systems.

As part of their work, park ranger's must know about the trees, bushes and flowers that grow in the park and about the birds and animals that live there.

Activity 82

Birds, Bees, Flowers and Trees

Subject Area: Science
Materials: Paper and pencil, crayons or markers
Time: 30 minutes plus library time

Part I

Background:
- Expand this activity to include other trees, flowers, or birds that are native to your area.
- Plan a trip to a park if possible. If you have a state or national park nearby, be sure to include a visit with the park ranger.

Procedure:
Most states choose different symbols from nature to represent them. They may be flowers, trees, and birds that are commonly found in the state.

1. Does your state have a state flower? What is it? Draw a picture showing what your state flower looks like.
2. Does your state have a state tree? What is it? Draw a picture showing what the state tree looks like.
3. Does your state have a state bird? Draw a picture of your state bird.
4. The United States has a national bird. Do you know what it is? Draw a picture of the national bird.
5. With your class, try to find your state flower, tree and bird in the neighborhood around the school.

Process Questions:
1. Why does the park ranger need to know about the flowers, trees, animals and birds that live in the state?
2. What are you studying now that would help you become a park ranger? Why would it help?

Part II

Background:
This activity works well as a cooperative learning activity. Make sure that each group member takes part in presenting the report to the class.

Procedure:
Park rangers also need to know about poisonous plants.

1. With your class, list some poisonous plants you have heard about.
2. Working in a small group, choose a plant from the list to report on to the rest of the class. Look up information on the plant in the library. Try to find a picture of the plant to copy, or draw a picture of the plant from a description. Answer the following questions in your report:
   a. What does the plant look like?
   b. Where does the plant grow?
   c. What about the plant is poisonous?
   d. What happens to a person who touches the plant?
   e. What do the park rangers need to do to help a person who has touched the plant?
3. Present your report to the class.

Process Questions:
1. What are some ways to prevent problems with poisonous plants? (Answers could include wearing protective clothing, knowing what the plants look like and avoiding areas where the plants grow.)
2. Besides park rangers, what other kinds of careers require knowing about flowers, trees and plants?

Miriam McLaughlin and Sandra Peyser

Chapter IV Science Activities

Pilot

Some pilots fly large planes that transport people and products all over the world. Others fly small planes that dust the crops for farmers or help firefighters put out forest fires. Helicopter pilots fly much shorter distances, sometimes transporting sick people to hospitals, or reporting on traffic conditions and road accidents for radio stations. Helicopters are also used to rescue people who cannot be easily reached in other ways. Pilots not only have to know how to operate their planes and helicopters, but how speed and weather affect flying conditions. Airline pilots must learn to operate the complex computers that help to fly large airplanes; and all pilots must know the laws that govern flying. Pilots are very well-trained and tested before they are given a license to fly.

Activity 83

Flying High

Subject Area: Science
Materials: Strips of paper
Time: 30 to 45 minutes

Part I

Background:
- Instruct the small groups to divide the research tasks for this activity.
- Locating and measuring some outside areas before the groups take their walks will help you to more easily direct this activity.
- After the groups have returned from their walks, demonstrate how to work the problem of walking speed.
- As an additional step in this activity, the groups can make bar graphs showing the speeds of the different modes of transportation.

Procedure:
1. With your small group, do some research to find out how fast a jet plane can fly. The speed is measured by the distance something can travel in one hour. Record that information on your Speed Data Sheet.
2. Continue your research to find out how fast a passenger train can travel. Record the information on your Speed Data Sheet.
3. Now, find out what is the fastest speed the law allows for a car to travel within your state. You are looking for your state's legal speed limit. Record the information.
4. With your group, take a walk outside for ten minutes. Have your teacher help you measure the distance you walked. There are 60 minutes in an hour, so to get your speed you will have to multiply the distance you walked by 6. Record the speed you walked on your data sheet.

Process Questions:
1. People do not always want to get to a place by the fastest method of travel. Why would someone choose a slower method?
2. Name some times when getting somewhere fast is important.

Career Development Activities for the Elementary Grades

Part II

Background:

- Using the following directions, practice making the helicopter from a paper strip.
- When demonstrating to the class, make sure that every student is keeping up with you. If a student has trouble making the helicopter fly, review the steps or have the student begin a new one.
- Ask the class for ideas on making the helicopter go faster. (It will build speed if you stand on a chair so that it has farther to fall. It will go faster if you attach a paper clip to the bottom.)
- Ask the class what would make the propeller turn in the opposite direction. (Reverse the direction of the blades and it will turn in the other direction).
- Ask the class what would happen if they had made their helicopters out of a much bigger strip of paper. Would it go slower or faster? You may want to experiment with a larger paper strip.
- Ask the class what force is causing the helicopter to fall to the ground. Ask what is causing the helicopters propellers to turn.
- Ask the class what keeps real helicopters from falling to the ground.

Procedure:

Follow the directions below, and your teacher's demonstration, and build and fly your own machine.

Directions

- Each class member receives a strip of paper 2" x 7".
- Hold the paper strip vertically.
- Fold the top over to approximately one and one half inches from the bottom.
- Crease the paper at the fold.
- Open the strip and hold it vertically again.
- From the top, tear the strip down the middle, just to the crease, creating two flaps.
- Fold one flap forward and one flap back.
- Crease the flaps at the fold and let the flaps loose.
- One quarter inch below the crease, tear the strip on either side toward the middle. Leave one quarter to one half inch attached in the middle.
- Fold the sides of the bottom of the strip toward the middle so that one side overlaps the other creating a stem.
- Fold the bottom of the stem up three quarters of an inch.
- Stand up, hold the strip up vertically by the stem.
- Let it go.

Process Questions:

1. Pilots are not only responsible for their own safety but the safety of their passengers. How do you think it feels to have so much responsibility?
2. Name some ways in which you have to assume responsibility.

Chapter IV   Science Activities

Meteorologist

Meteorologists are people who study the weather. They use tools like radar and computers to forecast weather and to watch out for dangerous storms. Some meteorologists work for television and radio stations and report on the weather. Others work in laboratories and schools that study weather patterns and ways the weather affects our environment.

Activity 84

Weather Words

Subject Area: Science
Materials: Paper, crayons or markers, magazines
Time: 30 to 60 minutes

Part I

Background:
You may want to partner your students at the beginning of this activity. If you do, ask them to share their answers with two other partners, and to tell their "bad weather" stories in groups of four.

Procedure:
1. Answer the following questions by looking up the underlined words.
    a. If the meteorologist <u>forecasts</u> a big storm, does that mean a storm is definitely coming?
    b. How bad is a tornado that causes <u>catastrophic</u> damage?
    c. Is it safe to be near the ocean during a <u>hurricane</u>? Why?
    d. What might happen if you get caught in a <u>blizzard</u>?
    e. Is it true that a <u>heat wave</u> can be dangerous for animals? Why?
    f. Find a partner and share your answers.
2. Take turns with your partner telling about an experience you have had with bad weather.

Process Questions:
1. What kinds of jobs are seriously affected by the weather?
2. What kinds of activities that you do with your family or class are affected by the weather?

Part II

Background:
- You may want to list the following questions for your students to include in their weather paragraph.
    1. What time of year does the weather most often occur?
    2. Where in the United States is this weather most common?
    3. What happens during this weather?
    4. What can people do to protect themselves during this weather?
- After your students have completed their collage, ask them to explain their pictures to the class.

Procedure:
1. Choose a kind of weather from the following list:
    Blizzard, Heat wave, Hurricane, Tornado, Thunderstorm
2. Find information about the weather you have chosen and write a paragraph describing what happens in the weather.
3. Make a collage of pictures that show what kinds of problems this weather may cause. Tape your paragraph to the bottom of your collage.

Process Questions:
1. Often during bad weather people seem very willing to help each other. What are some ways they help?
2. During what other times can you think of ways that people cooperate with one another?

Career Development Activities for the Elementary Grades

Gardener

Gardeners care for grass, trees, and flowers. They know what plants grow best in different areas and how to control the pests that can kill plants and trees. Gardeners are the people who keep the areas around our parks and public buildings neat and attractive. They work outside in all kinds of weather, planting, trimming grass and shrubs, watering, weeding and preparing soil.

Activity 85

How Does Your Garden Grow?

Subject Area: Science
Materials: Package of seeds, paper cups, soil, journals, pencils
Time: Periods of 20 minutes over several weeks

Part I

Background:

- This activity will take place over several weeks. Remember to allow time for your students to check their plants and write in their journals each day.
- Choose seeds that will do well in the light available in your classroom.
- Try to find enough variety so students can compare the growth of their seeds with those in other groups.

Procedure:

1. Make a small hole in the bottom of a paper cup. Write your name or initials on the cup.
2. Fill the cup almost to the top with potting soil. Tap the soil down lightly with your fingers. Do not pack it down.
3. Read the directions on your group's packet of seeds. The directions will tell you how deep to plant your seed. In three places on the soil press down with the eraser end of a pencil or your little finger to make places for the seeds. Be sure the places are no deeper than the directions say the seeds should be planted.
4. Divide up the seeds among the group. Each group member should plant three seeds in the three places they made in their soil.
5. Cover the seeds lightly with soil and gently tap the soil over the seeds.
6. Use a spray bottle to water your seeds. The soil should be moist but not wet.
7. Read the directions on your seed packet. The directions will tell you if the seeds grow best in sun, shade, or bright light. Choose the place in the classroom you believe will be best for your seeds.
8. Begin a journal by writing the day and date that you planted the seeds in a small notebook. Each day check your seeds. If the soil appears dry, spray the soil until it is moist again. Write in your journal if you water the soil that day. If you see no change, just write 'no change' in your journal and the date.

Chapter IV   Science Activities

9. Be sure to record the first day and every other day you see signs of leaves or growth. Describe what the growth looks like. When the plants are big enough, measure them every day and record the changes. If one or two of the seeds are not doing well, you may wish to remove them to give the strong plant room to grow.

10. In your journal, write the answers to the following questions:
    - How many days passed from the time you planted your seeds until the time you saw the first growth?
    - Once the plants started growing, how much did they grow each day?
    - How many days passed from the time you saw the first growth until the time the plants grew their second sets of leaves?
    - Did you notice any other changes to the plants as they were growing?

11. Compare the answers you gave with the answers of others in your group. The answers should be nearly alike. If someone in the group has a plant that grew less or more than the others, try to figure out why. For example, compare the number of times that student watered his or her plant with other group members watering records.

12. Work with your group to prepare a report on the growth process of your plants. Include any differences in growth among the group members' plants.

13. Once the plants are between two and three inches high you can plant them outside or in a larger pot.

Process Questions:

1. If you are a person who prefers staying indoors and keeping clean, should you choose gardening as a job? Why or why not?
2. Name some tools a gardener would use.

Part II

Background:
- This activity will continue over a 4- to 6-week period.
- Choose seeds with a relatively short germination period. Be sure the seeds are suitable to the light conditions in your classroom.
- Having your students research the effects sunshine, water and the nutrients in the fertilizer have on plants would be an additional step in this activity.

Procedure:

1. Follow the directions in the first six steps of part I for planting your seeds. Choose one of your group's cups to water every day. Write 'water every day' on a piece of paper and place the cup on the paper. The person who planted that cup will be responsible for the watering.

2. Choose another cup to receive a small amount of fertilizer, once after the first growth appears and once after the leaves appear. Write 'fertilizer' on a piece of paper and place the cup on it. The person who planted that cup will be responsible for fertilizing. That person should water this cup as needed.

3. Choose another cup to water once every 3 or 4 days. If a weekend interferes, the watering should be delayed until the next week. Follow the same process, writing 'water every 3 or 4 days' on a piece of paper and placing it under the cup.

4. One cup will be watered when the soil begins to feel dry. Write 'water as needed' on a piece of paper and place it under the cup.

5. All of these cups should be placed in the location which has the kind of sunlight suggested in the directions on the seed packet.

6. A fifth cup should be planted and placed out of any sunlight. Water the fifth cup as needed. If your group is small, you may have to share responsibility for one of the cups.

7. Write in your journal the day you planted the seeds and the instructions you have for caring for them. Whatever cup you planted is the one you will take care of throughout this experiment.

8. Continue to observe the progress of your seeds each day. If nothing changes, write 'no change' in your journal. If you water or fertilize, note that you did so in your journal.

9. When the first growth appears, observe the changes in your plant and measure the growth each day. Record this information in your journal.

10. After a period of four to six weeks, work with your group to compare the progress on each plant for which your group had responsibility. Write the information in your journal.

    Answer the following questions with your group and write your conclusions in your journal.

    - How does the plant that was watered daily compare with the other plants? What is different? What is the conclusion of the group after comparing this plant with the others?
    - How does the plant that received no light compare with the other plants? What is the conclusion of the group after comparing plants?
    - How does the plant that was fertilized compare with the other plants. How is it different? What can the group conclude from these observations?
    - How did the plant that was watered every three or four days do? Did it do better or worse than the plant that was watered every day? Did it do better or worse than the plant that was watered as needed? What can the group conclude from these observations?

11. Prepare a report on your findings to share with other groups.

Process Questions:

1. Where do gardeners learn what they need to know about plants?
2. Is there a difference in the information a professional gardener needs to know and what a home gardener should know?

Chapter IV

Oceanographer

Oceanographers study the oceans. They may do research on the currents and tides or explore the ocean floor. Some oceanographers study the water in the oceans, researching the elements and nutrients contained in the water. Oceanographers work in laboratories near the ocean or travel around the world to do their research.

Activity 86

Oil and Water

Subject Area: Science
Materials: Handout, vegetable oil, oatmeal, containers, paper towels
Time: 45 to 60 minutes

Part I

Background:
- Cut the story page handout into strips along the dotted lines. Give a set of strips to each small group.
- Discuss with the group the problems an oil spill can cause to the environment.

Procedure:
1. Using the story strips given to you by your teacher, work with your group to put the story in an order that makes sense.
2. Raise your hands when you have completed the story.
3. Take turns reading the story aloud.

Process Questions:
1. Why do you think it is important to clean up an oil spill as quickly as possible?
2. What other jobs, besides cleaning up oil spills, do oceanographers do?

Science Activities

Part II

- Vegetable oil works fine for this activity.
- Review the steps the students took in doing the activities. Compare these steps to an actual spill.
- Have paper towels or other absorbent material on hand for students to use to get rid of the oil.

Procedure:
1. Fill a clear plastic cup half full with water.
2. Pour the oil provided by your teacher into the cup.
3. Observe the water as you pour.
4. Record on your data sheet what happened.
5. Do the following experiments and record what happens on your data sheet.
   - Slosh the water and oil gently around inside the cup.
   - Stir the water and oil together with a stick or spoon and then wait a few seconds.
   - Look inside the cup from the top. What do you see?
   - Add a few drops of food coloring to the cup. What happens?
   - Sprinkle a few flakes of oatmeal into the cup. What happens?
5. Imagine pouring oil into a bowl of goldfish. What would happen to the fish? Explain on your data sheet what might happen and why.
7. Imagine that you are not allowed to pour the oil out of your cup. What else could you do to get rid of it. Experiment and record your findings on your data sheet.

Process Questions:
1. What other kinds of 'accidents' can you name that affect the environment?
2. What kind of man-made pollution affects the environment?

Educational Media Corporation®, Box 21311, Minneapolis, MN 55421-0311

149

Career Development Activities for the Elementary Grades

Handout—Activity 86

Oil and Water

An Oil Spill

An oil tanker was going through the Antarctic Ocean.

It was carrying a load of oil to a small country in South America.

Suddenly the tanker hit an iceberg.

The iceberg made a large hole in the side of the tanker.
Thousands of gallons of oil spilled into the ocean.

It spread in a thick layer over the surface of the ocean.

The oil was so thick in fact, it cut off the oxygen to the ocean water.

Fish and plants that depended on the oxygen in the water began to die.

Other sea life were dying as well.

Experts came from all over the world to see exactly what kind of damage the oil spill was causing.

Bill Walker was one of the expert oceanographers who was called in.

Bill took water samples and sent them back to his lab.

He also took samples of plants growing in the ocean near the oil spill.

Bill continued to work as the oil spill was being cleaned up.

When Bill was ready to return to his lab, he gathered samples of some of the fish that had been killed by the oil spill to take with him.

What he learned from studying these samples in the lab will help the workers still trying to clean up the ocean and shoreline where the oil was spilled.

Bill will return to the oil spill many times before all the oil is gone.

150 Miriam McLaughlin and Sandra Peyser

Chapter IV   Science Activities

Plumber

Plumbers install and repair the pipes that bring water into houses and other buildings and take waste water out. They decide where the pipes should go, install them and then connect them to the sinks, toilets, and bathtubs in our houses. They also connect pipes from the house to the sewage pipes or septic system that takes the used water away. Plumbers also help to conserve water by fixing leaks and dripping faucets.

Activity 87

Water Water Everywhere

Subject Area: Science, art
Materials: Drawing paper
Time: 30 to 45 minutes

Part I

Background:

To enhance this activity, discuss the kinds of repairers needed for the other problems on the list.

Procedure:

1. With your class, discuss some of the problems people have in their homes that need a repairer. Examples include:

   Squeaky or stuck door

   Dripping faucet

   Shingles blown off the roof

   Toilet won't flush

   Broken window

   Torn sofa cushion

   Clogged drain in the sink

   Light switch doesn't work

   Water coming from bottom of refrigerator

2. Decide which problems might need a plumber to fix them.

3. With your class, brainstorm the kinds of tools plumbers might use to make the repairs.

4. Draw a picture showing the problem before the plumber fixed it and after. For example, draw a dripping faucet on one side of the paper and a dry faucet on the other side.

Process Questions:

1. Have the class share experiences they have had with plumbers coming to their homes.

2. After a month of a dripping faucet, what happens to the water bill?

Part II

Background:

You can enhance this activity by discussing other places that need plumbers besides homes.

Procedure:

1. Divide one large piece of paper down the middle.

2. On one side of the paper draw the inside of a modern house that has all the plumbing in the bathroom, kitchen and laundry room.

3. On the other side of the paper, draw a picture of a house that doesn't have plumbing.

   Is there a bathtub? Where is it?

   Is there a toilet? Where?

   Is there a kitchen sink? Where?

4. Using a red pen or pencil, write the letter 'p' on each item in the modern house that would need a plumber to install or fix it. Do the same on the house that doesn't have plumbing.

5. With your class, discuss the differences in the two houses.

Process Questions:

1. What kinds of information do plumbers need in order to do their jobs?

2. What did people do before indoor plumbing?

3. Are there places that still use outdoor plumbing?

Optometrist

Optometrists test eyesight and decide what kind of glasses will help their customers see better. They are different from ophthalmologists because they do not have medical degrees and cannot treat eye injuries or diseases. They often make the lenses and sell the eye glasses and contact lenses they prescribe. Optometrists also repair and adjust glasses.

Activity 88

How Far Can You See?

Subject Area: Science, Writing
Materials: Handout
Time: 30 to 45 minutes

Part I

Background:
- Part I and Part II can be combined.
- When introducing this activity, stress the importance of people like optometrists that help us take care of our sight and other senses.
- This activity can be enhanced by using an object like an apple. Ask students how many senses they use when they eat an apple. Go through the steps:
- The students sees the red apple.
- They feel the smooth skin.
- They smell the apple smell.
- They take a bite and hear the crunch of the apple in their teeth.
- They taste the apple.

Procedure:
Sight is one of our five senses. It is through the senses that we learn about the world.

1. Read the list of words on the left side of the page. These words are associated with one or more of the five senses. The five senses are listed on the right side.
2. Draw a line between each word and the sense you think is associated with it. There may be more than one sense associated with a particular word.
3. Think of other words associated with the different senses and add them to the list.
4. Which of the words were connected to more than one sense?

Process Questions:
1. How does the lack of any of the senses change person's life?
2. Explore with your students which sense they think they could best do without.

Part II

Background:
Explain to students that when someone loses the sense of sight they are considered handicapped. However if a person does not have a sense of smell they are not considered handicapped. Your students may want to explore this idea in their essays.

Procedure:
1. Working with the list on the handout, put a line under all the words associated with sight.
2. Make a list of the activities that people do that require sight.
3. Write a short essay on the difficulties someone faces who is visually impaired. Share your essay in small groups.

Process Questions:
1. What have scientists discovered or invented to help people who have lost one of their senses?
2. Name some important people in history who were hearing or visually impaired.

How Far Can You See?

1. Read the list of words on the left side of the page. These words are associated with one or more of the five senses. The five senses are listed on the right side.
2. Draw a line between each word and the sense you think is associated with it. There may be more than one sense associated with a particular word.

perfume	
soft	
sweet	**Sight**
voices	
smooth	
color	
prickly	**Taste**
roar	
stink	
music	
faces	
odor	**Touch**
bitter	
flowers	
hot	
laughter	
deodorant	**Hear**
salty	
whistle	
book	
slippery	**Smell**
cold	
sunset	
picture	
seasoning	
computer	

Astronomer

Astronomers study the universe. They do research on the sun, moon, stars and planets. They work with special equipment that can photograph and record images at great distances far greater than the eye can see. Through their work, astronomers help us to understand the planet earth and its place in the universe.

Activity 89

Shining Stars

Subject Area: Science
Materials: See below
Time: 45 to 60 minutes

Part I

Background:
You can enhance this activity by having small groups or partners research and report on one planet.

Procedure:
1. Draw a small circle in the center of the paper. This circle represents the sun.
2. The nine planets listed below orbit around the sun:

MERCURY	PLUTO	JUPITER
EARTH	VENUS	MARS
NEPTUNE	URANUS	SATURN

3. Find out where each planet's orbit is in relation to the sun. For example, which planet orbits closest to the sun and which is farthest away?
4. Draw and color the planets in the correct place around the sun.
5. With your class, answer the following questions:
   a. Is the planet earth close to the sun or far away? _____
   b. Of the nine planets, which is the largest? _____
   c. If earth is always orbiting around the sun, why don't we see the sun all the time? _____

Process Questions:
1. Is life on other planets? Discuss your thoughts.
2. What is the occupation of persons who may someday travel to other planets?

Chapter IV

Science Activities

Part II

Background:
- This activity is especially effective if students choose different constellations and project them at the same time in a large darkened room. Be sure to follow a star chart so that each constellation is in its proper location in the 'sky.'
- Students put their star charts upside down on the containers to get mirror image patterns of the constellations. The constellations will then appear normal when projected.
- MATERIALS

   Cardboard containers, preferably the round cylinder type that usually contain oatmeal.

Procedure:
1. Find a picture of a star constellation or star chart in a book about astronomy.
2. Place the bottom of your cardboard container on a piece of paper and trace around it.
3. Copy the star chart onto the piece of paper staying inside the lines you have just traced. Use a pen or marker to do the drawing.
4. Carefully lay your drawing over the bottom of the container, FACE DOWN. You should be able to see the stars through the back of the paper. The traced lines on your paper should be even with the edges of the container bottom.
5. Using a nail, punch holes through the paper and the container bottom exactly where you see the stars on the paper.
6. Remove the paper. Check the bottom of the cardboard container to be sure you can see through the holes.
7. Go to a dark room, insert a flashlight into the open end of the container, tilt the flashlight slightly so it is not shining directly through the holes.
8. Project your constellation onto a wall and enjoy your miniature planetarium.

Process Questions:
1. Why do you think early civilizations worshipped the sun, moon and stars?
2. Why is mankind still fascinated by the sky and all it contains?

Career Development Activities for the Elementary Grades

Bakery Worker

Bakery workers make breads, cakes, cookies, and pies that are sold in bakery shops or to restaurants. They must know how to read recipes and measure and mix ingredients. Some bakery workers know how to decorate cakes and cookies. Bakery workers bake with large amounts of flour, sugar and yeast.

Activity 90

Bake Me a Cake

Subject Area: Science
Materials: See activity
Time: 45 to 60 minutes

Part I

Background:
- This activity works best if you use parent volunteers to work with the small groups.
- Send a note home with your students asking their parents for donations of ingredients and supplies.
- If you do not have access to an oven, a toaster oven will work.
- This activity and other recipes are wonderful tools for teaching measurement.

Procedure:
1. Working with your small group, assemble the supplies and ingredients on the handout.

Process Questions:
1. What kind of bakery items does your family make? Do you help?
2. Name some other stores that have bakeries inside them.

Part II

Background:
- Glucose is the principle food of yeast and is contained in the corn syrup. When yeast comes in contact with glucose, fermentation begins immediately. Yeast can also get glucose from table sugar and from corn starch but must break them down into simpler sugars before fermentation can occur.
- Ask your students how their observations support this idea.

Procedure:
1. Yeast is used by bakers to make bread rise. It is a one celled plant that cannot make its own food in the way that plants containing chlorophyll do. Yeast must get its food from its surroundings. Yeast is inactive until conditions are favorable. When conditions are right, yeast springs to life and begins the process of fermentation. Two products fermentation produces are alcohol and carbon dioxide. It is the carbon dioxide in the yeast that causes bread to rise.
2. To observe the process of fermentation, work with your small group to assemble the supplies on the handout and follow the directions.

Process Questions:
1. How is a bakery worker like an artist?
2. Where can you learn the skills of a bakery worker?

Chapter IV

Science Activities

Handout—Activity 90

Bake Me a Cake

Part I

Biscuit Recipe

1. Assemble the following:

    mixing bowl, small bowl, measuring spoons, measuring cups, spatula, mixing spoon, rolling pin, ruler, small glass, small cookie sheet or small flat pan, wax paper, paper towels.

    1 cup self-rising flour, another 1/2 cup self rising flour, 1/2 cup shortening, 1 1/2 teaspoon lemon juice, 1/2 cup milk.

2. Thoroughly clean your work surface.

3. Take turns with other group members measuring and adding ingredients according to this recipe:

    - In a small bowl, combine 1/2 cup of milk and 1 1/2 teaspoons lemon juice. Stir to mix. The milk will curdle.
    - Put one cup of self-rising flour in mixing bowl.
    - Add 1/2 cup of shortening.
    - Pour in milk and lemon juice mixture and stir until the flour and shortening are blended together. You should have a very stiff dough. If dough is sticky, add a small amount of flour and mix.
    - Sprinkle flour on a piece of wax paper on your work surface. Remove dough from mixing bowl and pat into a flat round.
    - Fold the flat round of dough in half. Fold it again into quarters. Press the dough into a flat round again. This process is called kneading. Knead the dough 10 times. You may have to flour the surface of the wax paper several times during the kneading process to keep the paper from sticking to the dough.
    - Spread flour on the rolling pin and on the work surface. Roll the dough out flat. It should be between 1/2 and 3/4 inch thick.
    - Dip the top of a small glass into flour and then press it into the dough. Do this until all the dough has been used.
    - Lift the rounds of dough with a spatula that has been dipped in flour and place the rounds on a cookie sheet.
    - We will bake them in a 400 degree oven for 5 to 8 minutes.

Part II

1. To observe the process of fermentation, work with your small group to assemble the following supplies.

    small glass bowl, measuring cups, measuring spoons, 3 small glasses, 3 spoons, wide dish or pot with 3 or 4 inch sides, 1 package of dry yeast, warm (not hot) water, 1 tablespoon sugar, 1 tablespoon corn syrup, 1 tablespoon cornstarch, 1 cup very warm (not hot) water, 1/2 teaspoon sugar.

2. Measure 1/2 cup of warm water into a small glass bowl. Sprinkle yeast over the water and stir to dissolve.

    Divide the yeast mixture between the three glasses.

    Put 1 tablespoon of sugar in the first glass, 1 tablespoon of corn syrup in the second glass and 1 tablespoon of cornstarch in the third glass. Stir each glass with a different spoon.

    Place the three glasses in a dish or pot. Carefully pour in enough very warm water to come halfway up the sides of the glasses. Take care not to let any water get into the glasses during this part of the experiment.

3. You have provided different surroundings containing food for the yeast. The material the yeast uses for food is called a substrate. When the yeast and the substrate come into contact, fermentation begins. Fermentation can be determined by the size of the bubbles in the foam produced in the glasses and the rate at which the bubbles form.

4. Record your observations. Include the answers to the following questions in your report.

    - Which glass starts fermentation first? Which substrate does that glass contain?
    - Which glass shows the steadiest rate of fermentation? Which substrate does the glass contain?
    - Can you smell the alcohol produced by fermentation. Is the smell stronger in one glass than in another? Which one?

Career Development Activities for the Elementary Grades

Furniture Worker

Furniture workers make the furniture for our homes. In manufacturing companies, furniture workers may operate machines that make one part of a piece of furniture, like the legs of a table, or the table top. The smoothing and finishing of the furniture may also be part of a furniture worker's job. Some furniture workers are craftsmen who design and make the entire piece of furniture themselves, using small machines and hand tools.

Activity 91

Table Talk

Subject Area: Science, Reading
Materials: Paper, pencils
Time: 45 minutes

Part I

Background:
To enhance this activity, have your students make a flow chart of the process of furniture making described in the story.

Procedure:
1. On the handout is a story about a table. The sentences are out of order. Working with your small group, put the sentences in an order that makes sense.
2. Rewrite the story with the sentences in the correct order.

Process Questions:
1. What materials were used to make the tables in your house?
2. What rooms in your house have tables?

Handout Answers:
Order of sentences:
  d.
  e.
  a.
  b.
  g.
  c.
  f.

Part II

Background:
This activity requires at least four different kinds of chairs. You will want to include a wooden or partly wooden chair, a plastic chair, a steel or other heavy metal chair, and an aluminum chair. You could also include a chair made out of fabric like a bean bag chair. Most of these chairs will be available in the school.

Procedure:
1. Wood is the oldest material from which furniture is made. Now there are many other materials to choose from. Make comparisons among the different chairs on display in the classroom.
2. With your class, discuss the positive and negative characteristics of each of the chairs.
3. From this information, list with the class, some conclusions you could make about the different materials used in the chairs.

Process Questions:
1. Why is wood still so popular with furniture makers?
2. Why are old, wooden chairs called antiques, highly prized?

Chapter IV — Science Activities

Handout—Activity 91

Table Talk

Part I

1. Here is a story about a table. The sentences are out of order. Working with your small group, put the sentences in an order that makes sense.
2. Rewrite the story with the sentences in the correct order.

   a. At the furniture factory a furniture worker put the lumber through a special machine to make it smooth and even.

   b. Another machine cut the lumber into the right size for a tabletop.

   c. The furniture worker then sanded and coated the tabletop to make it very smooth and shiny.

   d. A truck picked up the log and carried it to a saw mill.

   e. A truck picked up lumber from a sawmill and took it to a furniture factory.

   f. Legs were attached to the tabletop and they were sanded and coated to match.

   g. The furniture worker measured the table top according to an order from a customer.

Part II

Write the following observations about each chair:

- Material chair is made of. _____

- Appearance of chair (describe the color, style). _____

- Durability of the chair (will it rust, will it break easily)? _____

- Comfort (how does it feel when you sit in it)? _____

- Movability and storability (is the chair heavy or light, does it fold for storage)? _____

- Personal opinion (do you like or dislike this chair and why)? _____

Chemical Lab Technician

Chemical lab technicians help chemists and chemical engineers design and develop products by doing experiments and tests. For example, they may test soil and water for chemists who are working on new ways to control pollution, or keep notes on an experiment to develop a new kind of packaging material. Some technicians work with dangerous chemicals and poisons and must wear protective clothing while they work.

Activity 92

Experimenting

Subject Area: Science
Materials: Part I: Small glass, vinegar, chalk
Part II: Baking soda, small box, small plastic bags, an onion
Time: 45 to 60 minutes

Part I

Background:
- This experiment may be done in small groups.
- Explanation: vinegar is an acid. Acids react chemically with limestone, the mineral in chalk. Limestone changes to new substances when it comes in contact with acid. One of these substances is carbon dioxide gas, which students saw in the form of bubbles rising from the chalk after it was immersed in the vinegar. The acid that comes in contact with the statues is in the form of acid rain. Acid actually affects all minerals, not just limestone, but not as rapidly as it affects limestone. Any statues containing limestone deteriorate faster than the others.

Procedure:
1. Imagine that you are a chemical technician in Washington DC. Some of the statues in the parks there are showing signs of wear and some are not. You perform an experiment to find an explanation for this problem.

2. Fill a small, clear glass half full of vinegar (Note: vinegar is an acid). Add a piece of chalk (Note: chalk is made of limestone, a mineral also found in the stone in some statues). Observe what happens to the chalk and record your observations. Can you draw any conclusions about what is happening to some of the statues in the park.

Process Questions:
1. Name some statues that are in the parks or in front of buildings in your town.
2. What material are they made from and have some deteriorated more than others?

Part II

Background:
- Encourage your students to be creative in their ideas for applying the learning from the experiment to the problem of air pollution in buildings.
- Explanation: the used baking soda smells like onions. Other chemicals stick to the surface of baking soda. Students have heard the term absorb which means taking in other materials. Paper towels, for example, absorb water. Baking soda absorbs other chemicals. Gas is given off by the onion. The gas molecules stick to the surface of the baking soda. If there were no absorbent chemical available, the gas molecules would stay in the air.

Chapter IV   Science Activities

Procedure:
1. Imagine that you are a chemical lab technician in a laboratory working on the problem of air pollution in buildings. You demonstrate a way to clean the air by performing an experiment.
   - Working with your small group, pour one cup of baking soda into a small box. The box should have a lid.
   - Remove one tablespoon of the baking soda from the box, put that portion in a small plastic bag and seal it. Mark the bag "unused."
   - Place several pieces of onion on a small dish and place the dish in the box that contains the remaining baking soda.
   - Cover the box and let it stand for one day.
   - Remove one tablespoon of baking soda from the box, put that portion in a small plastic bag and seal it. Mark the bag "used."
   - Working with your group, open the bags, one at a time, and smell the contents. Look at the contents. Write the group's observations. What does your group conclude from these observations? Write the group's observations.
2. Brainstorm with your group how the learning from this experiment might be applied to the problem of air pollution in buildings.
3. Share your group's conclusions and brainstorm ideas with the class.

Process Questions:
1. Why do some families put a box of baking soda in the refrigerator?
2. Name some pleasant and unpleasant smells.

Career Development Activities for the Elementary Grades

Biomedical Engineer

Biomedical engineers design and build artificial parts for human bodies. They must know how body parts work and what materials can be safely used to make the parts. The parts they build replace diseased and damaged organs, like hearts and lungs and limbs like arms and legs. Biomedical engineers save and improve people's lives through their work.

Activity 93

The Human Body

Subject Area: *Science*
Materials: *Paper and markers*
Time: *45 to 60 minutes*

Part I

Background:

This activity works well with a study of the human body and disease, smoking and drug abuse.

Procedure:

1. Make list of all the internal organs of the body.

2. Working with an outline of the human body, draw in the organs from your list where they belong in the human body. You may have to use different colored pens or pencils where organs overlap.

3. As a class, discuss the job of each of these organs. Answer the following questions:
   - What happens in the body if the heart is damaged or diseased?
   - What happens if the lungs are damaged?
   - What kinds of behavior that human beings participate in might damage the lungs?
   - What organs might be damaged from using drugs?

Process Questions:

1. What can human beings do to protect different body parts?

2. What do you think is the most important organ in the body? Why?

Part II

Background:

- There are no right or wrong way to do this activity. Students should be encouraged to be creative with their ideas.
- If there is a teacher in your school with an artificial body part who is willing to share their experiences (and in the case of an artificial limb, allow students to view the body part), invite the person to speak to the class.

Procedure:

1. *You are a biomedical engineer who must design an artificial organ for the human body. Choose an organ or body part you want to design and find a picture and information on how the organ or body part works.*

2. *Make a drawing of the replacement organ or body part.*

3. *Write an explanation of the drawing at the bottom of the paper. Explain each part of your drawing including the function of the part.*

4. *Include the materials you think the body part could be made of and why you chose those materials. You will need to do research on materials that would be compatible with the needs and location of that body part. For example, if you choose the heart to design, you will want to use light weight material that is flexible and will not deteriorate. If you choose a hand to design and you want the hand to move, you may want to choose materials from which mechanical devices are made.*

5. *Share your designs with the class. Explain to the class how your part will work when it is connected to the human body.*

Process Questions:

1. *What kind of difference can an artificial body part make in a person's life?*

2. *Why do biomedical engineers need to be very creative?*

Chapter IV   Science Activities

Laundry and Dry Cleaning Worker

Laundry and dry cleaning workers operate the machines that wash and dry dirty clothes, sheets and towels, uniforms and table linens. They often work with chemicals that help remove stains and disinfect laundry. Many laundry workers have jobs in companies that provide businesses and organizations with clean uniforms or sheets and towels every day. Others work in small businesses that serve people who need their personal belongings washed or cleaned.

Activity 94

Mr. and Mrs. Clean

Subject Area: Science
Materials: None
Time: 10 minutes

Part I

Background:

You may want to have your students do Part I and II as a homework assignment to involve the parents.

Procedure:

Hotels, restaurants, hospitals, day care centers, beauty/barber shops and homes send out or do laundry every day.

1. Match the following laundry items with the place that sends it out. You may use the items more than once.

Hotel	napkins	curtains
Home	sheets	trousers
Hospital	towels	uniforms
Restaurant	diapers	dish cloths
Beauty Parlor	aprons	dresses
Barber shop	tablecloths	
Day Care Center	shirts	

2. Compare your lists with other class members.

Process Questions:

1. Why do people who work in hospitals or restaurants need to wear clean uniforms to work every day?
2. Why do beds in hospitals have to be changed every day?

Part II

Procedure:

Laundry workers divide clothing into colors before washing.

1. Using the lists of colors below, decide which colors can be washed together. Make separate lists for each group of colors.

tan	black
dark brown	light blue
white	bright green
navy blue	pale yellow
red	light gray
pale pink	bright orange
off-white	medium brown
beige	white with blue flowers
purple	pink & gray stripe
dark gray	

   Badly stained clothing usually goes to the dry cleaners.

2. Make a list of stains that are hard to remove from clothing, such as grape juice.
3. Make another list of the types of clothing that usually go to a dry cleaners such as heavy coats.

Process Questions:

1. What are some differences between washing and dry cleaning?
2. Why does a dry cleaner need to know about chemicals?

Educational Media Corporation®, Box 21311, Minneapolis, MN 55421-0311   163

Career Development Activities for the Elementary Grades

Biologist

Biologists study plant and animal life. Some biologists explore the areas where different plants and animals live and do research on plant and animal development and diseases. Some biologists work in laboratories doing experiments with plants and animals and others may travel to different parts of the world to study the plants and animals that live in those areas.

Activity 95

Leaves and Flowers

Subject Area: Science
Materials: Plastic cups, food coloring, carnations
Time: 30 min.- 2 hours

Part I

Background:
- If you use seeds, you may wish to talk about the different seeds that come from trees and plants before your students begin their collections.
- Help them identify the flowers, leaves, or seeds they find.

Procedure:
1. Collect eight different leaves, flowers, or seeds, around your home or school yard. Choose what you will collect according to the time of year. If it is spring, you may want to make a collection of wildflowers. Fall is a good time to find leaves and seeds.
2. Each time you collect an item, write where you found it.
3. Glue or tape your collection onto paper. Write where each item was found underneath. If you know what the item is, write it's name. For example, if you found a flower you know is a dandelion write "dandelion" underneath the flower on your paper.

Process Questions:
1. Compare the different kinds of leaves, flowers and seeds that each student has found.
2. Discuss why these particular leaves, flowers and seeds grow in the climate of your area.

Part II

Background:
- This experiment should tie to a study of plants and specifically to capillary action in plants.
- Carnations work well for this experiment because their stems are fairly sturdy.
- Choose tall, clear plastic cups.
- Trim the flower stems to a length that stands up in the cups before distributing them to students.

Procedure:
1. Fill two clear plastic cups with water.
2. Color the water in one glass only, using food coloring. The color of the water should be a deep red, blue, green or orange.
3. Put a white carnation or other white flower in each cup.
4. Put the two cups, one containing clear water and one containing colored water close together.
5. Wait a few hours or overnight.
6. Working with your partner, write a small paragraph explaining what happened to the flowers and why it happened. You may need to look up the term 'capillary action' in a science book in order to write your explanation.

Process Questions:
1. What occupations profit from this scientific theory?
2. How does this theory help a florist?

Chapter IV

Chemist

Chemists work in companies that produce products made of chemicals. They do research for these companies, developing and testing new products. Companies that produce plastics, cleaning products, drugs, certain fabrics, pesticides, some foods and many other products all use chemists. Chemists also work in government jobs, testing for harmful chemicals in the air we breathe, the water we drink and the food we eat.

Activity 96

Pollution

Subject Area: Science
Materials: See activity
Time: 45 to 60 minutes

Part I

Background:
- Ask your students what kinds of dirt pollute the air and list them on the board. Keep the list posted in the classroom until the conclusion of the experiment.
- At the conclusion of the experiment, ask them if there is something near or around their home that is not on the list.

Procedure:
1. Test for pollution in the air around your home, using the following procedure:
   - Take home a 5 x 7 unlined index card or piece of paper and a small bag containing vaseline.
   - Spread the paper with a thin coating of vaseline. Leave 1/2" around the edge of the paper free of vaseline.
   - Tape the paper to the outside of a window. Leave it for seven days. Observe the paper each day for changes in color. See if it has attracted particles of dirt or dust and write down your observations, including the date you observed, on a sheet of paper.
   - Carefully remove the paper from the window, cover it with clear wrap and return it to class.
   - Write your conclusions about air pollution around your home at the bottom of your observation sheet.

2. Share your conclusions about pollution in your home with your class.

Process Questions:
1. What effect does air pollution have on the human body?
2. How can you help stop air pollution?

Part II

Background:
- Prior to this experiment, discuss with the class how pesticides are applied to farm land. (Note: many pesticides are sprayed on the land by airplane or special machinery.)
- You may enhance this activity by having students repeat the experiment by spraying the paint and dirt. They will discover that there is no run off until the dirt is saturated with water.

Procedure:
Some water pollution is caused by the rain washing pesticides from the farmlands into the rivers and streams. Over a period of time, the pesticides begin to damage animal and plant life in the water. Pesticides also make the water unsafe for people to swim in or to drink.

1. Work with your group to study the concept of water pollution with the following experiment.
   - Collect the materials you will need: green or blue powdered tempera paint, dirt or sand, funnel, coffee filter, jar, water, measuring cup, measuring spoon, stirring spoon
   - Place the coffee filter in the top of the funnel. Place the funnel into the top of the jar.
   - Scoop the dirt into the coffee filter.
   - Sprinkle the tempera paint on top of the dirt in the filter.
   - Pour 1/2 cup of water over the dirt and paint in the filter.
   - Observe the water as it drips through the filter. Working with your group, write your observations on a piece of paper.

2. Discuss your conclusions with your group.

Process Questions:
1. What kinds of trash do swimmers and boaters throw into lakes and streams?
2. What does water pollution do to the fish?

Geologist

Geologists research the history and function of the earth through studying the materials that make up the earth. Geologists study rocks and fossils to learn how humans and animals lived many years ago. Some geologists do research that helps us understand ways we can protect the environment. Others explore the effects of water on earth and rock formations. Dinosaur bones have been discovered by geologists during their explorations.

Activity 97

The Good Earth

Subject Area: Science
Materials: Drawing paper, art materials, magazines
Time: Two 45-minute periods

Part I

Background:
Check the media center to find out what information is available on geology. Make the list of features according to what the media center has available.

Procedure:
1. Cut out pictures from magazines of different earth features such as:

   valleys   mountains   lakes
   rivers   deserts

2. Using an outline map of the United States, draw the features where they belong on the map. You will need to use the encyclopedia to find out where to draw the features.

3. Draw at least five of the earth's features on the map.

4. Share your map with the class.
   - How many mountain ranges did the students find? How many rivers? How many deserts?

Process Questions:
1. Discuss with your class which part of the US has the most natural land formations.
2. Where in the US is the potential for the most earthquakes?

Part II

Background:
Your students may also draw pictures instead of a three dimensional representation.

Procedure:
1. Choose a mountain range in the United States.

2. Look up information about the history of the mountain range you chose. Answer the questions below.
   a. Are there mines in your mountain range?
   b. What kind of mines?
   c. Are there any tourist attractions in the range you chose?
      Name them.
   d. Are there rivers? Name one.

3. Make a three dimensional representation of your mountain range to present to the class using clay or other materials.

Process Questions:
1. Discuss how geologists use natural land formations to determine the age of the earth.
2. Are there any mountain ranges in your part of the US? Have you visited them? Discuss.

Chapter IV Science Activities

Steel Worker

Steel workers build the metal frameworks for skyscrapers and bridges. They move huge steel girders into place. Once they have placed the girders, they bolt them together. Steel workers often work high above the ground. They move around on the metal frameworks, and sometimes sit on the steel girders to eat or to rest, hundreds of feet in the air. Steel workers could not do their job if they were afraid of heights.

Activity 98

On the Beam

Subject Area: Science
Materials: See below
Time: 45 to 60 minutes

Part I

Background:
- You can enhance this activity by having small groups or partners research and report on one planet.
- Mark a 9 ft. by 6 in. area on the playground with masking tape or find a long board or log of similar dimensions to use for this activity.

Procedure:
1. We have marked an area on the playground that is 9 feet long and 6 inches wide. Pretend this area is a steel girder and you are the steel worker, walking along the girder high in the air.
2. Line up with your class and take turns walking on the 'girder'. Remember, if you step over the line that marks the side of the 'girder' you will fall off.
3. If you are unable to make it all the way to the end on the first try, keep trying until the teacher calls time.

Process Questions:
1. Discuss how important it is for the steel worker to have balance and coordination.
2. Discuss your own personal fear of height or any other fears.

Part II

Background:
Be sure to use straight plastic straws. You may allow students to use pencils for their upright girders, to make the base stronger.

Procedure:
1. Use plastic drinking straws for girders and tape for bolts to build the frame for a building.
2. The building will be five inches across the front and back and six inches along the sides. You can make the building as tall as you want. However, it must be able to stay upright on it's own.
3. Display your building frame to the class. Tell what the building would look like when finished. Would you make it brick or stucco? What might the building be used for?

Process Questions:
1. Why are precise measurements and bolting important? What would happen if the girders were not properly measured or bolted?
2. Ask your students how the frame of a building is like the human skeleton?

Career Development Activities for the Elementary Grades

College Teacher

College teachers work in colleges and universities. They teach advanced subjects that college students must take to earn their degrees. Most college teachers have doctorate level degrees in the fields in which they teach. College teachers also write and do research in their fields.

Activity 99

College Courses

Subject Area: Science, Math, Social Studies
Materials: None
Time: 45 to 60 minutes

Part I

Background:
You may want to add these words to the weekly spelling list.

Procedure:
1. Below is a list of some subjects taught in college.

   Chemistry,   Psychology,   Literature,
   History,   Calculus

2. Choose one of the subjects to look up in the dictionary and encyclopedia.

3. Write a short paragraph to explain what the subject is about.

Process Questions:
1. How is teaching in college different from teaching in elementary school?
2. How is the subject you chose tied to a particular career?

Part II

Background:
Have volunteers teach a fact to the class.

Procedure:
1. Choose a subject from the list in Part I. It should be different from the one you chose for Part I.

2. Do research on the subject in the media center. Find five facts a college teacher might choose to teach his/her students. List the facts on a piece of paper.

3. You may choose to teach one of the facts to the class.

Process Questions:
1. How did you decide which facts to put on your list?
2. What are other ways college professors teach facts besides telling them to students?

Chapter IV

Science Activities

Forest Technician

Forest technicians work in our national and state parks and forests. They maintain the hiking trails, watch for damage to the forest and assist visitors. They must be familiar with the trees and plants that grow in the parks and be able to recognize diseases and pests that attack trees and plants. They often assist foresters in developing new growth for forests and parks.

Activity 100

Save a Tree

Subject Area: Science
Materials: Paper or small notebook
Time: 45 to 60 minutes

Part I

Background:
- Choose a park, preferably with woods and trails for the class hike. Invite parents to participate.
- If your park has a ranger, forester or technician, ask them to speak to the class when they arrive at the park.
- Your park may provide information about the trails and ponds. Obtain the information prior to the hike if possible.

Procedure:
1. Working with your class, plan a hike for the class. First decide with your teacher, where and when you can go.
2. Make a list on the board of rules for safe hiking. One rule, for example, is having a partner.
3. Brainstorm a list of trees, plants and animals you might see.
4. On the day of your hike, count the number of trees, plants and animals you see. Also note the colors and sizes.
5. When you return from your hike, discuss the following questions:
    - How many different varieties of trees, flowers, and animals did you see:
    - How could a forest technician have been helpful to the class before or during the hike?
    - What would you do differently before going on a hike next time?

Process Questions:
1. What can citizens do to keep their parks looking nice for hikers?
2. What are some other fun activities to do in forests and parks?

Part II

Background:
Conduct the Part II hike as a scientific excursion.

Procedure:
1. Plan the hike as described in Part I.
2. Also list local trees, plants and animals that you may be able to identify during your hike. For example, what is your state tree? See if you can identify it during your hike. What other trees are common to your area? With your class, discuss how you can identify certain trees and plants. Record the information in a small notebook you will take on your hike.
3. During the hike, make notes about what you observe. Do you see insects? What kind? What are they doing? If you don't know the name of something you see, write or draw a description of it in your notebook. For example, if you can't identify a certain tree, draw the shape of a leaf of the tree and write a brief description. Look up the tree when you get back to the class.
4. After the hike, share your most interesting observations. See if other class members can help you identify some of the plants or insects you saw. Look up those that class members couldn't identify.

Process Questions:
1. What was the most interesting tree, flower or animal you found on your hike?
2. Talk about any hiking experiences you may have had.

Machinist

Machinists make the metal parts for the machines used in factories. The machines they work with either perform tasks or produce products. The machinist must know how to read blueprints of machines and must understand how machines operate. They use welding torches and cutting and shaping tools to make the parts. Different kinds of metal cut and melt differently, and machinists must know which metals will work best in the parts they make.

Activity 101

The Wonderful Machine

Subject Area: Science
Materials: Chart paper, pencils, markers, plus items listed in Part II
Time: 45 minutes

Part I

Background:
- Your students may come up with their own ideas for machines, if you wish.
- Using chart paper gives every student access to the design as the group works.
- Enhance this activity by taking a field trip to a manufacturing plant in your area, to see how machines make products.

Procedure:
1. Working with your small group, plan a design for one of the machines listed below.
    - lollipop making machine
    - shoelace making machine
    - pencil making machine
    - bubblegum making machine
    - baseball making machine
    - ruler making machine
    - bicycle tire making machine
    - pizza making machine
    - T-shirt making machine

2. Using pencils and chart paper, sketch a design of the machine your group chose. Be sure all group members' ideas are part of the design. Keep in mind that one end of the machine should have a place to put in the materials used to make the product and the finished product should come out the other end of the machine. Otherwise, there is no right or wrong way to design your machine. (You may want to sketch the design on a small piece of paper first and then transfer it to the chart paper.)

3. Once you have sketched the design on chart paper, trace over the design with colored markers. Write labels for the different parts of the machine and tell what they do. You can write that information on the side of the chart paper and use arrows to point to the parts described.

4. As a group, show your design to the class and explain how your machine works.

Process Questions:
1. What machines do you use daily that make your life more pleasant?
2. What machines could you turn off and not miss?

Chapter IV — Science Activities

Part II

Background:
- Discuss with your class the difference between machines that perform tasks and machines that produce products. For example, farm machinery is designed to perform tasks. Ask students other kinds of machines they can think of that do tasks. Note that some machines may do both.
- Collect the following materials for students to use in their machine models:

    aluminum foil, large nails, florist wire, florist tape, rubber bands, paper clips, pipe cleaners, paper towels, tissue paper, plain paper, string, empty thread spools, small wood pieces, chips, index cards, wire cutters, scissors, scotch tape, glue
- You can enhance this activity by having students research how certain machines work.

Procedure:
1. *With your small group, brainstorm a list of ideas for machines that would make life in the classroom easier.*
2. *Draw a sketch of the machine to use as a guide for making a model (prototype).*
3. *Using the materials supplied by the teacher, build a model of the machine.*
4. *Using a large index card, write the name of your machine and an explanation of how the machine would work. Write all group members names on the card.*
5. *Display your group's machine in the classroom with the index card in front of it.*
6. *Take time to visit the displays of other groups.*

Process Questions:
1. *Was there much leisure time before the invention of machines? Why or why not?*
2. *What did the invention of machines do to leisure time?*

Career Development Activities for the Elementary Grades

Medical Technologist

Medical technologists perform chemical tests with blood, tissue and other body substances. The tests can show changes in the body that may indicate disease. Medical technologists also match blood samples for transfusions. When people are in accidents or have surgery, they may lose a great deal of blood very quickly. The replacement of lost blood is called a transfusion. The blood type used in the transfusion must be the same or compatible with the blood type of the patient receiving the new blood. Medical technologists work in hospitals and laboratories. They use special machines and microscopes to do their work.

Activity 102

Looking and Learning

Subject Area   Science
Materials: Microscope, newspaper, tape
Time: 30 to 45 minutes

Part I

Background:
- To enhance this activity, have your students work with magnifying glasses, noting what they see with and without the aid of the glasses.
- For the second step of this activity, read the questions aloud while they are standing approximately three feet away from the newspaper.
- Another enhancement of this activity is a discussion of how lenses work to magnify objects.

Procedure:
1. Medical technologists use microscopes to look at samples of body tissue and fluid. Microscopes magnify the size of substances many times. The increase in size allows the technologist to see the parts of the substance.
2. Working with your small group, look at a newspaper that is taped to a wall of the classroom. Stay in your seat while you are looking at it. Answer the following questions:

- Can you see the newspaper?
- Can you read it?
- If you can read it, what parts can you read?
- Do you notice any special details about the paper?

3. Choose someone from your small group to stand and go closer to the paper. Your group member should stand three feet away.
4. Your teacher will ask all the standing group members the same questions as you answered before and allow each standing group member to answer.
5. Choose another group member to go to the newspaper and stand close enough to touch their nose to the paper. They should then return to the group and answer the same questions again, aloud for the group. If there is time, all group members, one at a time, should go to the newspaper and stand close enough to touch their noses to the paper.
6. With your teacher discuss what happened as people moved closer to the newspaper. Talk about what you saw when you were very close to the newspaper. Did you see the individual letters of the words? What other details did you see?

Process Questions:
1. How does a microscope help medical technologists do their jobs?
2. Discuss any other equipment that a medical technologist may use.

Chapter IV — Science Activities

Part II

Background:
- This activity can be greatly enhanced by visiting a laboratory or blood bank.
- Your students should have opportunities to experiment with the microscopes before they begin work with the slides. If you do not have access to slides of dry blood, have them make their own slides of other substances or objects. Do not allow them to use fresh blood.
- To enhance this activity, have your students research the components of blood and why there are different types.

Procedure:
1. As a class, discuss the parts of a microscope.
   - *The part you look through is called an EYEPIECE. Sometimes it is called the OCULAR.*
   - *Underneath the eyepiece is The BODYTUBE, which helps focus the microscope on the slides.*
   - *At the top of the bodytube, just below the eyepiece, is the COARSE ADJUSTMENT KNOB. This knob moves the body tube up and down in order to achieve a focus.*
   - *The REVOLVING NOSE-PIECE is at the bottom of the bodytube. It rotates the lenses.*
   - *Just below the revolving nose-piece are the OBJECTIVE LENSES that magnify the slides.*
   - *Below the objective lenses is the STAGE, which is the platform on which the slides rest.*
   - *The slides are held in place by STAGE CLIPS that are on the side of the stage.*
   - *The ILLUMINATOR is below the slide. It lights up the slide so it can be seen more clearly.*

2. *In your small groups, practice looking through a microscope at a prepared slide. The slide should be of a small bug or plant, so that you can easily tell if you are focusing accurately.*

3. *Once you have mastered using the microscope, view some slides containing dry blood samples.*

4. *Discuss the appearance of the blood samples under the microscope in your small group. What characteristics of the blood samples might be different in someone with a disease? Note that the medical technologists samples would be fresh.*

Process Questions:
1. *Why must medical technologists be sure of what they see when looking at a sample of someone's blood?*
2. *What would happen if they gave the doctor the wrong results?*

Career Development Activities for the Elementary Grades

Welder

Welders use blowtorches to permanently join metal parts. Blowtorches are tools that create intense fire and heat with strong blasts of air. When a blowtorch is directed at metal it quickly melts or softens the metal, which allows it to be joined to another piece of metal. Once the metals cool, they are permanently attached, or welded, together. Welders must wear protective clothing and glasses to do their work. They do welding on airplanes, trains and cars, join beams in buildings and bridges and do welding jobs in factories and manufacturing plants.

Activity 103

Heat and Fire

Subject Area: Science
Materials: Magazines, scissors, dictionary, index cards, pencils
Time: 30 minutes

Part I

Background:
You may have to help your students with the concept of flux.

Procedure:
1. Cut out magazine pictures of cars, trains and airplanes.
2. Look up the word flux in the dictionary.
3. Circle or underline all the places on the pictures where parts may be put together by welding and where there might be some flux.

Process Questions:
1. What are some other ways that things are joined together besides welding?
2. What would happen if two parts of a car became unwelded?

Part II

Background:
- This activity is based on the learning activity "Each One Teach One." You will collect and redistribute the fact cards.
- Ask your students what they learned about one of the positive uses for heat and fire.

Procedure:
1. With your class, brainstorm a list of the useful ways—besides welding—to use heat and fire.
2. Research three facts about this positive use. Each fact should be among the most interesting you can find.
3. Write each fact on a separate index card. The fact should not be more than two or three lines long. Turn the index card in to your teacher.
4. The teacher will give you a new index card with a fact on it. The fact should not be one you wrote.
5. Read the fact, then find a partner and teach the fact to your partner. Your partner will also teach a fact to you.
6. Share the new fact you learned with you class.
7. Repeat this activity, using a new fact.

Process Questions:
1. How is the gold in jewelry fused together?
2. How did ancient doctors use heat and fire?

Chapter IV   Science Activities

Optical Technician

Optical technicians make prescription eye glasses. They cut, grind and shape lenses according to the prescription provided by an eye doctor. After they have shaped the lenses, optical technicians fit them into eye glass frames. Some optical technicians make lenses for telescopes, binoculars, microscopes and other optical instruments.

Activity 104

Experiments with Light

Subject Area: Science
Materials: Flashlight, waxed paper, construction paper
Time: 30 to 45 minutes

Part I

Background:
- To enhance this activity, talk about how the human eye uses light. Have your students add that information to their drawings.
- Another enhancement for this activity is having them read an eye chart in a fully lighted classroom, and then gradually reducing the light. Have students note what is happening to the pupils of their eyes that allow them to adjust to the darker room.

Procedure:
1. How well people see depends on how much light enters the eye, and the parts of the eye the light reaches. Light enters the eye through the pupil. To see how the pupil of the eye controls the amount of light the eye receives, do the experiment that follows with your small group.
   - Make your class room as bright as possible, turning on all lights and opening blinds or shades.
   - Shut one eye and keep it shut. Look in a mirror. The pupil of your open eye should be very small, because the eye has more than enough light available.
   - Open the shut eye while still looking in the mirror. The pupil of your other eye should be large, because the eye was exposed to little or no light.
   - Continue to watch the pupil of the recently opened eye. It should get smaller as it adjusts to the light in the classroom.
2. Working with your small group, make a drawing of the human eye. Label each part.

Process Questions:
1. What happens to your eyes when you go quickly from a dark room into the bright sun?
2. What is the purpose of sunglasses?

Career Development Activities for the Elementary Grades

Part II

Background:
- This activity works well as an introduction to the study of light as energy.
- Enhance this activity by exploring the concept of reflected light or by adding vocabulary such as transparent, translucent and opaque.
- You can also enhance this activity by having your students research eye diseases and how those diseases affect the light the eye receives.

Procedure:
1. Perform the following experiments in your small group. Each group member should keep a data sheet on each experiment.
   - Light travels in a straight line through space. Confirm this fact by shining a flashlight in a darkened room. Write what you see on your data sheet.
   - Light beams are invisible unless they are reflected off something else. To confirm this fact, shine a flashlight in a darkened room. Clap two erasers together directly underneath the light, so that chalk dust rises up into the light. Record what you see on your data sheet.
   - Light is energy. Matter takes up space, energy does not. Confirm this fact by turning the lights on and off in your class room. Do you have more space in the room when the lights are off? Write what you see on your data sheet.
   - Light travels through some matter more easily than others. Shine a flashlight through glass. Write what you see on your data sheet. Shine a flashlight through waxed paper. Write what you see on your data sheet. Shine the flashlight through black construction paper. Write what you see on your data sheet.
   - Shine a flashlight on a piece of furniture in a darkened room. What happens to the light? Write your observations on your data sheet.

2. With your class, discuss the observations you made about light.
3. Using the concept that light is necessary for us to see, explore what the lenses in eyeglasses do with light.

Process Questions:
1. Why is it important to take care of your eyes?
2. How have contact lenses changed the optical industry?

Chapter V

Music and Art Activities

Career Development Activities for the Elementary Grades

Clothes Designer

Clothes designers develop ideas for clothing using sketches or the computer. They also select colors and materials to use with the designs they create. A designer tries to create clothes that are useful, attractive and fashionable so that people will want to buy them. Clothes designers may work for themselves, creating and selling their own designs or they may work for a company that makes and sells a large variety of clothing.

Activity 105

Lookin' Good!

Subject Area: Art
Materials: Paper, crayons or markers
Time: 30 to 45 minutes

Part I

Background:
- You may want the class to brainstorm the different kinds of materials used in clothing before they begin their drawings. (If possible, point out the different kinds of materials from the children's own clothing.)
- Instruct your students to draw the clothing as separate pieces, rather than drawing the clothes on a figure.
- Encourage your class to include details in their drawings and accessories they might need for particular kinds of weather.

Procedure:
1. Think of a special occasion when you really want to look good!
2. Design an outfit to wear for that occasion. Be sure the outfit is warm enough or cool enough for the time of year.
3. Choose the materials you will use for your outfit. You may want special buttons or decorations on your outfit.
4. With the rest of your class, post your design on the wall.
5. Standing next to your design, tell your class what occasion you chose. Explain the special features of your design.

Process Questions:
1. How do your clothes affect the way you feel?
2. Some people wear uniforms to school or to work. How would you (or do you) feel about wearing a uniform?

Part II

Background:
- You may want your class to brainstorm the kinds of activities young people are involved in now and how those activities might change 100 years from now.
- Give them the option of drawing the clothing on a figure or as separate pieces.

Procedure:
1. Design an outfit young people might wear 100 years from now. Remember that the clothing must be useful as well as attractive and fashionable.
2. With your class, post your design on the wall.
3. Stand in front of your design and tell the class why you chose the design. What will the young person be doing while wearing this outfit?

Process Questions:
1. Why does a clothes designer need basic skills such as reading, writing and mathematics?
2. Why do clothes designers need good decision making skills?

Chapter V — Music and Art Activities

Musician

Musicians play musical instruments, sing, or compose music. They usually have a strong interest in music which they develop through years of training and practice. Musicians who play instruments often work in orchestras and bands, performing in concerts or providing music for singers and dancers. Those musicians who compose music are usually able to sing or play an instrument as well

Activity 106

I've Got Rhythm

Subject Area: Music
Materials: Records, tapes or CDs
Time: 30 to 45 minutes

Part I

Background:

- Choose some music that has obvious rhythms. Marching songs are a good choice.
- Keep the rhythms simple at this level. Once your students begin to sense the rhythms, you can make them more complex.
- You may want to count aloud, so that they can hear the beats in each rhythm. You can also shake your hand to the beat.

Procedure:

1. The two basic components of music are the sounds and the rhythms. With your class, listen to the music; play and clap the rhythm. Continue to clap until everyone has the same rhythm.
2. Without the music, listen to your teacher clap a rhythm, then clap the rhythm yourself. Continue to clap the rhythm, until the whole class is together.
3. Volunteer to lead a rhythm. You may want to practice by yourself first. If you have trouble clapping a rhythm, think of a song you know, and clap the rhythm of that song. You may want to practice with the following example:

1	2	3	4	1	2	3	4
Clap	Clap	Clap	Clap	Clap	Pause	Clap	Pause

   Repeat

   (Notice the rhythm is in four time, which means there are four beats for each part of the rhythm.)

Process Questions:

1. What is your favorite kind of music?
2. Why do you like that particular kind?

Part II

Background:

- You may wish to bring some music to class that has more complex rhythms for your students to listen to before they develop their own.
- The rhythm bands will be more interesting if you can provide such things as blocks of wood, empty tin cans, cardboard boxes, and metal spoons. Sandpaper also makes an interesting sound.

Procedure:

1. Practice expanding the rhythms from Part I. For instance, the example in Part I could be expanded by adding the following

1	2	3	4	1	2	3	4
Clap	Pause	Pause	Pause	Clap	Pause	Clap	Pause

2. Lead the class in your expanded rhythm. They must be able to clap the rhythm all the way through. If they clap the example in this activity they would begin with 4 claps, then clap pause clap pause, then one clap and four pauses, and finally clap pause clap pause.
3. After several students have had opportunities to lead the class in expanded rhythms, move to your small group.
4. In your group, decide what you will use to make a rhythm band. I may have some materials you can use for instruments. You can also create your own using pencils as if they were drum sticks, finger and toe tapping, and books rubbing together.
5. Once you have decided on your instruments, develop the rhythm you will play with your group. Practice playing the rhythm.
6. With your group, perform the rhythm for the class.

Process Questions:

1. How do people develop a love of music?
2. Can people like more than one type of music? Why or why not?

Career Development Activities for the Elementary Grades

Graphic Designer

Graphic designers design books, magazines, advertisements and even packaging for products. They put pictures and words together in ways that will get the attention of people. Graphic designers know a great deal about colors and use a computer to do some of their work.

Activity 107

Make a Pretty Picture

Subject Area: Art
Materials: Magazines, paper, paste
Time: 45 minutes

Part I

Background:
- You may want to make a sample design to show your students.
- Encourage them to move their arrangements around the paper to see where they look best.

Procedure:
1. Using a variety of magazines, cut out parts of advertisements in the magazines that appeal to you. Choose things you like the color or shape of or things that look interesting to you. You may want eight or ten different pieces.
2. Make an arrangement of the pieces on paper. Rearrange the pieces until you get an arrangement you like; then paste them to the paper in that arrangement.
3. Share your design with your class. Explain why you chose those pieces of advertisements and why you arranged them the way you did.

Process Questions:
1. Why would a graphic designer need to know about how things are arranged?
2. What are you learning in art class that would help you become a graphic designer?

Part II

Background:
- Explain the words "ad copy."
- Tell your students that some graphic artists also write the copy for the ads they design.

Procedure:
1. Design an advertisement for one of the products listed below. You may draw the ad or use cutouts or both.
2. Write something on the ad that helps sell the product.
3. Share your ideas with the class.

   Product List

   toothpaste, pizza, baseball hats, video games, roses, comic books

Process Questions:
1. How do some people relieve stress through art?
2. How might a graphic designer show feelings in a design?

Chapter V Music and Art Activities

Painter

Painters apply paint and other mixtures to the surfaces of different structures or buildings. They decide on the right kinds of paint to use by considering the kind of surface being painted, the location (inside or out, kitchen or living room) and the desires of their customers. Painters know how to create colors by mixing paints and what colors go well together. Painting is physical work and painters must be able to stand for long periods of time and to reach and bend easily.

Activity 108

What Color Will You Use?

Subject Area: Art
Materials: Paint chip card, paint, paper
Time: 20 to 40 minutes

Part I

Background:
You may wish to expand this activity to a discussion of pigments.

Procedure:
1. Painters often have to mix colors. Using your paint palette, combine two colors to make the following:

   ORANGE   GREEN   PURPLE

2. Experiment with your paints. What other colors can you make?
3. Try to mix colors to match a paint sample from a paint store. What do you have to think about when mixing the colors? Below your sample, list the colors necessary to make it.
4. On a piece of paper, paint an unusual rainbow. Use colors not usually found in a rainbow.

Process Questions:
1. Dependability and promptness are two important work qualities. How do they apply to a painter?
2. Who can be a house painter?

Part II

Background:
A parent who has recently had a house painted may be a good resource for this project.

Procedure:
1. Each small group will be painting a house in a new subdivision. Your group will have to figure out:
   a. What colors to use (some consultation with other groups will be necessary since the houses are next to each other)
   b. How much paint will be needed for a two story house
   c. What kind of ladders you will need
   d. What size of paintbrushes you will need for the walls, trim, doors.
2. Make a presentation to the rest of the class about your findings.

Process Questions:
1. How can a painter use a computer in his job?
2. How do math skills figure into the job of a painter?

Photographer

Photographers use cameras to take pictures of people, animals, plants, objects, places and events. They often specialize, becoming experts at taking pictures of certain subjects, like nature or sporting events. They not only know how to use a variety of cameras, but they understand how to judge the lighting and what kinds of film works best for different photographs. Taking good pictures takes practice, and photographers must learn what makes a good picture. They try to say something or create a feeling with the picture. Newspapers, magazines, companies that advertise their products, and individuals all use photographers. Photographers often work alone, taking pictures for people on special occasions, or developing an artistic style to their photographs.

Activity 109

Hold that Pose

Subject Area: Art
Materials: Magazines, glue, paper
Time: 45 to 60 minutes

Part I

Background:
- You may want to find some pictures before this class to demonstrate what you mean by a picture telling a story or creating a feeling.
- If your students have trouble identifying feelings in the pictures, ask them how they would feel if they had a little puppy like the one in the picture, for example.

Procedure:
1. Working with your small group, look for photographs in old newspapers and magazines. Cut out five of the pictures your group finds.
2. Paste each picture on a piece of white paper.
3. Decide as a group if the picture tells a story. Below the picture, write the story you think the photographer was trying to tell.
4. Decide as a group if the picture creates a feeling like happiness or sadness. Write the feeling below the picture.
5. Share your pictures with the class. Explain how your group decided what story the picture told and what feeling it created.

Process Questions:
1. Why does a photographer need to know about feelings when trying to capture a mood in a picture?
2. How can you tell by a person's face what they are feeling?

Part II

Background:
- Ask the photographer to bring samples of the work they have done as well as equipment to demonstrate to your students.
- If there is a camera available in the school, you may want to have small groups of children take some pictures to share with the class.

Procedure:
1. With your class, make a list of questions you would like to ask a photographer.
2. Invite a photographer to class and ask your questions.
3. Ask the photographer to demonstrate the camera equipment and how it is used to take pictures.
4. Ask the photographer to share pictures he or she has taken and explain the story or feeling he or she was trying to create in each picture.

Process Questions:
1. What personal characteristics does a photographer need to have?
2. Why is patience important for a photographer?

Chapter V Music and Art Activities

Radio and Television Announcer

Radio and television announcers present news, interview guests, choose and play music and do commercials. Announcers that work as disc jockeys know a great deal about the music they play and the people who perform the music. Announcers reporting the news or weather often research and write their own material. They must be good communicators and learn to speak clearly and in pleasant tones of voice. The most successful announcers seem to have a special kind of energy and enthusiasm that people like to listen to or watch.

Activity 110

On the Air

Subject Area: Music, Reading, Writing
Materials: Paper, pencils
Time: 30 to 60 minutes

Part I

Background:
Your students may need help with topics for their stories.

Procedure:
1. Think about an event that happened at school in the last week. It can be a PTA meeting, an assembly, or an interesting activity in your classroom.
2. Write a short news report for a radio or TV show about the event. Be sure to include:
    a. what happened
    b. where it happened
    c. when it happened
    d. who was involved
3. Take turns reading your news stories.

Process Questions:
1. What do you think is the most difficult part of being an announcer?
2. What part do you think is the most fun?

Part II

Background:
You may want to brainstorm a number of products with your class before they begin.

Procedure:
1. Think of a product that students your age might use and write a 30-second commercial for that product.
2. The commercial can be in the form of a jingle, song, poem or straight talking.
3. Be sure to include a reason that students would want to buy this product.
4. Perform your commercial for the class as if you were on the radio or TV.

Process Questions:
1. Discuss some commercials you have heard. What makes you want to buy a product?
2. How can you tell if a commercial is aimed at children or young people?

Career Development Activities for the Elementary Grades

Telephone Operator

Telephone operators assist people making phone calls. Most phone calls are dialed directly and a computer places the call and charges the person making the call. People who use an operator need information or special assistance. Large organizations may use operators to answer and direct the calls that come into the building. Hospitals often have operators to connect callers to patient's rooms or to someone who can provide information about a patient. Telephone operators also provide assistance to callers in emergencies.

Activity 111

This is the Operator

Subject Area: Art
Materials: Paper, crayons or markers
Time: 20 to 45 minutes

Part I

Background:
- If there is time, ask for volunteers to role play for your class.
- You may want to introduce the telephone book during this activity.

Procedure:
1. Discuss as a class how you ask a telephone operator for a number.
2. Find a partner; one person will be the operator and the other will be the caller. Then switch roles.
3. You may use the following for your role play:
   a. the phone number of a friend
   b. the phone number of the local library
   c. the phone number of your school
   d. a number you want to call.

Process Questions:
1. What skills are necessary to be a good telephone operator?
2. Why are these same skills necessary in any conversation?

Part II

Background:
- There are several ways to do this activity. Students can work in small groups, listen to you read the poem once, and then attempt as a group to draw Sammy.
- Your students can also work on their own, read through the poem once, close their books and draw Sammy.

Procedure:

A telephone operator must listen carefully, hear what is said, and record it accurately.

1. Listen to the poem, "Sammy Sweet," as I read it aloud.
2. Draw a picture of Sammy Sweet as he is described in the poem.

Sammy Sweet

Have you ever seen old Sammy Sweet
Whose ears are bigger than his feet?
He is very tall and very thin
With a purple bump upon his chin.
He has black hair that sticks straight out
And enormous hands that he waves about.
When Sammy walks around the town
He's always dressed all in brown.
With a yellow tie and one red shoe
The other shoe is always blue.
It's not hard to find this fella
Just watch for his big green umbrella.

3. Share your pictures with the class.

Process Questions:
1. Why do all of the pictures look different?
2. What would happen if emergency medical people got the information from the operator as confused as the pictures of Sammy?

Chapter V | Music and Art Activities

Autobody Repairer

Autobody repair people fix the dents, scratches, rust, and holes on the bodies of cars. They know how to replace fenders, smooth surfaces and paint the cars that are damaged. Many autobody repairers work with automobile mechanics . They are often involved in repairing cars that have been in accidents.

Activity 112

Paint Job

Subject Area: Art
Materials: Pictures from magazines, paint, markers
Time: 30 to 60 minutes

Part I

Background:

To enhance this activity, you can visit a car in the parking lot of the school. Your students can then note some parts that may not be visible or noticeable and discuss the replacement of these parts.

Procedure:

1. Draw or cut out a picture of a car. Place the picture at the top of a plain piece of paper.
2. Write the name of each part of the car on the same paper and draw an arrow to point to that part. Point out as many parts as you can.
3. Underline the names of parts that might have to be replaced.
4. At the bottom of the paper, write the name of the part again and one or more reasons it might have to be replaced. For example, the reasons you might have to replace a windshield are because it is cracked or completely broken.
5. Discuss with your class your reasons car parts are replaced.

Process Questions:

1. What were some of the most common repairs found by the class?
2. How does an autobody repairer fix a broken windshield while the car is in your driveway?

Part II

Background:

You may have your students use graph paper to draw and color their cars more precisely.

Procedure:

1. Draw the shape and style of a car you would like to own.
2. Using paint, markers, or crayons, give your car a fancy paint job.
3. Display your car to the class and tell the kind of car you drew and why you chose the "paint job" you gave it.

Process Questions:

1. Why does an autobody repairer have to have a knowledge of color?
2. Is this a good job for a person who likes cars? Explain.

Career Development Activities for the Elementary Grades

Jeweler

Jewelers design and make jewelry. They often work in stores that sell the jewelry they make. Some jewelers also make repairs, fixing watches that don't run and replacing broken clasps on necklaces and bracelets or replacing missing gemstones in rings. Other jewelers work alone and sell their designs to small shops and galleries.

Activity 113

Creative Jewelry

Subject Area: Art
Materials: See list below
Time: 45 to 60 minutes

Part I

Background:

You will need a large variety of magazines or pictures.

Procedure:

1. Cut out pictures of different kinds of precious stones from magazines. Be sure to include diamonds, rubies, emeralds, sapphires, and garnets.
2. Using the pictures of precious stones as guides, design some jewelry for yourself or a member of your family. You can design a ring, a bracelet, a necklace, or a watch. Share your designs with the class.

Process Questions:

1. Where are some places that you or your family member could wear the jewelry that you designed?
2. How do you think jewelry designers get their ideas?

Part II

Background:

- You may want to ask your students to volunteer to bring supplies from home or send a written request to parents.
- Jewelry can be mounted on a sturdy piece of cardboard for display.

  Supplies: Scissors, small pliers, glue, large paper clips, small paper clips, colored paper clips, and other materials.

Procedure:

1. You will be designing and making paper clip jewelry. Some of the materials you may want to use will be available in the classroom. You may wish to bring other materials from home.

Suggested Materials

Plain large paper clips

small pieces of colored paper

colored paper clips

plastic flowers

buttons

narrow ribbon or yarn

large beads

2. Collect the materials and work at a table with your small group. Each group member will make their own piece of jewelry, but the group will share the materials.
3. Paper clips link together easily to make chains. They also can be bent or opened up and buttons or beads threaded onto them. Experiment with the different materials to decide what you like.
4. Create your jewelry. Take turns with other class members displaying your jewelry and pointing out special design features.

Process Questions:

1. Discuss what other pieces of jewelry could be made out of paper clips.
2. What other materials could be used to make jewelry?

186   Miriam McLaughlin and Sandra Peyser

Chapter V Music and Art Activities

Artist

Artists paint, draw, create or sculpt pictures or objects. They convey feelings and thoughts through their art work. Artists often interpret the everyday things they see and hear through their paintings and sculptures in ways that may cause others to see these things differently. All cultures, from the earliest civilizations have had artists who interpreted the world for others.

Activity 114

Rainbow of Colors

Subject Area: Art
Materials: Paper, crayons, paint
Time: 30 to 60 minutes

Part I

Background:
- Explain the concept of primary colors.
- To enhance this activity, allow your students to make other colors like pink, brown, and aqua.

Procedure:
1. On two pieces of paper, draw two rainbows with a pencil.
2. Using paint or crayons, color one rainbow using only primary colors. Color the other rainbow using primary colors and the colors you make.
   - Mix yellow and red together. What color do you make? _____
   - Mix blue and yellow together. What color do you make? _____
   - Mix blue and red together. What color do you make? _____

Process Questions:
1. What other mediums do artists use beside paint?
2. Tell about a visit you made to a museum or art gallery. What famous works of art did you see?

Part II

Background:
- The more mediums your students have to choose from, the more interesting this activity will be.
- You can enhance this activity by bringing in pictures of famous works of art for your students to discuss.

Procedure:
1. From the list below, choose a feeling that you want to convey in some form of art work.
2. Choose the medium from the choices the teacher offers you that you think will best convey the feeling.
3. In your art work you may do something realistic or symbolic. Be sure any colors or designs you use are consistent with the feeling.

   Anger, joy, sadness, pleasure, love, fear, excitement, confusion, silliness.

4. When you have completed your work, give it a title and display it in the classroom.

Process Questions:
1. Why are so many artists called "starving artists?"
2. What can artists do while waiting for some of their work to sell?

Career Development Activities for the Elementary Grades

Computer Graphics Specialist

Computer graphics specialists are artists who use computers to do their art work. They work with all kinds of software, making the pictures and adding the colors that make the software more interesting to people who use it. Computer graphics specialists also design video games. They can create cartoon characters, colorful backgrounds, and movement, all on the computer.

Activity 115

Take a Byte

Subject Area: Art
Materials: Paper, magazines, colored pencils or pens
Time: 30 to 60 minutes

Part I

Background:

To enhance this activity, your students can design and color their own letters.

Procedure:

1. Cut letters from magazines to spell the words below:

Fun Quiet Fast Tall

The letters should have shapes and colors that look like the words. For example, small letters that are green or blue remind you of quiet. You would look for small green or blue letters in magazines to spell the word "quiet."

2. Glue the letters on a piece of paper, spelling out each word.
3. Share your words with your class. Explain why you chose the letters you did for each word.

Process Questions:

1. Why would someone with artistic ability choose to be a computer graphics specialist?
2. How is drawing on the computer different from drawing on paper?

Part II

Background:

Make a model so that your students can see how the finished product will work.

Procedure:

1. Working in the blocks below, draw something getting bigger or growing in four steps. For example, if you chose to show a tree growing, you would start in block one with a tiny plant, block two would show a sapling (a tree the height of a bush), block three would be a small tree, and block four a full grown tree.
2. Cut out the block strip.
3. Take a plain strip of paper and cut two slots in it. The slots should be as far apart as the width of one block and the height of the block strip.
4. Insert the block strip in one slot in the paper and out the other.
5. Now, beginning with the first block, pull the strip through the slots and watch your drawing grow.

Process Questions:

1. Where are graphic artists likely to work?
2. What kind of computer skills does a graphic artist need?

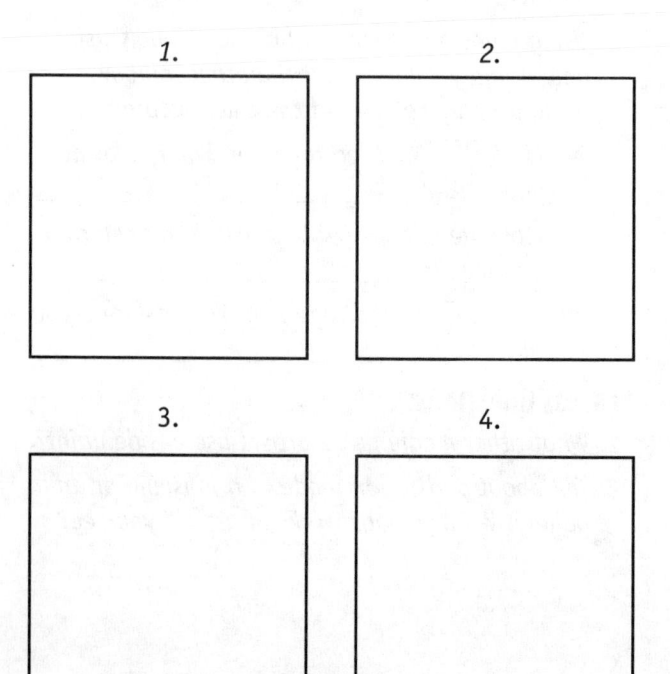

1.

2.

3.

4.

Chapter V   Music and Art Activities

Clothing Pattern Maker

Clothing pattern makers work with clothing designers. They make patterns from the designs and other workers use the patterns to make the clothes. Because there is a pattern, the same clothing design can be made over and over again. When we see several pieces of clothing in the store that look exactly the same, it is because the pattern maker made a pattern from one clothing design.

Activity 116

Patterns

Subject Area: Art
Materials: Old sheets, magic markers, fabric paint
Time: 45 to 60 minutes

Part I

Background:
- Send a request home for donations of old sheeting, tee shirts, or other material.
- Enhance this activity by having students cut out parts of their designs, so that the coloring of the design is uniform.
- Fabric paint is the ideal medium for this activity. Colored markers will work too. When paint is dry it becomes stiff and so does not work well with fabric.

Procedure:
1. *Patterns are used to make clothing, designs on walls, furniture, and other items. Patterns for clothing are often attached to the material and used as a guide for cutting. Other patterns are traced on material and cut out or colored in some way. Follow the directions to make a pattern that will be used as decoration for a piece of material.*
2. *Think of a design you could use in rows or scattered to decorate a piece of material. Draw the design on a piece of paper. It should be small so that you can repeat it several times on the material.*
3. *Once you have the design you want, copy it onto a piece of cardboard. Cut the design out of the cardboard.*
4. *Decide where you want to put your design on the material. You should put the design in at least three different places on the material. You may want to put a row of designs on the material or place it on different parts of the material. Once you have decided, mark the areas where you will place your design with a pencil.*
5. *Trace the design onto the material in each place you marked.*
6. *Once the design is traced, color the designs with magic markers.*
7. *Share your design with the class.*

Process Questions:
1. *How did the pattern help you put the design on your fabric?*
2. *Name some other places where you see patterns.*

Career Development Activities for the Elementary Grades

Part II

Background:
- You may want to bring examples of logos to class.
- Encourage your students to portray the positive qualities of their groups in the logos.

Procedure:
Many designers put their initials or a logo on their clothing.

1. As a class discuss the logos you are familiar with, on sports clothing, for example.
2. Working in your small group, decide on a logo for your group. The logo should help to describe your group and must represent all group members.
3. Use tracing paper and pencils to design your logo. With your group, decide on the colors to use in your logo.
4. Trace the logo onto a piece of cardboard. Carefully cut the inside parts of the logo where you wish to add color. You should leave a little cardboard around each space you cut out. Next, cut the logo around the edge.
5. Lay the logo on a piece of paper and attach it with paper clips. Draw around the logo with a pen that is one of the colors in the logo. Color the inside of the logo in the areas that are cut out.
6. Remove the logo pattern from the paper. Add any other touches you have decided upon with your group. Each group member should make a copy of the logo using the process described above.
7. Share your group's logo with your class. Explain why your group chose the logo.

Process Questions:
1. What do you want the logo to say to the rest of the class about your group?
2. What does the pattern represent in your logo?

Broadcast Technician

Broadcast technicians install, test, repair and maintain electronic equipment used in radio and television. They also operate this equipment to transmit radio and television programs. Broadcast technicians work with cameras, microphones, and lights to make sure the programs transmit properly. They are the people who operate the control panels that make the programs we see and hear run smoothly.

Activity 117

You're On

Subject Area: Arts
Materials: Audio and video recorder
Time: 45 to 60 minutes

Part I

Background:
- Review the operation of the tape recorder with your class.
- If you do not have enough recorders for each group, allow your students to record in shifts throughout the day.
- Ideally, they should be in a quiet place, away from the classroom, to do their recording.

Procedure:
1. Working with your small group, use an audio tape recorder to survey your group.
- The survey question is "Should elementary students be able to decide when and where they do their homework?"
2. The group will rotate responsibilities so that each group member has an opportunity to work the recorder, ask the survey question and answer the question.
3. When you operate the recorder, check the volume, be sure both the interviewer and the person being interviewed are close enough to the microphone to be heard and that there is enough tape to record the question and answer. When the recorder is ready, signal the interviewer to ask the survey question.
4. Continue this activity until each person in your group has had a chance to do each job.
5. Play back the recording with your small group. Talk about what worked or did not work well during the recording. For example, if you recorded in the classroom, there may have been background noise that interfered with the recording. Discuss what you would do differently and what you would do the same if you recorded again.
6. Share your recording with the class. Tell the class what your group learned about recording during this activity.
7. After the class has heard all the recordings, decide what the consensus of the class was about the survey question.

Process Questions:
1. Why do some people dislike being recorded?
2. Why are some people more natural in front of the recorder?

Career Development Activities for the Elementary Grades

Part II

Background:
- Review the operation of the camcorder with the class. Your students should be allowed to hold it, find the volume and focus and practice taping if they wish.
- Have them do their taping in shifts. Allow them to go to another room to tape if that is possible.

Procedure:
1. Working in groups of three, use a camcorder to survey group members.
- The survey questions is " How do you feel about fast food restaurants replacing cafeterias in schools?"
2. The group will rotate responsibilities so that each student has a chance to operate the camcorder, ask the question and be interviewed.
3. When it is your turn to operate the camcorder, check the focus and volume. Hold the camcorder steady. When you are ready, signal the interviewer to ask the question.
4. Continue this process until all students have had an opportunity to do each job.
5. Play the tapes as a class. Discuss the techniques for using the camcorder that worked and those that did not work.
6. Discuss what the consensus of the class was regarding the survey question.

Process Questions:
1. Why is the job of broadcast technician so important to the production of a T.V. show?
2. Tell about a time you watched a show with bad audio or video.

Chapter VI

Physical Education, Health and Safety Activities

Career Development Activities for the Elementary Grades

Military Officer

Military officers are in charge of different sections of the Army, Navy, Marines, Air Force, or other branches of the service. Many military officers are responsible for groups of people who are learning how to become part of the military. The officers train these people, teach them to use different kinds of military equipment and help them to become physically fit. Because military people may be involved in dangerous activities, they must be disciplined, follow orders the officers give them and abide by the rules made to protect them.

Activity 118

Forward March

Subject Area: Physical Education
Materials: None
Time: 20 to 60 minutes

Part I

Background:
- Your class should perform this activity on the playground or large indoor space.
- You may want to lead the whole class in a march after they have marched in their small groups.
- Marching music is very helpful if it is available.

Procedure:
1. Read through the list of marching commands below with your small group. Talk about any actions you are not sure about.
2. Practice each command so that all group members agree on what to do.
3. Take turns with other group members being the military officer who calls the commands. The rest of the group will march.
4. When it is your turn to be the officer, decide on which commands on the list you will use with your group.
5. To begin, have your group form a line. Set the march rhythm by saying Hup 2, 3, 4 as the marchers march in place. Marchers should start with the same feet at the same time.
6. Start your march. Be sure you give the marchers time to respond after each command. Each officer will have one minute to call commands.

Command List

Attention!—Stand up straight with eyes ahead, hands at sides.

Forward march!—Start marching.

Halt!—Stop marching.

Right face!—Turn right.

Left face!—Turn left.

Eyes right!—Look to the right while marching straight ahead.

Eyes left!—Look to the left while marching straight ahead.

Process Questions:
1. Why is it important for one person to set the rhythm?
2. What would happen if there was no one giving the commands?

Chapter VI

Physical Education, Health and Safety Activities

Part II

Background:
- This activity works best in the gym or on the playground.
- To extend this activity, choose exercise leaders for every school day for a month. Have each leader plan a 15-minute period using some of the exercises he or she learned in small group. At the end of the month, have a discussion on the exercise program.

Procedure:
1. Choose an exercise you know about and find out how the exercise helps you to become physically fit. You may have to visit the media center or ask the physical education teacher to get this information. Each member of your small group should choose a different exercise.
2. Tell your small group about the exercise. Explain how the exercise helps the body.
3. Demonstrate the exercise for your small group.
4. Lead your small group in ten repetitions of the exercise.

Process Questions:
1. Are the exercises easier to do now than when you first started?
2. Do you feel differently about exercise than you did when you started?
3. Has exercise helped you do other activities better or longer?

Career Development Activities for the Elementary Grades

Chef

Chefs are cooks who have had training in preparing and fixing all kinds of dishes. Chefs are usually in charge of the kitchens in restaurants and oversee all the planning and preparation of meals. They plan the menus the restaurant will serve, decide on purchases that must be made and often have staff people to whom they assign different parts of the preparation. They may have special dishes they always prepare themselves. Chefs make sure the meals the restaurant serves are attractive, nutritious and that the price of the meals more than covers the cost of making them.

Activity 119

What's Cookin'?

Subject Area: Health
Materials: Recipes
Time: 30 to 60 minutes

Part I

Background:

Discuss the idea that in small quantities some of the snacks such as cake may be acceptable.

- Expand this activity by bringing wrappers or packages of various snacks to the classroom. Work with students to read the nutritional information, noting fat, sugar, and salt content.

Procedure:

1. With your class, talk about healthy and unhealthy snack foods. Decide what makes a snack healthy or unhealthy.

2. Below is a list of snacks that can be unhealthy. Beside each unhealthy snack write the name of a healthy snack you could eat instead.

   chips (taco, potato, corn)
   cheese puffs   candy
   ice cream   doughnuts
   cake   cookies
   soda   pie

3. Share your ideas for healthy snacks with your class.

Process Questions:

1. Why is it important to eat nutritious snacks?
2. How is learning to fix snacks a step in learning how to cook meals?

Part II

Background:

If you have the facility to cook, this activity is a wonderful way to involve parents.

Procedure:

1. With your class, discuss the different food groups and how they contribute to healthy bodies. You may have to look for this information in your media center.

2. Using the chart below, work with your small group to plan three nutritious meals for one day. Write each item included in your menu under the correct food group on your chart. You may have to divide some foods. For example, cheese toast would be included under grains and dairy products.

Chart

FRUITS & VEGETABLES

GRAINS & PASTA

MEAT, EGGS, FISH

DAIRY PRODUCTS

3. Share your meal plan with the rest of the class.

Process Questions:

1. How did your group cooperate to make this meal?
2. Why is meal planning important?

Chapter VI

Physical Education, Health and Safety Activities

Dietitian

Dietitians plan meals. They know how different kinds of food affect the body. Dietitians plan school lunch menus and make sure the cafeteria serves balanced, healthy meals. They know what vitamins and nutrients different foods contain and how much people need each day to stay healthy. They also work in hospitals, nursing homes and with doctors, planning meals for people on special diets.

Activity 120

Eat Healthy

Subject Area: Health
Materials: Handout
Time: 45 to 60 minutes

Part I

Background:

- Your students should be notified several days before this activity to ask their families to save empty packages and cans. Tell them to be sure to wash out the cans or empty the packages of crumbs before bringing them to school. If you are unable to give students notice, you may ask them to bring unopened packages and cans that will be returned at the end of the activity. You may wish to bring some products yourself to ensure that there is a variety of food.

- This activity will take at least one class period. If you wish to shorten the activity, have students work in groups and divide the cans and packages among the groups. They will have fewer labels to read and the activity will move much faster.

Procedure:

1. Today, the makers of packaged and canned foods are required to list the nutritious value of the foods on the can or package label. Bring at least two empty or unopened cans or packages from home that still have the labels on them. Place these products at the front of the room.

2. Work with your small group to check your answers. You may have to go back and look at the products again if your answers do not agree with the rest of the group's answers.

Process Questions:

1. Why do most people staying in hospitals need special diets?
2. How can reading labels help families plan more nutritional meals?

Part II

Background:

- You can enhance this activity by taking your class to a grocery store to do their research. Assign your students to do their comparisons in different product areas to get a variety of comparisons to share in class.

- If the packaging brought to class does not have enough similar products to do comparisons, you may have to supplement the supply.

Procedure:

The nutritional values of cans or packaged food are broken down by serving size. It is difficult to know which product is better unless you compare serving sizes. For example, one brand of cereal may list 120 calories per serving. The serving size listed is 1/2 cup. Another cereal lists the calories per serving as 150. The serving size listed on this package is 1 cup. That means that you get 150 calories by eating one cup of the second cereal and 240 calories by eating one cup of the first cereal.

1. Using the products from Part I, find two similar foods that list two different serving sizes. Record the names of the products on Handout Part II.
2. Complete Handout Part II.
3. Share your findings with your class.

Process Questions:

1. Why do babies need good nutritionally balanced diets?
2. Why do young people between 12 and 19 need good nutritionally balanced diets?

Educational Media Corporation®, Box 21311, Minneapolis, MN 55421-0311

Career Development Activities for the Elementary Grades

Handout—Activity 120

Eat Healthy

Part I

1. Which product(s) has the most calories per serving? _____

2. Which product(s) has the lowest sodium content? _____

3. Which product(s) has the highest fat content? _____

4. Which product(s) has the lowest fat content? _____

5. Which product(s) contains the most vitamin C? _____

6. Which products contain more than 2% protein? _____

7. Which product(s) has the least nutritional value over all? _____

8. Which product(s) contains the most sugar? _____

Part II

1. Compare each nutritional value listed on the labels beginning with the number of calories. Which product actually contains fewer calories? _____

2. Which product contains the most sodium and/or total fat per serving? _____

3. Which product lists the most nutrients per serving (protein, vitamins, calcium, iron, etc.)? _____

4. Which product is lower in sodium per serving? _____

5. Based on the information you gain from this comparison, which product do you think is the healthier food? _____

Chapter VI

Emergency Medical Technician

Emergency Medical Technicians drive ambulances and respond to emergency calls. They are trained to make quick decisions that will help injured victims before they get to the hospital. They may use first aid to stop bleeding or put a temporary splint on a broken bone. Sometimes they have to follow instructions given by a doctor over the radio in order to save a victim's life. Emergency medical technicians are on hand when there are fires, car accidents, serious storms and floods and any time you call 911 for medical help.

Activity 121

What Would You Do?

Subject Area: Health
Materials: Paper, pencils
Time: 20 to 45 minutes

Part I

Background:
- This activity is a good introduction to a discussion of safety in the home.
- You can enhance this activity by inviting an EMT to discuss safety issues.

Procedure:
1. Using a plain piece of paper, draw a house. You can make a simple box with a triangle on top for the roof.
2. Draw lines in the box showing the rooms in the house. Where ever you made a room, write the name of the room. Include a living room, kitchen, bedroom and bathroom.
3. Draw at least two smoke detectors in your house.
4. Draw a first aid kit in the room where it should be kept.
5. Draw telephones in your house. Write the number you would call if there was an emergency at your house.
6. Share your pictures with your class.

Process Questions:
1. Why do we need smoke detectors?
2. What can you do in an emergency if you do not have a telephone?

Physical Education, Health and Safety Activities

Part II

Background:
Send a note home with your students asking families to work with their children in filling out the Fire Safety Sheet. Ask that the whole family be involved in the fire safety plan.

Procedure:
Do your family members know what to do if there is a fire in your house?
1. Take the Fire Safety Sheet home and answer the questions on the sheet with your family.
2. When you return to class, use the information on your Fire Safety Sheet to make a fire safety poster for your home.
3. Title your poster: IN CASE OF FIRE.
4. Measure your poster paper and divide it into six equal sections. In each section write what one thing your family decided to do in case of fire. Decorate or draw pictures for each section on the poster.

Process Questions:
1. Discuss the fire safety rules for your school.
2. Why do schools and other public buildings have regular fire drills?

Fire Safety Sheet

- Do we have a smoke alarm? _____
- Is it working ? _____
- When should we call the fire department ? _____
  _____
- If there is a fire in the kitchen, how will we get out of the house? _____
- If we are on an upper floor and there is a fire on the stairs, how will we get out? _____
  _____
- How will we know that the whole family is out safely ? _____

Educational Media Corporation®, Box 21311, Minneapolis, MN 55421-0311

Career Development Activities for the Elementary Grades

Pharmacist

Pharmacists work in drugstores and hospitals. They are responsible for giving the patients the medicine the doctors prescribe. They mix the ingredients for medicines, count out the pills, and explain to patients how to take the medicine safely. Pharmacists know a great deal about drugs and how drugs affect people.

Activity 122

Read the Prescription

Subject Area: Health
Materials: Handout, paper, pencils
Time: 30 to 45 minutes

Part I

Background:

You may want to put different medication names on the board for your students to use on their labels.

Procedure:

1. You are a pharmacist working in a drugstore. A person comes in with a prescription from their doctor for cough medicine. You must type up the label for the bottle.

2. Write the information that will need to go on the label:
   a. name of pharmacy and phone number
   b. your name as pharmacist
   c. the name of the doctor
   d. the name of the medication
   e. instructions of how much to take and how many times a day to take it. Also, how many days it should be used.
   f. the patient's name and the date the prescription was filled.

Process Questions:

1. Why do pharmacists have to be very careful when typing up their labels?
2. What might happen if the pharmacist gave a person the wrong medication?

Part II

Procedure:

Medicines are drugs. People take medicine to treat illnesses. They must follow the instructions the doctor and pharmacist give them to take the medicine safely. See if you can decode the rules for taking medicine listed on the handout.

Process Questions:

1. Are there other rules you can think of for the safe use of medicine?
2. Where should medicine be stored?

Answers to pharmacy quiz:

1. Never take more medicine than the doctor said to take.
2. Never use someone else's medicine.
3. Always have an adult with you when you take medicine.
4. Never try taking medicine to see what might happen.
5. Never give someone else your medicine.
6. Always make sure your medicine is out of reach of little children.

Chapter VI

Physical Education, Health and Safety Activities

Handout—Activity 122

Read the Prescription

Medicines are drugs. People take medicine to treat illnesses. They must follow the instructions the doctor and pharmacist give them to take the medicine safely. See if you can decode these rules for taking medicine.

1. x w more# than the & said to w.

2. x % someone else's #.

3. o have an = with @ when @ w #.

4. x try taking # to see what might !.

5. x + someone else your #.

6. o make sure your # is ^ of reach of little *.

Secret Code

* children	& doctor
w take	% use
@ you	x never
o always	# medicine
= adult	! happen
^ out	

Career Development Activities for the Elementary Grades

Dentist

Dentists help us to care for our teeth and gums. Most dentists take care of the teeth of everyone in a family, checking "baby" teeth, filling cavities and capping and replacing teeth that have been damaged. They also treat infections and diseases of the teeth and gums. Some dentists specialize in mouth surgery or in straightening teeth. The dentist who puts braces on teeth is called an orthodontist.

Activity 123

Smile

Subject Area: Health, Math
Materials: Handout
Time: Two 30- to 45-minute periods

Part I

Background:
- This activity offers a good opportunity to discuss dental care, regular brushing, and dentist visits.
- To enhance this activity get a poster or model of a set of teeth and discuss the different ages when teeth grow in.

Procedure:
1. Fill in the worksheet.
2. Compare your answers with your class.

Process Questions:
1. Why is it important for very young children to begin going to the dentist?
2. Discuss when you first learned how to brush and take care of your teeth.

Part II

Background:
- Enhance this activity by inviting a dentist to donate blank dental charts.
- Encourage your students to ask their dentists to show them their charts.

Procedure:
1. Draw a picture of a set of teeth.
2. Name each tooth. Find molars, cuspids, bicuspids, etc..
3. Now work with your drawing as if it were a dental chart.
   a. Show two cavities in the teeth by coloring small dark spots where the cavities are located.
   b. Show three fillings by using a lighter color and marking where the fillings are located.
   c. Show where three teeth are capped (they should not have fillings or cavities) by placing x's on those teeth.
   d. Two teeth in front look a little crooked. Write what you could do to fix those teeth and draw arrows to the teeth that need to be fixed.

Process Questions:
1. Discuss how pedodontists (children's dentists) have made dental visits less scary for children.
2. Discuss what happens to the teeth of adults who do not take good care of them.

Chapter VI
Physical Education, Health and Safety Activities

Handout—Activity 123

Smile

a. Count how many teeth you have. _____

b. Are any teeth missing. Check where they are located in your mouth.

    top right side ___   bottom right side ___

    top front ___   bottom front ___

    top left side ___   bottom left side ___

c. Do you remember the last time you visited the dentist? __ yes   __ no.

d. What did the dentist do? _____

e. How can you tell if you have a cavity? _____

f. What does the dentist do to fix a cavity? _____

Career Development Activities for the Elementary Grades

Dental Hygienist

Dental hygienists clean and examine teeth. They usually work with dentists, preparing patients teeth for the dentist's treatments. They clean the teeth, floss them, take X rays, examine them and record their examination findings. Dental hygienists also instruct patients on how to take care of their teeth and gums.

Activity 124

Take Care of Your Teeth

Subject Area: Health, Art
Materials: Handout, teeth picture, poster paper, markers or paint
Time: 30 to 60 minutes

Part I

Background:
- Introduce the concept of dental health to your students, by asking them if they know what to do to take care of their teeth. You may want to have a hygienist visit with the class, to talk about what they do.
- Discuss with your students how commercials and billboards get their messages across, prior to beginning this activity.
- Make sure they have access to bright paints or markers.

Procedure:
1. In your small group, list the things people do to take care of their teeth.
2. Design a poster that encourages your students to care for their teeth, using the ideas from your list. Make sure the poster is eye-catching and easy to understand. You should use as few words as possible. Your poster should look like a small billboard.
3. Share your poster with the class. Put the posters in the hallways of the school to promote dental health.
4. Fill out the handout.

Process Questions:
1. Why do families encourage children to take care of their teeth?
2. Why do small children have to brush baby teeth if the teeth are going to fall out?

Part II

Background:
- Dentists have wonderful charts and pictures of teeth you can use for this activity.
- Invite a dental hygienist to teach the students about teeth and use the activity to evaluate what they learned.

Procedure:
1. Look at the teacher's picture of a set of teeth. Using the picture as a guide, draw a set of teeth on a piece of paper.
2. Fill in the statements on the worksheet. If your class has not discussed the different kinds of teeth and what they do, you may have to do research to find the answers.
3. Write the names of the different teeth on your drawing. Add braces or show a tooth missing if you wish.

Process Questions:
1. At what age is a person likely to have no teeth?
2. At what age would a person most likely be missing one or two front teeth?
3. Why do most people who have braces, get them as children?

Answers:
a. 32 teeth
b. back and sides, grinding food
c. incisors, bite
d. front sides, tearing and gnawing
e. to replace teeth that are missing
f. braces

Chapter VI

Physical Education, Health and Safety Activities

Handout—Activity 124

Take Care of Your Teeth

Complete the following statements:

a. Adults have _____ teeth in their mouths.

b. Molars are located at the _____ part of the mouth. We use molars for _____ .

c. The teeth in the very front of the mouth are called _____. We use them to _____ .

d. Cuspids and bicuspids are teeth located _____ of the mouth. We use bicuspids for _____ .

e. False teeth are used _____ .

f. Appliance for straightening teeth is called _____ .

Career Development Activities for the Elementary Grades

Respiratory Therapist

Respiratory therapists help people with breathing problems. People can live for a few days without water and a few weeks without food, but they cannot live without oxygen for more than a few minutes. Respiratory therapists use large machines to give patients the oxygen they need to live. Many people with heart or lung problems depend on respiratory therapists to help them breath.

Activity 125

Take a Deep Breath

Subject Area: *Physical Education*
Materials: *Handout*
Time: *20 to 30 minute exercise periods*

Part I

Background:

- It is important for your students to take time for their observations. It may be helpful to use a stop watch to time the observation and data recording for each activity.
- Mark a specific distance on the playground for them to jog and to run so that observations of different students will be comparable.

Procedure:

1. Find a partner and sit next to that person. You will be observing how the human body gets the oxygen it needs to function.
2. Using the data sheet, write your observations of your partner's breathing while he/she is sitting down. Take turns observing each other and writing what you see.
3. Next, walk with your partner to the playground. Observe your partner's breathing as you walk. Once you get to the playground, write your observations on the data sheet.
4. Next, take turns with your partner running a measured distance across the playground. The first time each of you runs, it should be at a slow jog. Write what you see after your partner has finished the slow jog. Then run the distance again as fast as possible. Write what you see when your partner has had a turn running fast.
5. Return to the classroom, and share your observations and conclusions with other students.

Process Questions:

1. What conclusions were you able to draw from your data?
2. What physical limitations are put on people with breathing problems?

Part II

Background:

- You may wish to have parent permission before introducing this activity. Cooperation of family members is essential to the success of this activity.
- Be sure your students choose activities appropriate to their environments. For example, if students live in an area where walking or running is unsafe, you may need to arrange for them to borrow aerobic tapes and tape players to use at home.
- Demonstrate appropriate stretching exercises for warming up and for cooling down.
- Check with students and look at journals each week to see how they are doing.
- To enhance this activity, you may wish to include a lesson on taking pulses and what the pulse rate means.

Chapter VI Physical Education, Health and Safety Activities

Procedure:

1. Choose a physical activity from the list below. This activity should be one that you do not do often now, but would be willing to do for one month.

Walking	Jogging	Running
Aerobics	Bike Riding	Swimming

   You should have access to anything you need to do the exercise. For example, if you choose swimming, you should have access to a pool and if you choose aerobics, you should have a video tape of exercises.

2. Once you have chosen your activity, talk to your family about your exercise plan. Be sure that your family considers your choice of exercise a safe and healthy one. Decide with your family how you will fit your exercise into your schedule.

3. Write a chart in your journal of how you will train for one month. Be sure to include the days and times you plan to train. The example below is a typical training schedule.

   Week I. Four times a week, for at least twenty minutes each time. Monday, Wednesday and Friday from 4 to 4:30 p.m., Saturday from 10 to 10:30 a.m.

   Week II. Four times a week for at least twenty-five minutes each time.

   Week III. Five times a week for at least twenty-five minutes each time

   Week IV. Five times a week for at least thirty minutes each time.

   Allow five minutes at the beginning of each exercise period to warm up; according to your teacher's instructions.

   Allow five minutes at the end of each exercise period to cool down according to your teacher's instructions.

4. Record information in your journal each time you exercise.

5. At the end of one month, study your journal and answer the following questions:

- Did the length of time you were able to exercise increase? By how much?
- Did your breathing change during the exercise as the month progressed? Explain.
- Did the exercise require less effort over time? Explain.
- Did you feel differently after exercise as the month progressed? Explain.
- Have you noticed any changes in your activities at the end of this month? What are they?

Process Questions:

1. Why does breathing often become easier after a person has exercised for awhile? (exercise builds lung capacity).

2. Why do people feel more energetic when they exercise regularly? (body builds strength, lung capacity, and uses energy more efficiently).

Career Development Activities for the Elementary Grades

Handout—Activity 125

Take a Deep Breath
Data Sheet

Part I

Sitting
- Can you see your partner breathing? _____
- Can you hear your partner breathe? _____
  How does your partner look, flushed skin or shining eyes? _____
- Is your partner perspiring? _____

Walking
- Can you see your partner breathing? _____
- Can you hear your partner breathe? _____
  How does your partner look, flushed skin or shining eyes? _____
- Is your partner perspiring? _____

Slow Jog
- Can you see your partner breathing? _____
- Can you hear your partner breathe? _____
  How does your partner look, flushed skin or shining eyes? _____
- Is your partner perspiring? _____

Running
- Can you see your partner breathing? _____
- Can you hear your partner breathe? _____
  How does your partner look, flushed skin or shining eyes? _____
- Is your partner perspiring? _____

Part II

Record the following information in your journal each time you exercise.

Date _____

Length of time you exercised. _____
Observations: _____
_____
How are you breathing (easy, hard, panting, gasping)? _____
How much work is required to do the exercise (hard work, some work, effortless)? _____
How does your body feel during the exercise (sluggish, heavy, light, weightless)? _____
How are you feeling fifteen minutes after you cool down (very tired, tired, comfortable, energetic)? ___
_____

Miriam McLaughlin and Sandra Peyser

Chapter VI

Physical Education, Health and Safety Activities

Security Guard

Security guards protect businesses, neighborhoods and buildings from intruders and other dangers. Some security guards sit at reception desks in the entryway of buildings. They check people in and out of the buildings and may even check the bags or packages the people are carrying. Other security guards work at night and spend their time checking the rooms in the buildings and walking the grounds.

Activity 126

Guard Duty

Subject Area: Health
Materials: None
Time: 30 to 45 minutes

Part I

Background:
- This activity explores the concept of fear and how your students can deal with it.
- During the discussion part of this activity, explore the idea that loud noises, unusual movements, and strangers are not always dangerous. Explain to students that knowing ahead of time how they will handle scary situations helps them to be less afraid.
- During the brainstorming part of this activity, ask them to think of other situations where they might be afraid. Some students, for example, may be afraid of the dark or of thunderstorms. Ask them what they can do to feel safe.

Procedure:
1. Working with your small group, answer the following questions.
   - Imagine you are a security guard who is alone in a building. You hear a loud crash. What should you do? How do you think you might feel?
   - If you were home alone and saw something moving outside your window, what would you do? How would you feel?
   - Imagine you are a security guard sitting at the front desk of a large building. A person you have never seen before tries to sneak past you. The person is carrying a large package. What would you do? How do you think you would feel?
   - You are at home alone and someone rings the doorbell. You look out the window and see someone you do not know. What would you do? How would you feel?
2. Discuss your group's answers as a class.
3. With your class, brainstorm some things that security guards can do to help themselves feel safe.
4. With your class, list the things you can do to feel safe.

Process Questions:
1. What other jobs are similar to that of security guard?
2. What training would be necessary to be a security guard?

Career Development Activities for the Elementary Grades

Part II

Background:
- Ask your students what the term common sense means.
- When writing the group's rules on the board, eliminate duplicate rules.
- Ask for volunteers to put the rules on chart paper for posting in the classroom.

Procedure:
1. *Most safety rules are common sense. Working with your small group, think of two or more common sense rules for staying safe for each of the situations described below and write them on a piece of paper.*
   - *When you are out with friends and a parent drops you off at the mall or the movies.*
   - *When you are home alone at night and all the lights go out.*
   - *When you are walking back from your friend's house in the dark.*
   - *When someone you do not know well offers you a ride.*
2. *Think of two other situations that might cause you to be afraid or in danger. Write two or more common sense safety rules for these situations.*
3. *List each group's ideas on the board. Brainstorm any other rules of common sense that you want to add to the list.*

Process Questions:
1. *How are the duties of a night security guard different from those who guard during the day?*
2. *How has airport security changed over the years?*

Nurse

Nurses take care of people who are sick or injured. Most nurses work in hospitals, providing the care the patients' doctors prescribe. They give medicine and shots, change bandages, check temperatures and blood pressures and assist the physicians with operations and medical procedures. They teach patients about their illnesses and injuries and how to care for themselves. Nurses can be found working in hospitals, emergency rooms, doctor's offices, schools, manufacturing plants, nursing homes and in community health organizations.

Activity 127

A Need for Nurses

Subject Area: Health
Materials: Handout, chart for each child
Time: 20 to 45 minutes

Part I

Background:
You may want to list some simple medications like aspirin for the class.

Procedure:
1. As a class list the qualities someone should have to be a good nurse. Name some of the places that nurses work.
2. Pretend you are a nurse in a hospital and must fill out a chart for one of the patients on your ward. You are working the 7:00 a.m. to 3:00 p.m. shift. Under the part called "instructions," write down any tests (like blood tests or X rays) the patient must have and the times they should take their medications.

Process Questions:
1. What do you think is the hardest part about being a nurse?
2. What is one of the most rewarding parts?

Part II

Background:
- Instruct your students to read the paragraph carefully.
- To increase the difficulty of this activity you may want them to spell and define the terms as you read them aloud.

Procedure:
1. Read the paragraph on the handout and write definitions for the terms listed below.

Process Questions:
1. Discuss any positive experiences you have had with nurses.
2. What do you think is the job of the school nurse?

Career Development Activities for the Elementary Grades

Handout—Activity 127

A Need for Nurses

Part I

Medical Chart—Treelane Hospital

Date: _____ _____ Nurse: _____

Patient's Name _____ Room Number _____

Doctor's Name _____

Current Medications _____

Instructions:

8:00 a.m. _____

9:00 a.m. _____

10:00 a.m. _____

11:00 a.m. _____

12:00 p.m. _____

1:00 p.m. _____

2:00 p.m. _____

3:00 p.m. _____

Part II

The emergency room nurse was attending to a woman with a leg wound. The wound was bleeding severely, and the nurse had to apply a tourniquet to stop the bleeding. A tourniquet is a long piece of cloth or cord that is wrapped around the leg just above the wound. It is tightened to close the vein or artery that is carrying blood to the wound. Once the nurse had stopped the bleeding he checked the woman's blood pressure by wrapping a blood pressure cuff around the woman's arm and pumping air into it. The blood pressure cuff measures how hard the heart is working to pump blood through the body. While the nurse did this, he also listened to the woman's heart beat through a stethoscope.

A doctor came in and examined the wound. She and the nurse cleaned the wound and applied a dressing to it. A dressing is made up of gauze pads and tape. The dressings are sterile, meaning they have been through a process that makes them germ-free. Often the doctor puts some medication on the wound before applying the dressing. The doctor also ordered a shot of antibiotics for the woman. Antibiotics are types of medicine that fight infection. The nurse took a syringe and filled it with fluid containing the antibiotics. A syringe is a needle attached to a tube. It is used to give shots. The woman was required to stay in the emergency room for several hours so the nurse could monitor her condition. The nurse monitored the woman by checking her blood pressure regularly and being sure the wound did not start bleeding again. Finally the woman went home.

Write definitions for the following terms:

Stethoscope	Tourniquet
Monitor	Dressing
Sterile	Antibiotics
Syringe	Blood Pressure Cuff

Chapter VI | Physical Education, Health and Safety Activities

Robotics Technician

Robotics technicians are responsible for repairing robots. The robots these technicians take care of work in factories doing the repetitive tasks people used to do. Any factory where there are jobs that are done again and again may use robotics machines to do those jobs. For example, in factories that make soft drinks, robotics machines fill the bottles as they move down a conveyor belt. In potato chip factories, robotics machines fill the bags with potato chips and may move them to other robotics machines that seal the bags. These machines can do the work faster than people can because they do not need to eat or sleep and do not get tired and bored. The robotics technicians keep the machines in good working order.

Activity 128

The Production Line

Subject Area: Physical Education
Materials: Paper, pencils
Time: 20 to 45 minutes

Part I

Background:

You can make the task more visual by placing a chair in the center/front of the classroom to represent the robot. Use a desk or a table on the side of the room and a box or wastebasket to represent the machine at the back of the room.

Procedure:

1. Using a plain piece of paper, draw your idea of a robot. The robot must have at least two arms and be able to move about. Draw a light on your robot showing when it is 'on' or 'off'.

2. Under the picture of your robot, draw a control panel. The panel should show all the controls used to make the robot move. For example, you will have a control for moving forward, back and sideways, and one for arm movement. Be sure to include controls for any movement you think the robot should do.

3. Your robot must now perform a task. It must pick up a machine part from a table on the left side of a room, carry it to a place at the back of the room and place the part in a machine. On another piece of paper, write the control commands you must give the robot to accomplish this task.

4. Discuss the control commands with your class.

Process Questions:

1. What else would you like to have a robot do?
2. How do robots make life easier for us?

Educational Media Corporation®, Box 21311, Minneapolis, MN 55421-0311

Career Development Activities for the Elementary Grades

Part II

Background:

- Write the names of the following machines on separate slips of paper. Place the slips in a box and allow each small group to draw one. Remind students to keep their assignment a secret from other groups.

  Bottle capping machine, grapefruit packing machine, pill bottle filling machine, chicken plucking machine, milk bottle filling machine, cookie packaging machine

- Encourage applause for each group's demonstration.

- Allow your students areas in the classroom or hall to build their machines and practice their demonstrations.

- Encourage them to let the groups complete their demonstrations before guessing aloud what machine the group demonstrated.

Procedure:

1. With your small group, draw one name of a machine from the slips of paper the teacher passes out. Keep the name of your machine a secret from other groups.

2. Go to a corner of the classroom or into the hall and decide how your group can make the machine using all group members. You will build and act out what the machine does without speaking. You can make noises. You can also use simple props like chairs or pieces of paper. Other groups will guess what kind of machine your group is portraying.

3. Once your group has decided what to do to demonstrate your machine, practice the actions. Try to keep other groups from seeing what you are doing.

4. Demonstrate your machine in front of other groups. Students watching should not guess out loud what kind of machine your group is until you have completed your demonstration.

5. Applaud all efforts.

Process Questions:

1. What would happen to the machine if someone in your group did not cooperate?

2. What happens in the classroom when one or more people do not cooperate with the group process?

Chapter VI **Physical Education, Health and Safety Activities**

Military Enlisted Personnel

Military enlisted personnel are in the military service. They may belong to the Navy, Army, Air Force, or Marines. They fight for our country during wartime and protect us in times of war and peace. They learn to do particular jobs in the military. Enlisted personnel are trained to fire guns, work on battle ships and aircraft carriers, drive tanks or serve as support for fighter jets and submarines. Some of them have jobs in offices where they do the paper work necessary to run the military. Military enlisted personnel work in teams and support each other in doing the tasks they are assigned.

Activity 129

Balloon Ball

Subject Area: Physical Education
Materials: Balloons
Time: 20 minutes

Part I

Background:
- This game works best in a gym or other open area. The playground does not work as well because of wind and the irregular ground that may cause the balloons to pop.
- Have a small prize on hand for the winning group. It should be something the group can share.
- Students enjoy this game. You may want to do a two out of three contest.

Procedure:
1. Working as a team means depending on team members to do their parts. Play the following game with your small group.
   - Stand in a circle with your small group. Make sure you are away from desks and chairs.
   - When I say "go," toss your balloon in the air. Work as a team to keep the balloon from landing on the floor, without using your hands. You may use your heads, bodies and feet.
   - Once your balloon touches the floor, your group is out and should sit down.
   - The group who keeps it's balloon in the air the longest is the winner.

Process Questions:
1. Would you have done better keeping the balloon off the floor alone? Why or why not?
2. When are some other times it is good to work as a team?

Part II

Background:
- This activity is best done in a gym.
- Have a small prize available that the winning group can share.
- Your students may want to go for 2 out of 3 to determine a winner.

Procedure:
1. With your small group, lay on the floor in a circle, with your head toward the center of the circle.
2. When I say "go", toss your balloon in the air. You must keep the balloons in the air without using hands or arms. You may use heads, bodies and feet.
3. When your balloon touches the floor, your group is out and must sit up.

Process Questions:
1. Name some times in the class that you work as a team.
2. Name some times at home that you work as a team.

Career Development Activities for the Elementary Grades

School Counselor

School counselors are helpers to students. When students have problems that get in the way of learning, school counselors help them deal with these problems in healthy ways. They talk with students, parents and teachers and visit classrooms. They work with individual students and small groups, teaching them problem solving, communications skills, and how to handle conflict. Counselors also help students make decisions about their futures.

Activity 130

Negotiating and Mediating

Cluster: *Education and Social Services*
Subject Area: *Health, Reading*
Materials: *Handout*
Time: *45 to 60 minutes*

Part I

Background:
- During the discussion of everyday conflicts, stress that it is a normal part of life. Focus on some of the unhealthy ways people deal with conflict.
- Ideally, your students will be able to identify some of their own conflicts to role play.
- Remind them to use good listening skills when practicing negotiation.

Procedure:

1. Counselors teach students to negotiate or mediate the conflicts they have every day of their lives. Conflict is normal; it is the way conflict is sometimes resolved that causes problems. With your class, discuss the conflicts that occur in everyday life. For example, when you were getting ready to leave for school this morning, perhaps your mother wanted you to wear a jacket and you didn't think you needed one. Talk about the conflicts people have with their friends, brothers and sisters, teachers and coaches as well as with their parents.

2. With your class, brainstorm a list of the different ways people resolve conflicts.

3. Look at the list. Decide with your class how many of these ways of resolving conflicts have a winner and a loser. For example, if you yelled at your mother and ran out of the house without your jacket, who was the winner in the conflict? Who was the loser?

4. Negotiation is a way of resolving conflicts that allows both sides to win. For negotiation to be successful, both sides must be willing to talk about the conflict. Choose a partner and practice negotiation by following the steps of negotiation.

5. After the role play discuss the negotiation process with the class. Answer the following questions:

   What parts of negotiating were hard for you?

   Did you find a good and fair solution to your problem? What was it?

Process Questions:

1. What can you do if someone yells at you when you are trying to negotiate a problem?

2. Why is it important to have the skills to work out your own problems with your friends?

Chapter VI — Physical Education, Health and Safety Activities

Part II

Background:
- There are several good resources available for training students to be mediators. Peer mediation is used in many schools as one part of a program for reducing violence. The program requires strong leadership, commitment from administration and faculty and extensive training for student mediators.
- These activities are intended for students to experience positive ways of resolving conflicts.

Procedure:
1. If a conflict cannot be resolved through negotiation, try mediation. Mediation involves a third person who helps the disputants work through the problem. Mediators must be thoroughly trained to mediate for other students. Form groups of three and think of three conflicts your group members have had with other people that your group can role play. Write them down.
2. Decide who in your group will be the first mediator. The other two will be the disputants. Mediators should follow these guidelines:

   Do not take sides.

   Do not tell the disputants what to do to solve their problem.

   Practice good listening skills.

   If the disputants do not abide by the ground rules, cancel the mediation.
3. Choose one of the conflicts from your group's list. Disputants should each represent a different side of the conflict. Follow the Steps for Mediators to mediate the conflict as the disputants role play.
4. Repeat this process, giving each group member an opportunity to mediate. Use a different **conflict each time.**
5. As a class, discuss the mediation process. What is difficult about mediation? When does it work best?

Process Questions:
1. How can mediating a problem instead of going to court help save the taxpayers money?
2. How can mediating a problem in a school keep students from being suspended?

Career Development Activities for the Elementary Grades

Handout—Activity 130

Negotiating and Mediating

Part I

Steps in Negotiation

a. Choose a conflict from the Conflict List to role play or think of one you or your partner have experienced. Decide who will be partner A and who will be partner B.

b. Before you start the negotiation, you and your partner must state out loud that you agree to talk about the problem.

   Partner A "I agree to talk about this conflict."

   Partner B "I also agree to talk about this conflict."

c. Each partner must agree not to interrupt while the other person is telling his or her side of the story.

   Partner A "I agree not to interrupt while you are talking."

   Partner B "I agree not to interrupt while you are talking."

d. Start the negotiation. Partner A should tell their side of the story while partner B listens. Then Partner B should talk while partner A listens.

e. Brainstorm possible solutions. Think of as many ways of resolving the problem as you can. For example, if you were negotiating with your mother about wearing a jacket you might suggest that you wear your jacket on Tuesday and Thursday and go without it on Monday, Wednesday and Friday. Your mother might suggest you wear it every day, except in July and August. Another solution might be to wear the jacket to school on cool mornings and put it in your book bag when the day gets warmer.

f. Once you have brainstormed all possible solutions, find one that both of you can agree on. You may have to combine two ideas to get the solution that you both like.

g. Once you have reached a solution, each partner should state the solution out loud.

   Partner A "I agree to....."

   Partner B "I agree to....."

h. Shake hands with your partner.

Conflict List

- You say it is your turn to use the basketball. Your partner says it's their turn to use the ball.
- You said you loaned your friend the pen and he was supposed to give it back. Your friend says you gave it to him to keep.
- You think you should get a raise in your allowance. Your parent thinks you get enough allowance now.
- Your brother took your bike without asking and you needed it. He says you used his bike last week when he was planning to ride to a friend's house.
- Your friend wants to copy your homework. You don't want your friend to copy your work.

Handout—Activity 130 (cont.)

Negotiating and Mediating

Part II

Guidelines
Mediators should follow these guidelines:

Do not take sides.

Do not tell the disputants what to do to solve their problem.

Practice good listening skills.

If the disputants do not abide by the ground rules, cancel the mediation.

Steps for Mediators
- Sit in between the disputants
- Introduce yourself. Shake hands with the disputants.
- Read the ground rules aloud to the disputants.

Ground Rules
Be willing to solve the problem

Tell the truth

Listen without interrupting

Be respectful; no name calling or fighting

Take responsibility for doing what you say you will do.

- Ask the disputants one at a time if they agree to abide by the rules.
- Ask the disputants, one at a time, what happened. If the other disputant interrupts, remind him or her of the ground rules.
- After each side has told his or her story ask the disputants, "What ideas do you have for solving this problem?" Get disputants to come up with as many ideas as possible.
- Ask disputants which idea they think would work best to solve the problem. Review the idea. Ask each disputant to tell what they will do to help solve the problem.
- Ask disputants how they can avoid the same problem in the future.
- Congratulate disputants for solving their conflict. To avoid rumors, ask them to tell their friends that the problem is solved.

Career Development Activities for the Elementary Grades

Preschool Teacher

Preschool teachers work with three and four year old children teaching them basic skills. They may help children learn to tie their shoes, wash their hands, or hold a pencil. They make use of games, songs, artwork, computers and special play areas to teach the children. Preschool teachers are also responsible for the safety and well-being of the children in their care. They must be sure the children get the food and rest they need, and have plenty of time for play.

Activity 131

Learn a Skill

Subject Area: Physical Education and Music
Materials: None
Time: Two 30-minute periods

Part I

Background:

- The first part of this discussion should allow time for sharing. Learning to button, tie, and count are all skills three and four year olds learn.

- In the second part of this activity, help your students to understand how children learn by using examples from the first part of the discussion. For example, children may have learned how to pedal a bike by someone showing them how to pedal. Get as many ideas as possible for how children learn. Students will use these ideas in designing their game.

- When partners are teaching the rest of the class, instruct the class to be respectful of the teaching partners and applaud all efforts.

Procedure:

1. With your class, talk about what you were like when you were three and four years old. What did you do during the day? What were your favorite toys? Do you remember what you learned when you were that age?

2. Working as a class, make a list of skills small children need to learn. Talk about how children learn new things and write those ideas next to the list. For example, a child might learn a new skill by trying it several times.

3. Working with a partner, choose one of the skills and invent a short game to teach the skill. Be sure you use some of the ideas listed on the board in your game. For example, in your game you could have the child try the skill several times.

4. With your partner, practice the game and then teach it to the rest of the class.

Process Questions:

1. Why don't we expect 3 and 4 year olds to do many paper and pencil activities?

2. What does it mean to be uncoordinated?

Part II

Background:

- Be sure that your students work through the first two steps of Part I before starting on this activity.

- If you have access to a preschool, you can enhance this activity by taking your students to the class to teach their songs to the children.

Procedure:

1. If you have not done Part I of this activity, do #1 and #2 from Part I now.

2. Working with your small group, write a song that teaches a skill to three and four year olds. Use the information on the board to guide your writing. You may want to choose a tune the group knows and add new words. "Twinkle, Twinkle Little Star," "Old MacDonald Had a Farm" and "Row Row Row Your Boat" are a few suggestions.

3. Once your group has written the song, practice it once or twice quietly.

4. Teach your song to your class.

Process Questions:

1. Why do small children like songs?

2. Why do small children like to sing the same song over and over again?

Chapter VI Physical Education, Health and Safety Activities

Firefighter

Firefighters put out fires that are a danger to people, houses, buildings and land. They must pass physical as well as written tests to become firefighters because they must handle heavy hoses and ladders, move large pieces of wood and metal and carry people to safety. Firefighters take care of the fire trucks, and the equipment they use to put out fires. Some of their time is spent helping people to understand how to prevent fires.

Activity 132

To the Rescue

Subject Area: Health & Safety
Materials: None
Time: 45 to 60 minutes

Part I

Background:
- This activity requires a visit to a fire station. Arrange the visit and ask that small groups of students be permitted to interview individual firefighters. The number of firefighters available for interview and the number of small groups of students should be the same.
- Your students should be encouraged to ask questions about the other work firefighters do besides fighting fires.

Procedure:
1. Working with your small group, plan a trip to the fire station. Write a list of questions you will want to ask a fire fighter. When you return to class, each group member will write a biography of the fire fighter the group interviewed. You may want to know what the fire fighter does when they have time off or what the fire fighter does at the station house during work hours.

2. In preparation for your visit, make a copy of the list of questions the group will ask. Leave a space after each question where you can write the answer. Decide in your group, which group member will ask which question. Everyone should have a turn.

3. When you return from your fire station visit, work on your own to write a biography of the fire fighter your group interviewed.

4. Share your biography with your small group. Discuss how the biographies are alike and how they are different. Think of two new things you learned about being a fire fighter.

5. Tell the class about the firefighter your group interviewed and the new things your group learned about being a firefighter.

Process Questions:
1. What are some positive uses for fire?
2. Why does the job of firefighter require extensive training?

Educational Media Corporation®, Box 21311, Minneapolis, MN 55421-0311

Career Development Activities for the Elementary Grades

Part II

Background:
- The class discussion of fire hazards is important to this activity. A hazard may be something like a lighted cigarette, or something that puts the people in the building at risk if there is a fire, like an inadequate or broken fire escape.
- You may want students to do this activity in small groups. You can also assign groups of students to different areas of the school. They will then do their reports only on their assigned areas. The class can pool their information to determine the fire safety level in the school.

Procedure:
1. With your class, brainstorm a list of fire hazards. Discuss why the items listed are fire hazards. For example, why is a pile of oily rags a fire hazard? Talk with your class about where some fire hazards in the school may be located.

2. With your class, go on a field trip around the school checking for fire hazards. Take a pad of paper and a pencil with you to record your findings. You will want to look for anything that could cause a fire and also those things that could cause injury to students and teachers if the school was on fire. For example, a locked exit door might be a hazard if students and teachers could not get out of the burning building. Also, look for those measures the school has put in place to protect students and teachers in case of fire. For example, school buildings have fire extinguishers placed in different areas of the school.

3. When you return to your class, write a report on fire safety in your school, using the notes you took on your field trip.

4. As a class, discuss the level of fire safety in your school. Is the school very safe or are there changes that should be made to make it safe.

Process Questions:
1. Why do schools and office buildings have regular fire drills?
2. Why do firefighters have periodic safety renewal courses?

Chapter VI   **Physical Education, Health and Safety Activities**

Physical Therapist

Physical therapists work with people who have problems that limit their ability to move. These people may have suffered an injury or have a disease that affects their bones and muscles. Physical therapists test the strength of these people and then help them with special exercises to build the strength in their muscles. They also teach handicapped people to use wheelchairs, canes, crutches and walkers.

Activity 133

On the Go

Subject Area: Health
Materials: Canes, walkers, wheelchairs, crutches
Time: 30 minutes—all day

Part I

Background:
- You may want to decide on the exercises the children will lead and assign them to the different groups.
- Enhance this activity by having your students research the different kinds of exercise and how each kind affects the body.

Procedure:
1. Working with your small group, think of five different exercises a person could do sitting down. Decide what each exercise would do for a part of a person's body. For example, squeezing a ball, even a ball of paper, strengthens fingers and hands. Practice each exercise. A different group member should lead each time. Check how you feel after the exercise. Does the exercise stretch your arm muscles, does it loosen joints like elbows and knees?
2. Move your chairs to the front of the room. Take turns with your group leading the class in an exercise. Each exercise should be done no more than five times. Tell the class what the group thinks the exercise does for a person's body and why.
3. After each group has had opportunities to lead exercises, discuss the experience. Was it easier or harder to exercise sitting down?

Process Questions:
1. How does exercise help your muscles stay limber?
2. Why do young people need as much exercise as older ones?

Career Development Activities for the Elementary Grades

Part II

Background:
- This activity offers students a remarkable experience. It requires the donation of wheelchairs, crutches, canes and walkers for the duration of the experience. If you do not have enough devices to go around, have students use the devices in two hour shifts during the school day.
- Giving your students this experience also requires the cooperation of the principal, teachers and staff at the school.
- Write the words "crutches," "cane," "walker," and "wheelchair" on individual slips of paper. The number of paper slips should correspond to the number of devices you have available.
- If at all possible, have a physical therapist come to the class to explain the use of these devices.
- Stress to your students that if there is an emergency of any sort at the school, they are to abandon their devices and follow the normal emergency procedures.

Procedure:
1. You will be experiencing what it is like to be physically handicapped. Draw a slip of paper to find out what kind of device you will use during this experience.
2. Each device is for a different kind of handicap.
   - Wheelchairs are for people whose legs cannot support their weight or who cannot move their legs.
   - Canes are for people who need assistance walking. These people usually walk very slowly.
   - Walkers are for people whose legs can support a limited amount of weight. Their arms support most of the weight.
   - Crutches are usually used by people who have only one leg that can move and support them.
3. Practice using your device. For the period of time you are assigned, you will depend completely on this device.
4. After you have experienced a few hours or a day as a physically handicapped person, write an essay telling about your experience.
5. Share the essay with the class.

Process Questions:
1. How did this experience change your view of a handicapped person?
2. What was the most difficult part of the experience?

Chapter VI

X ray Technologist

X ray technologists operate X ray machines to take pictures of the interior of the body. These machines use radiation to take the pictures. The X rays are used to diagnose medical problems. X ray technologists take the x rays of patients as they are requested by the patient's doctors and develop the pictures.

Activity 134

Hold that Pose

Subject Area: Health
Materials: Handout
Time: 30 to 45 minutes

Part I

Background:
- Tell your students that many people who work in the field of medicine must deal with people who are in pain or afraid.
- When reviewing the best responses, discuss why some of the other responses are not good ones to say to people who are in pain or worried.

Procedure:
1. Doctors order X rays for people with broken bones and other injuries, and for people who have diseases. They also order X rays to find out why a patient is ill. Many of the people doctors send to the X ray technologists are very worried about what might be wrong or are in pain from an injury. Technologists must help these people relax in order to do their work.

   Working with your small group, read the situations on the handout and decide, as a group, on the best response.

Process Questions:
1. Ask your students if they have ever had X rays taken and what the experience was like.
2. Discuss any experiences with broken bones.

Physical Education, Health and Safety Activities

Part II

Background:
Tell your students that people in the medical field must deal with people's feelings as well as their bodies.

Procedure:
1. Complete the Part I activity, before doing Part II.
2. Working in small groups, read the situations on the handout and write what your group thinks the X ray technologist should say.

Process Questions:
1. Ask your students to share experiences that they have had when someone said the right thing or was reassuring.
2. If they are able to share negative experiences when someone said the wrong thing, ask the class for ideas of better things to say.

Educational Media Corporation®, Box 21311, Minneapolis, MN 55421-0311

Career Development Activities for the Elementary Grades

Handout—Activity 134

Hold that Pose

Part I

Working with your small group, read the situations below and decide, as a group, on the best response.

- James has a toothache. The X ray technologist must get an x ray of the tooth so the dentist can see what is wrong. James is worried about his tooth, and complains about the ache. He asks if everything is alright. Choose the technologist's best response and write why you chose it.
    a. Nothing to worry about.
    b. Don't you ever brush your teeth?
    c. You have a cavity.

    Why _____

- Wilandra comes into the X ray department with an injured arm. The doctor has ordered an X ray to see if it is broken. It hurts when the technologist moves it slightly and Wilandra says "OW". Choose the technologist's best response and write why you chose it.
    a. Sorry, I know this hurts.
    b. Don't be such a baby.
    c. How can I do my job if you don't cooperate?

    Why _____

- Kelly's parents bring her in for an X ray. Kelly was hit in the head with a baseball and they want to be sure she is alright. They tell the technologist they are very worried. Choose the technologist's best response and tell why you chose it.
    a. You shouldn't let her play baseball, she's much too small.
    b. As soon as I have some information I will come and tell you.
    c. It doesn't look serious.

    Why _____

Part II

Working in small groups, read the situations below and write what your group thinks the X ray technologist should say.

- A student comes into X ray on a stretcher. He has been in a car accident. He asks the X ray technologist "Am I gonna be alright?"

    Response _____

- A little girl and her mother come in for an X ray. The little girl has had her fingers shut in a door. She is crying. The mother is very scared. She says "I think those fingers are broken, don't you?"

    Response _____

- A man comes to X ray from the emergency room. He is in great pain. Every movement he makes causes him to groan.

    Response _____

- An athlete comes in to have her teeth X rayed. Her front teeth have just been knocked out while she was playing her sport. Some of her other teeth may be damaged as well. She says "Oh, what am I going to do? I look awful."

    Response _____

Chapter VI — **Physical Education, Health and Safety Activities**

Physician

Physicians help people stay well and they care for people who are sick or injured. Primary care physicians may take care of entire families, delivering their babies, bandaging cuts and treating the illnesses they get, like measles, mumps and the flu. Physicians also do physical examinations on children and adults, making sure that their bodies are healthy and functioning properly. Some physicians are specialists, and only take care of certain parts of the body, like the eyes or feet. We are very dependent on physicians to help us live long, healthy lives.

Activity 135

Jeopardy

Subject Area: Health
Materials: Index cards, pencils
Time: 45 minutes

Part I

Background:

- Your students may need some time to do research to prepare for this game. Assign each student a category. The categories are listed below.

    Doctor's Office, Medicine, Tools Doctors Use, The Human Body, Illnesses

- Keep index card piles separate. Read the answers written by the students on the right side of the room to the students on the left and vice versa.

- Remind your students that they should respond to each answer you read, with a question. If they are not able to respond correctly once they are called on, the answer goes to the other side of the room. One person on that side wrote the answer and should know the correct question.

- Keep score by making chalk marks on the board for each group's correct answers.

Procedure:

1. Jeopardy is a game where the answer is given and the contestants have to provide the question. The questions are divided into different categories and there are three contestants who provide the questions to the answers the host reads. This game of jeopardy will be a little different from the one you have seen played on television or in your home.

2. Working on your own, think of one answer and question for your assigned category. You must think of the answer and question on your own and not share it with anyone else. You may have to look information up in a dictionary or encyclopedia. The following is an example of an answer and question:

- If your category is Doctor's office, one answer could be "this person assists the doctor and takes temperatures and blood pressure." The question for this answer is " What is a nurse" ? Write your question and answer on an index card.

3. Divide the class in half. One side of the classroom will compete against the other side. Pass your index card to the front of the room on your side. There should be two piles of index cards at the front of the room.

4. I will ask a question, of one side of the room, using the index cards from the other side. Once I have read the answer, raise your hand if you know the question. If you put your hand up and do not have the right question, the other side will get a chance to answer. Your side will get one point for each correct answer. You may want to consult with other students on your side of the room before you answer.

5. Once you have completed the game, share with your class what new information you learned about physicians.

Process Questions:

1. How did this game help you learn about the medical profession?
2. How have new medicines prolonged life?

Part II

Background:
- Assign the categories to your students and proceed with the game exactly as it is described in Part I.
- The categories for this level are as follows:
  Childhood Diseases, Medical Equipment, Body Organs, Medical Specialists, Legal and Illegal Drugs

Procedure:
1. Follow the exact format of Part I, using the categories assigned.
2. Once you have completed the game, share with your class any new information you learned about the field of medicine.

Process Questions:
1. Discuss some positive experiences you or your family have had with physicians.
2. Discuss how immunizations have lessened the threat of childhood diseases.

Chapter VI

Receptionist

Receptionists greet visitors, give directions, respond to questions and answer phones for businesses and organizations. They are often the first people visitors or customers see and talk to in the organization. Some receptionists also provide security for buildings, making sure visitors have identification cards, and checking the workers in when they arrive.

Activity 136

First Impressions

Subject Area: Safety
Materials: Index cards, magazines, scissors
Time: Several days in shifts

Part I

Background:
- Set the number of picture index cards each group can make.
- Encourage your students to say the first word that comes to their minds when they see a picture.
- Groups should rotate going first, since students may be influenced by what other group members say.

Procedure:
1. Visitors and customers often get their first impressions of a business or organization from the receptionist. People are often judged by the first impression they make. Working with your small group, select and cut out pictures of people from magazines that present a variety of looks. The pictures should show a variety of hairstyles, clothing and facial expressions.

2. Paste the pictures on individual index cards. Place the cards face down in the center of the table.

3. Choose one group member to go first. That person will draw an index card, look at it, and say the first word that comes to mind. The person should pass the card to the person sitting next to them and that person should say the first word that comes to mind. The picture should be passed all the way around the group, so that each group member has a chance to say something about the picture.

4. When it is time to draw the next index card, a different group member should go first. Each group member should have at least two opportunities to start the activity.

5. Once the groups have finished giving first impressions of each picture, discuss with the class whether first impressions are fair or unfair.

Process Questions:
1. As a class, discuss why it is important for a receptionist to make a good first impression.
2. What do hair, makeup and clothes have to do with making an impression?

Part II

Background:

- It will be necessary to have the cooperation of principal and staff to accomplish this activity.
- A table can be set up just outside the office door or adjacent to the counter, for the three receptionists.
- Review the school rules and policies for students. Do visitors have to sign in at the office? Do they have to wear name tags? What are the rules when parents come to pick up their children?

Procedure:

1. With you class, form groups of three. Each group of three will serve as the receptionists outside the school office for a period of time during the day.
2. Provide instructions on how the receptionist groups will perform their duties.
3. The receptionists must abide by all school policies and be prepared to make a good first impression.
4. Once you have served as a receptionist, write a short summary of the experience.
5. Share your experience with your class.

Process Questions:

1. What was the hardest duty you had as the receptionist?
2. What did you like best about the job?

Psychologist

Psychologists study how people think, feel and behave. Some psychologists work with people to help them change their behavior. Others do tests and experiments that help determine what kind of personality a person has or how intelligent they are. They work with police departments, schools and universities, hospitals and for private clinics. The work psychologists do helps us understand why human beings behave the way they do.

Activity 137

What Do Psychologists Think

Subject Area: Health
Materials: None
Time: 30 to 45 minutes

Part I

Background:
- This activity is performed in the style of a talk show with you serving as host. Humor and applause should be a part of the activity.
- Caution your students to ask appropriate questions. Reserve the right as host to ask students to sit down if their questions are inappropriate.

Procedure:
1. Psychologists are often asked to appear on talk shows to help the people on these shows with their problems. Working on your own, think of a question you could ask psychologists on a talk show about the topic listed below.

   Show's Topic: PARENTS AND KIDS

2. Write your question on a piece of paper, so you will remember it if you are called on during the show.

3. I will be the host. Three students at a time will sit at the front as the guest psychologists.

4. When I call on you, stand and ask your question. One psychologist should give an answer. When the next student asks a question, a different psychologist should answer. Once all three psychologists have answered one question, a different group of students should take their seats.

5. Continue this activity until each class member has had a chance to answer one question.

6. As a class, discuss why a real psychologist would probably have provided more helpful answers.

Process Questions:
1. What are some of the duties of psychologists in schools?
2. Why do some people ask for advice and others do not?

Career Development Activities for the Elementary Grades

Part II

Background:
- This is an exercise in active listening. To enhance this activity, have students role play active listening using the statements below.
- You may want to review other components of active listening.

Procedure:

1. Psychologists seldom offer advice to the people who come to them. Usually, they listen and ask questions that help the people think things out for themselves. For example, if a teenager said to a psychologist, "I am very angry with my Mother," the psychologist might respond with a question like "Why do you think you feel that way?" Working with your small group, think of questions that could be responses to the following statements. All the questions should be different.

   "I am really worried about the Math Test."

   "I'm not going to make the team!"

   "I can't believe I got an A."

   "This is the second time I missed the bus. My mom will kill me!"

   "I don't understand why I wasn't invited to the party!"

   "I wish it was the last day of school instead of the first."

2. Share your questions with your class. Discuss what kind of responses the questions might bring.

Process Questions:

1. Why will people tell strangers their problems before their own family and friends?
2. Why don't psychologists offer advice?

Chapter VII

Computer Skills Second Language

Career Development Activities for the Elementary Grades

Desktop Publisher

Desktop Publishers work on computers. They work with books, newsletters and other written material to make the finished publications look good. They know how to use the computer to create headlines and titles and to move sentences and paragraphs around the page. In addition to having strong computer skills, desktop publishers are skilled at writing and spelling.

Activity 136

Computer Whiz

Subject Area: Computer Technology, Writing
Materials: Computer, pencils, and paper
Time: 30 to 60 minutes

Part I

Background:

To save time, enter the story starters on diskettes prior to the class. Students can then load a story starter file using a word processing program, rather than typing it in.

Procedure:

1. Access a word processing program on your computer or use a pencil and paper for this activity.
2. Choose a story starter from the list below and type the sentence into your computer or write it at the top of your paper.
3. Complete the story with at least three more sentences.
4. Choose a title for your story and type it in.
5. Check the following and make any corrections:
   - Have you capitalized the proper nouns and the first letter of the first word of each sentence?
   - Is the title capitalized?
   - Are there any misspelled words?
   - Is your punctuation correct?
6. Print your story and check it again.
7. Share your story with your class.

Story Starters

- Once upon a time there was a boy named Will who lived near a deep, dark forest.
- One day a magician came to the town where I live.
- Susan was the best baseball player in fourth grade.
- There once was a rabbit who left his home in the woods and hopped all the way to the city.
- I was walking home from school one day and found a crown of jewels, barely hidden under some leaves.

Process Questions:

1. Why is it important for a desktop publisher to know about spelling, punctuation and grammar?
2. What are you learning in school that could help you be a desktop publisher?

Chapter VII

Part II

Background:
- To save time, enter the article Survey at Wilson School on diskettes prior to class.
- Copy a corrected form of the article for each student, or write the corrected article on chart paper so that students can check their own corrections.

Survey at Wilson School

Students at Wilson School have been busy doing a survey. The survey is a study of how students spend their free time. Wilson students found that fifth and sixth graders spend most of their time playing video games.

The students at Wilson are making graphs of the survey. They plan to send the graphs to students in another city. The students at Wilson School are very excited about this project.

Procedure:
1. Type the following article into your computer exactly as it is written below. If you are not using a computer, you may use paper and pencil.

   survey at wilson school

   students at wilson school have been busy doing a survey. the survey is a study of how stoodents spend their free time. wilson students found that fifth & sixth graders spend most of there tine playing video games

   the student at wilson are making graphs of the survey. they plan to send the graphs to students in another citee. the students at wilson school are very excited about this project

Computer Skills Second Language Activities

2. Correct the misspelled words and punctuation in the article. Check for capitalizations. Center the title of the article and indent each paragraph.
3. Save the article.
4. If you are working on a computer see if you can:
   - underline the title
   - change the size of the type
   - make the title darker than the rest of the article
   - count the number of words in the article.
5. Print the article and compare it with the model.

Process Questions:
1. How has the computer changed the whole publishing business?
2. How has desktop publishing helped small business people?

Career Development Activities for the Elementary Grades

Computer Programmer

Computer programmers set up programs on the computer. The programs are in the form of complicated codes and the computer programmers must know the meaning of the codes to install the programs on the computer. They know how to install hardware and software, like the word processing software we use on the school computers. Computer programmers will continue to have many job opportunities as Americans become more and more dependent on computers.

Activity 137

Summertime

Cluster: Technology
Subject Area: Computer, Writing
Materials: Computer
Time: 30 to 45 minutes

Part I

Background:
- This activity is intended to give students practice in the basic skills of word processing. Be sure your students understand DELETE, SAVE, SPELL CHECK, PRINT.
- If you have computers available for all students, instruct students to work in their small groups to generate story starters. Once they have decided on the first line of the story, have them print a copy of the line for each group member. Students can then work on their own to complete their stories.
- You can enhance this activity by inviting a computer programmer to school to demonstrate their skills.

Procedure:
1. Computer programmers first had to learn how to use computers. They became familiar with using word processing before they went on to more complicated software. Working with your small group, bring up the word processing program on a computer.
2. Brainstorm a list of action words, adjectives and characters associated with summertime. Take turns TYPING the words into the computer. An example of an action word associated with summer is 'swimming', an adjective could be 'hot' and a character could be 'lifeguard'.
3. From the words your group has brainstormed, TYPE several sentences into the computer that could be used as story starters. An example of a story starter sentence is 'No lifeguard was on duty the day we went to the beach to go swimming'. Choose the story starter sentence the group likes best. DELETE the other starter sentences. DELETE the brainstorm list.
4. Discuss with your group how you want the story to go. Take turns with group members TYPING the sentences to complete the story.
5. SAVE the story.
6. Check the spelling and punctuation. If your word processing software has a SPELL CHECK, use it to check the spelling.
7. PRINT your group's story.
8. Share the story with your class.

Process Questions:
1. Computers have a SPELL CHECK. Does that mean you do not need to know how to spell?
2. How has using a dictionary been affected by the computer?

236   Miriam McLaughlin and Sandra Peyser

Chapter VII

Part II

Background:
- Enhance this activity by having your students work with a variety of print sizes, numbers, and margin changes and other tools. Also, you may want them to include dialogue in their stories. Be sure students have an opportunity to practice anything you add to this activity.
- Check your students' practice work before letting them go on to story writing.

Procedure:
1. Using the word processing program on your computer, perform the following tasks:
   - Type your name and center it near the top of the page, like a title. Put your name in bold print.
   - Go down two spaces and type your address and center it on the page under your name. Your address should have two lines.
   - Go down four spaces and change to another font. Tab in from the left side of the page, twice. Type the name of one of your parents.
   - Go down one space and tab in twice again. Type the name of a neighbor. The neighbor's name should be directly under your parent's name. Underline the neighbor's name.
   - Go down one space and tab in twice again. Type the name of one of your friends. Italicize your friend's name.
   - Go down one space and tab in twice again. Type the name of a brother, sister or cousin. Change the name to all CAPS.
   - Go two more spaces down the page, indent and type a sentence that describes your friend. Cut this sentence and paste it at the bottom of the page.
   - Print your work and check it.
2. On a new page write a short story about you and your friend. It should have at least two paragraphs. Be sure you title the story and center the title. Be sure you indent each paragraph. At the end of the story, drop down two spaces and tab to the right center of the page. Type your name.
3. Print the story and share it with your class.

Process Questions:
1. Why do computer programmers need a background in math and science?
2. Is computer programming a job for someone who likes to work alone? Why or why not?

Flight Attendant

Flight attendants make sure passengers are comfortable and safe during airplane flights. They greet the passengers and help them stow their belongings. Flight attendants are responsible for explaining all the safety features on the aircraft and what passengers should do in an emergency. They also serve food and drinks to passengers and tend to the needs of the pilots of the aircraft.

Activity 138

Coffee, Tea, or Milk

Subject Area: Second Language
Materials: Index cards, pencils
Time: 30 to 45 minutes

Part I

Background:

You can enhance this activity by inviting a flight attendant to visit the class.

Procedure:

1. Working with your class, list the ways flight attendants help passengers on airplanes. For example, flight attendants serve food and drinks.
2. Divide into small groups. Each group should choose one of the duties of a flight attendant from the class list to role play.
3. Practice the role play and perform it for the class.

Process Questions:

1. Discuss an experience you may have had in an airplane.
2. What skills would you need to be a good flight attendant?

Part II

Background:

- Write each word from the list below, and the name of the language on an index card. Be sure you have an equal number of "hello" cards and "goodbye" cards to distribute to your students.
- Instruct them to say the word as best they can.
- If you are currently studying a language, enhance this activity by having your students ask questions and receive responses in this language.

Procedure:

1. Some flight attendants work on international flights. They travel by plane to other countries and frequently have passengers on their planes that speak other languages. These flight attendants are often required to know at least one other language besides English. With your class, identify the languages you think are the most popular in the world.
2. Look at the index card the teacher has given you. The card has either the word hello or goodbye in another language. If you have received a hello card, move to the right side of the room and form a line. If you have a goodbye card, form a line at the left side of the room facing the hello line.
3. The first person in the right line should look at the first person in the left line and say hello in the language written on the card. After saying hello in the language, they should tell what language was spoken.
4. The first person in the left line should then look at the first person in the right line and say goodbye in the language on the card. The person should then tell what language was spoken.
5. Continue down the line, with each person saying hello or goodbye to the person opposite them.

Process Questions:

1. How would knowing a second language help a flight attendant?
2. Would knowing their language be a comfort to frightened passengers? Why or why not?

Chapter VII — Computer Skills Second Language Activities

Handout—Activity 138

Coffee, Tea, or Milk

Hello

O'la	Italian
Heda	German
Buenos dias	Spanish
Neno la kusalimu rafiki au mtani	Swahili
Aloha	Hawaiian
Salut	French
Comment allex-vous	French
Selamat datang	Malaysian
Zdravstvul	Russian
Sayonara	Japanese
Shalom	Hebrew
She you	Native American (Cherokee)

Goodbye

Do svidamiya	Russian
Arriverderci	Italian
Ciao	Italian
Auf wiedershen	German
Adios	Spanish
Au revoir	French
Selemat djalan	Malaysian
Farval	Swedish
Tidama	West African
Shalom	Hebrew
Konnichiwa	Japanese
Dan da go yue	Native American (Cherokee)

Bibliography

Brown, D., & Crace, R.K. (1995). A values-based model of career choice and satisfaction. *Career Development Quarterly*, 44-47.

Careers in action (1997). Frankfort, KY: Educational Associates

Campbell, C., Dahir, C.A. (1997). *The National Standards for School Counseling Programs* Alexandria, VA: American School Counselor Association.

Fitzgerald, L.F., & Betz, N.E. (1994). Career development in cultural context: The role of gender, race, class, and sexual orientation. In M. Savickas & R. Lent (Eds.) *Convergence in career development theories: Implications for science and practice* (pp. 103-115). Palo Alto, CA: Consulting Psychologists Press.

Gibson, R.L. (1972). *Career development in the elementary school*. Columbus, OH: Charles E. Merrill.

Harr, G.L. (1995). *Career guide*. Pacific Grove, CA: Brooks/Cole Publishing.

Herr. E.L. & Crammer, S.H. (1996). *Career guidance through the life-span: Systematic approaches (5th ed.)*. New York: HarperCollins.

Holland, J.L. (1992). *Making vocational choices (2nd ed.)*. Odessa, FL: Psychological Assessment Resources.

Holland, J.L. (1996). Exploring careers with a typology: What we have learned and some new directions. *American Psychologist*, 51, 397-406.

Hoyt, K.B., Pinson, N.M., Laramore, D. & Mangum, G.L. (1973). *Career education and the elementary school teacher*. Salt Lake City: UT: Olympus Publishing Company.

Lindsay, N. (1994). *Pathfinder-Exploring Career & Educational Planning for Junior High & High School Students*. Indianapolis, IN: JIST Works, Inc.

Looft, W.R. (1971). Sex differences in the expression of vocational aspirations by elementary school children. *Developmental Psychology*, 5, 366.

MacKay, W.R. & Miller, C.A. (1982). Relations of socioeconomic status and sex variables to the complexity of worker functions in the occupational choices of elementary school children. *Journal of Vocational Behavior*, 20, 31-37,

Mitchell, L.K., & Krumboltz, J.D. (1996). Krumboltz's learning theory of career choice and counseling. In D. Brown, L. Brooks, & Associates (Eds.). *Career choice and development (3rd ed.)*. San Francisco: Jossey/Bass.

National Occupation Information Coordinating Committee (NOICC) (1992). *The national career development guidelines project*. Washington, DC: U.S. Department of Labor.

Peyser, S. & McLaughlin M. (1998). *Character education activities for k-6 classrooms*. Minneapolis, MN: Educational Media Corporation.

Sharf, R.S. (1992). *Applying career development theory to counseling*. Pacific Grove, CA: Brooks/Cole Publishing.

Super. D. (1990). A life-span, life-space approach to career development. In Dr. Brown, L. Brooks, & Associates (Eds.) *Career choice and development*. San Francisco, CA: Jossey-Bass.

U.S. Department of Education (1994). *School-to-work: What does research say about it?* Washington, D.C: U.S. Government Printing Office.

Van Zandt, Z., Perry, N., & Brawley, K.T. (1993). *Get a life: Your personal planning portfolio for career development*. Alexandria, VA: American School Counselor Association.

Zunker, V.G. (1998). *Career counseling (5th ed.)*. Pacific Grove, CA: Brooks/Cole.